Quebec Society and Politics:
Views from the Inside

Dale C. Thomson
(Editor)

Quebec Society and Politics:
Views from the Inside

McClelland and Stewart Limited

McClelland and Stewart Limited
The Canadian Publishers
25 Hollinger Road, Toronto

ISBN 7710-8456-0

Contents

Contributors

Dale C. Thomson – Director, Center of Canadian Studies, Johns Hopkins University, Washington, D.C.; and Professor of Political Science, University of Montreal.

Léon Dion – Professor of Political Science, Laval University.

Michel Brunet – Professor of History, University of Montreal.

Jean-Charles Bonenfant – Professor of Constitutional Law, Laval University; former Librarian, Quebec National Assembly.

André Larocque – Assistant to the Parliamentary Leader of the Parti Québécois, Quebec National Assembly; formerly Lecturer in Political Science, University of Montreal.

André Gélinas – Professor of Public Administration, Ecole Nationale d'Administration Publique, University of Quebec.

Vincent Lemieux – Professor of Political Science, Laval University.

Maurice Pinard – Professor of Sociology, McGill University.

André Raynauld – Chairman, Economic Council of Canada; former Professor of Economics, University of Montreal.

Jacques Henripin – Professor of Demography, University of Montreal.

Norbert Lacoste – Director of Pastoral Service, Montreal Catholic School Commission; former Professor of Sociology, University of Montreal.

Gilles Lalande – Professor of Political Science, University of Montreal.

Daniel Latouche – Political Scientist, Centre d'études canadiennes-francaises, McGill University, and occasional lecturer, McGill University, Montreal.

Claude Morin – Professor of Intergovernmental Relations, Ecole Nationale d'Administration Publique, University of Quebec.

Raymond Breton – Professor of Sociology, University of Toronto.

Preface

In this age of information proliferation, every author must ask himself before preparing another manuscript: is this one really necessary? Does it offer something new to potential readers? We believe that this volume qualifies on both counts. The society and politics of Quebec are a rich subject, of particular significance for North Americans at the present time. The Province of Quebec, with its predominantly French-speaking population, has long been one of the most distinctive parts of the continent, but it attracted little attention because of its relative isolation and the hermetic nature of the French Canadian way of life. In the past decade or so, it has found itself much closer to the mainstream of world society and more exposed to external influences. Established institutions and patterns of conduct are disintegrating before the "winds of change" sweeping the entire globe, and new ones are gradually emerging.

This process is exhilarating for some Quebecers, disturbing and even painful for others. It is highly complex, and its outcome remains uncertain. It has generated tension between English- and French-speaking Quebecers, traditional and modernizing élites, social classes and occupational groups, members of families, and even within individuals. It is calling into question not only the form and nature of Quebec society, but the relationship between Quebec and the rest of Canada. Indeed, it is raising doubts about the future of Canada as a country.

There is little unanimity about the significance of current developments in Quebec. The perception of inside observers is frequently distorted by partisan feelings or lack of an overview; outside observers are rarely able to appreciate the many dimensions and forces involved. Perhaps the most that can be said at the present time is that Quebec society is seeking a new harmony, both within itself and in its relations with the larger human community. But, it can well be asked, is such a goal attainable in a period of human history when, as Léon Dion remarks in Chapter II, the only constant factor is continual change?

This volume has the limited objective of offering some insights into this complex situation. It grew out of a series of lectures delivered in the fall semester of 1971 at The Johns Hopkins University's Center of Canadian Studies in Washington, D.C. Ten French-speaking academics from Quebec were invited in turn to discuss Quebec society and politics from the viewpoint of their respective disciplines. Their lectures were so well received that it was decided to have them prepared in chapter form and to publish them. Subsequently, several additional chapters were added to reflect further dimensions of the subject. Only two participants have contributed more than one chapter: Léon Dion, who delivered the opening and closing lectures, and Gilles Lalande, who agreed to do double duty when one of the original participants failed to produce a written text. The editor was the only non-French Canadian participant in the project; his credentials for writing on Quebec are that he is a bilingual Canadian who has been on the faculty of the University of Montreal since 1960.

Although a range of academic disciplines and political leanings are represented in this volume, many facets and viewpoints have been left out. This situation reflects the complex nature of modern Quebec; it cannot be encompassed within one or even several books. We can only hope that the collection of statements that we have assembled will provide readers with new insights, particularly on how Quebec is viewed from the inside.

A number of people contributed materially to the preparation of this volume. Most of the chapters were written in French, and several persons participated in their translation. Four individuals deserve special mention. Elizabeth Richards of Montreal read the entire manuscript, checking some translations and doing others herself, and improving the quality of the text greatly with her exceptional mastery of the English language. Judith Webster of The Johns Hopkins' Center of Canadian Studies translated some chapters and typed various versions of others, proof-read them all and prepared the index. Amelia Rarick, my Research Assistant, read the printers' proofs, and in doing so, set an example of clarity and precision for all of us. Micheline Thibaud, devoted mainstay of the Center, assisted in innumerable ways. The Canada Council provided funds to meet translation costs.

1
Introduction
by Dale C. Thomson

Quebec is the most distinctive of the Canadian provinces, and that
distinctiveness is related essentially to the fact that 84 percent of French-
speaking Canadians, *i.e.*, those whose mother tongue is French, live there.
An additional 12 percent live in the contiguous provinces of Ontario and
New Brunswick, within easy communicating distance of Quebec. Thus
while Quebec and French Canada are not synonymous terms, the Province
remains, as it has been for three and a half centuries, the heartland of the
French-speaking community. Since French-speaking Canadians constitute
80.7 percent of the Province's population, they have a predominant influence on its society and politics, and the distinction between this majority
group and the Province itself occasionally becomes blurred.

Another factor that must be borne in mind in seeking to understand
current social and political trends in Quebec is the presence of two
themes that are not always easy to reconcile. One is the theme of
survival, which is as old as the first French settlement in North America, and has made an indelible imprint on the French Canadian character. It reflects the struggle to establish the colony of New France, then
the difficulties of a conquered people clinging to its own way of life, and
now the dilemma of a language group that constitutes a mere 2.5
percent of the population of the continent it inhabits. The other and
more recent theme is characterized by the French expression "*épanouissement*", roughly translated as "flourish" or uninhibited development according to one's potential. This concept is applied not only to
individuals, but to French Canadian society as a unit. The first of these
themes is defensive and even negative in connotation; the second, positive and expansionary. It has been argued that the Quiet Revolution, the
rapid modernization of Quebec society since the death of Premier Maurice Duplessis in 1959, has exorcised the preoccupation with survival, and
replaced it with the *leitmotiv* of *épanouissement*. However, both are still
clearly evident, and often reflected in a single statement. It is interesting
to observe how men such as Pierre-Elliott Trudeau and René Lévesque,
with contrasting political goals, seek to harmonize these themes in their
political programmes.

Quebec in Retrospect

Quebec society and politics have been fashioned over a period of three and a half centuries, and much of that historical experience is reflected in the current situation. Even under the French *régime*, the settlers or *habitants*, from whom most French Canadians are descended, had developed distinctive traits. They were generally independent-minded, tenacious, and inclined to irreverence of authority. Well integrated into the North American environment, their sense of identity as a group was so strong that, in the view of some historians, they already constituted a nation. When the colony was ceded to Great Britain in 1763, this feeling of solidarity was strengthened, first, because of resistance to the new rulers, and second, because of the greater need for self-reliance in a situation of adversity.

When the British took over the administration and defence of the colony, and the lucrative fur trade that was the mainstay of the economy, the French Canadians withdrew increasingly to the countryside and sought to maintain their way of life with a minimum of interference from their new masters. Primarily concerned with maintaining peace and stability, the Imperial authorities gave tacit support to this situation by recognizing their local laws and customs, including their religion and language; they also sought to associate representatives of the French Canadian lay and clerical *élite* with the administration of the colony. This French Canadian defensive strategy of withdrawal before the civil authorities, already manifest under the French *régime*, became a generalized political attitude that is still recognizable today, particularly with regard to the federal government. It also explains, at least in part, the indifference of French Canadians in the years after the Conquest to proposals to introduce representative institutions, demanded with increasing insistence by British immigrants.

When French Canadians received their first legislative assembly through the Constitutional Act of 1791 (which also divided the Province of Canada into two parts, Upper and Lower Canada, corresponding to present-day Ontario and Quebec), they saw it primarily as an instrument of survival of their group, a defence mechanism against the British authorities and the growing British population who controlled the Executive and Legislative Councils. They learned to use it with considerable skill, and notable parliamentarians emerged during this period. However, this polarization of the two language groups around two institutions within the same government eventually led to open conflict, in what is known in English Canada as the Rebellion of 1837, and in French Canada as the *"guerre des patriotes"*. This uprising was of

Quebec Society and Politics

limited scope and duration because, while there was probably wide-spread sympathy for it, few French Canadians rallied to the call to arms. Their instinct for survival restrained them from committing themselves to a cause that had little chance of success; isolation and passive resistance to change served their interests better. Their clergy encouraged them in this attitude.

The British authorities despatched Earl Durham, a liberal imperialist, to investigate the situation. He found, in his words, "two nations warring in the bosom of a single state," and proposed to eliminate one of them by absorbing it into the other – for their own long-range benefit, of course. Specifically, he recommended reuniting the Province of Canada under a single system of responsible government. With the strong influx of immigrants from the British Isles, the French element would soon be in a minority, he argued; and, since they were a people without history or culture, they could easily be converted through the full application of British parliamentary institutions into loyal English-speaking British subjects. However, assimilation was no longer possible, if, indeed, it had been at any time since the Conquest. The Act of Union of 1839 fused the two parts of Canada into one, although maintaining separate administrative departments in certain fields such as justice and education; and eliminated French as an official language. These steps did not alter the basic socio-political realities; French Canadians continued to speak French in the legislature and elsewhere, and demanded the full application of responsible government, a valuable vehicle for the defence of their interests. Indeed, they succeeded so well in making the system serve them that the demands for change that brought about the dissolution of United Canada in the 1860s came, not from French, but from English Canadians. The latter, having become the majority group, complained of excessive French Canadian influence in the government.

French Canadians did not actively seek Confederation. Conservative leader George-Etienne Cartier accepted the formula devised at the Quebec Conference in 1864 as necessary to meet English Canadian dissatisfaction, and Liberal leader Antoine-Aimé Dorion opposed it as too centralized; he advocated instead a "small federation" of Ontario and Quebec. The French Canadian vote on the plan in the Assembly of United Canada was 28 in favour, 22 against; the population as a whole was not consulted. Once the plan had been adopted, the Liberals agreed to give it an honest try, and the clergy urged public acceptance. In the general elections of 1867, Confederation was presented to French Canadians as a victory for the cause of survival, since it gave them control, through the Quebec legislature, of those subjects of legislation judged

Introduction   11 most important to preserve their identity.

In retrospect, the guarantees offered to French Canadians under the British North America Act, 1867, appear rather limited. Their language was recognized officially only in the Parliament of Canada, the Legislative Assembly of Quebec, and before the federal and Quebec courts. In Quebec, English and French were to be equal; in the other provinces, English was to prevail. The exception to this situation was the existing network of Roman Catholic schools throughout the country, which were to be protected by the constitution, and in many of which French was the language of instruction. In short, French Canadians became citizens of a country extending from sea to sea, but equal, as far as the protection of their language was concerned, only in the Province of Quebec. Furthermore, only in Quebec were they to be able to maintain their civil code, their system of education, and other attributes of their distinctive existence. Thus Confederation perpetuated the concept of Quebec as the homeland or bastion of French Canada. Even the capital, Ottawa, was an Ontario municipality, part of the outside world where they were vulnerable. In contrast, English Canadians could identify easily with all parts of the country, including Quebec; indeed, they were a majority in Montreal, and almost a majority in Quebec City. This feeling of identification only with the Province of Quebec was intensified in the decades following Confederation when the governments of several provinces attempted to suppress Roman Catholic separate schools; and when Louis Riel, French-speaking Roman Catholic Métis leader on the Prairies, was hanged in 1885 for his part in resisting the white man's (to many French Canadians: the English Protestant's) advance into the West.

In the century following Confederation, the British North America Act, 1867, served the cause of French Canadian survival well. Under conservative lay and clerical leadership, and protected by provincial autonomy and religious, linguistic, and social barriers, French-speaking Quebecers were able to maintain their way of life and group identity. Their elected representatives in Ottawa, for the most part, played a similarly protective role, often functioning more as delegates to an outside authority than as full-fledged participants in the governmental process. Indeed, those who took a more wholly Canadian stance, like Prime Ministers Laurier and St. Laurent, exposed themselves to denunciation as "traitors" and "sell-outs." The exceptionally high birth rate of French Canadians, stimulated by lay and clerical leaders under the slogan "the revenge of the cradle," enabled them to remain about 30 percent of the Canadian population, notwithstanding the massive inflow of immigrants to English Canada and the exodus to the United States during the nineteenth century of an estimated 800,000 of their own

Quebec Society and Politics

number. Thus, while they survived and grew under Confederation, French Canadians did not identify fully with all of Canada, nor did they share in the challenge and benefits of building a Canadian nation from sea to sea.

The Quiet Revolution

In a static world, this balance between internal and external forces, carefully inscribed in the Canadian Constitution, might have continued for several centuries more. However, as early as World War I new factors intervened. The loyalty of English Canadians to the British Empire led them to impose compulsory military service on French Canadians, most of whom did not consider that their interests warranted such a measure. The industrialization and consequent urbanization of Quebec, the economic crisis of the 1930s, and World War II had a similarly disruptive effect. Although the old model of Quebec society and politics endured relatively intact until 1959, the seeds of its destruction were sown decades earlier. In 1948, the painter Paul-Emile Borduas issued his manifesto, *Le Refus Global*, rejecting the constraints of a society that inhibited his artistic creativity. In 1949, a strike in the asbestos mines of Asbestos and Thetford Mines turned into a confrontation between the trade unions and a new, reform-minded *élite* on the one hand, and the traditional leadership on the other. Pierre-Elliott Trudeau, then a young socialist-oriented intellectual, subsequently wrote a penetrating analysis of that episode in which he declared that "our social framework – decrepit because conceived for a different era – was ready to burst apart."[1] In the 1940s and '50s, new Faculties of Social Science at Laval University and the University of Montreal, and groups of individuals such as those associated with the review *Cité Libre* and the *Institut canadien des affairs publiques*, were already preparing the next phase of Quebec's history.

By the time Premier Duplessis died in the summer of 1959, the conservative, paternalistic type of government associated with his name was irremediably undermined. Even though Duplessis' *protégé*, his successor, Paul Sauvé, had only to adopt the slogan "Henceforth" to signal the beginning of a new era, and to create a wave of enthusiasm and hope across the Province. However, he lived only one hundred days in office; and his successor, Antonio Barrette, was defeated after only a few months. It fell to Jean Lesage, new leader of the provincial Liberal Party, to introduce the next chapter of Quebec history with his own slogan, "It's time for change."

Prior to entering provincial politics, Lesage had served as a junior but very promising minister in the federal Cabinet of Prime Minister Louis St. Laurent, only changing his base of operations after the Liberals had been defeated in the federal elections of 1957. A hard-working, competent administrator, impatient for progress, he was able to rally behind him both the traditional Liberal vote and the reform-minded elements of the population, and was carried to power on the "winds of change" in June, 1960. He proclaimed a "quiet revolution" to transform Quebec into a fully modern state within a single generation.

Jean Lesage proposed to use the provincial government and administration, long underdeveloped because of French Canadian distrust of the state apparatus, which they associated with outside domination, as his vehicle of modernization and to harness traditional French Canadian nationalism to power it. With the Conservatives, not known in recent decades for their comprehension of French Canada, in power in Ottawa, he was able to attract to Quebec City new talent from the federal public service and to recruit many promising young persons who, under other circumstances, would have sought careers there. One of the leading members of Lesage's team, as Minister of Natural Resources, was René Lévesque, socialist and Quebec nationalist. In 1962, Lévesque played the leading role in bringing about the nationalization by the Quebec government of the Province's hydro-electric industry. Lesage capped that popular move by calling an election and increasing his party's strength in the Legislative Assembly. During the campaign, the Liberals made effective use of the slogan, *"Maîtres chez nous,"* or approximately, "Masters in Our Own House."

In identifying with both modernizing and nationalist trends in Quebec society, the Lesage Administration was attempting to synchronize the two themes mentioned early in this chapter, survival and *épanouissement.* In this way the past was to serve the cause of the present; the present to serve the causes of the past. This situation was soon to lead to concern in English Canada. Most English Canadians had welcomed the Quiet Revolution, seeing in it an indication that French Canadians were emerging from their long period of withdrawal, and were about to make a more positive contribution to Canada as a whole. Accordingly, they were disturbed to note the new and even more strident manifestations of Quebec nationalism, demands for greater Quebec autonomy, and increasing preoccupation by French Canadians with affairs in "their own" province. A new and hitherto unequalled wave of Quebec separatism nourished the unease of English Canadians, particularly since they tended to confuse all forms of nationalist expression in Quebec. Terrorist incidents, which began in 1963, intensified these feelings.

After he became Prime Minister of Canada in the spring of 1963 with strong support from Quebec, Lester B. Pearson sought to accommodate French Canadian modernizing aspirations within the Canadian federal system. He acknowledged that Quebec, as the homeland of French Canadians, was different from the other provinces – something English Canadians have always been reluctant to concede – and that it had particular needs and responsibilities. He also proved flexible in meeting Lesage's demands for increased financial resources and control over certain areas of government activity such as social welfare; but he did not alter the existing division of powers. He created the Royal Commission on Bilingualism and Biculturalism, to "recommend what steps should be taken to develop the Canadian Confederation on the basis of equal partnership between the two founding races, taking into account the contribution made by other ethnic groups." However, as Lesage soon found, modernizing nationalism is an unruly mount to ride; and Pearson, for his part, soon learned that it was hard to reconcile with existing institutions. The demands of the new generation of politicians and officials in Quebec City were increasingly difficult to meet within the present constitutional framework; they, in turn, were being urged on by highly vocal young nationalists who wanted nothing less than independence. The Leader of the Opposition, Daniel Johnson, attempted to outbid Lesage for nationalist support by proclaiming that federalism was dead, and calling for "equality or independence" for Quebec.

By 1965, the atmosphere of exhilaration and confidence had begun to give way to a greater sense of realism and even of disappointment, as exaggerated hopes failed to be realized. Most young Quebecers could identify with Lesage's "grand design"; fewer were prepared for the long, hard pull to achieve it. And since modernization is a destructive as well as a creative process, an increasing number of Quebecers were feeling threatened and even injured by it. Some of the prime intellectual movers of the Quiet Revolution, notably Pierre Elliott Trudeau and his closest associates, became concerned that the combination of head-strong Quebec nationalism and Ottawa's highly pragmatic flexibility was eroding the federal system. They determined to enter federal politics in the November, 1965, elections to halt this process, and make Ottawa a more effective counterweight to Quebec City.

Jean Lesage undertook the 1966 election campaign with a divided team, reflecting the increasingly fractionalized state of Quebec society and politics. Two separatist parties were able to draw off 8 percent of the extreme nationalist vote. Johnson's Union Nationale, still strong in the rural areas (favoured by the outdated electoral laws) and traditional sectors of society, was able to attract the support of sufficient nationalist and discontented elements to win a majority of seats in the legislature. The first phase of the Quiet Revolution was at an end.

Faced with the same forces, even within his own Cabinet, Daniel Johnson proved more dexterous than his predecessor. Maintaining essentially the same officials and government programmes, he allowed himself to be carried along by the momentum that had been generated since 1960, tacking and hauling as circumstances demanded, or in other words, playing on the themes of equality, independence, and even confidence in the federal system, with a masterly political touch. In his two years and four months in office before he died suddenly in October, 1968, did he lead Quebec along the path towards separation or strengthen its place within Confederation? Did he advance or retard the Quiet Revolution? Such was the nature of the man and his administration that it is difficult to say with precision. He did call for, and helped to launch, a thorough review of the Canadian constitution, during the course of which he declared he was "placing a bet" that Canada would survive. On the other hand, he created the setting for General de Gaulle's resounding cry, *"Vive le Québec libre,"* in July, 1967, which gave significant impetus to the separatist cause at a time when it was being overshadowed by the Canadian centennial celebrations. Daniel Johnson's successor as Premier, Jean-Jacques Bertrand, was a more committed federalist, and less able to contain the nationalist forces within the Union Nationale party. A victim of ill health and a sincere desire to reconcile Quebec's aspirations and Canadian federalism, he led his party to defeat in the elections of April, 1970.

By the time of the 1970 elections, the Quiet Revolution had been in progress for a whole decade, and had no longer the same exciting connotations. Jean Lesage had retired from politics, an out-dated politician to much of the electorate. The political vedettes were Canadian Prime Minister Pierre-Elliott Trudeau, who had swept Quebec on an unequivocally federalist platform in the federal elections of June, 1968; and René Lévesque, former minister in the Lesage Cabinet and leader of the Parti Québécois, a new separatist party formed through a merger of smaller ones. Since Trudeau had the more effective power base, and was clearly demonstrating that French Canadians could play an effective role in Ottawa, the balance of political forces was shifting once more in favour of federalism.

The new Liberal leader was Robert Bourassa, 36-year-old lawyer-economist first elected to the Quebec Legislature in 1966, but with no Cabinet experience. He had won the leadership earlier in the year by eschewing more divisive topics such as separatism, and giving priority to economic development as the prerequisite for attaining social and cultural objectives.

16

Rather than using Ottawa as a convenient foil to demonstrate his primary allegiance to Quebec, the customary strategy of Quebec politicians, he declared his intention to make the federal system work more effectively to the Province's advantage. While his slogan *"fédéralisme rentable,"* or "profitable federalism," had somewhat cynical overtones, it was in harmony with the desire of a majority of Quebecers to build a strong, modern Quebec, but within Canada.

In short, while Bourassa's platform appeared somewhat unlikely at first glance in view of the current wave of nationalism, it reflected a keen appreciation of political realities. This was borne out in the elections of April, 1970, when he led the Liberals to power with 72 of 108 seats in the Quebec Assembly. At the same time, Lévesque's Parti Québécois surged forward, winning some 24 percent of the popular vote but only seven seats. The *Ralliement Créditiste* made an equally impressive entry on the provincial political scene with twelve seats, wrested principally from the Union Nationale, the big loser in the contest; it emerged with only seventeen seats and 20 percent of the popular vote. Clearly, the Liberals had played the game of consensus politics with great success, but the voting pattern reflected a volatile political situation that gave little cause for complacency. The population was probably more divided on political issues than at any time in its history, and the aspirations engendered since 1960 seemed unlikely to be satisfied in the short run by Bourassa's down-to-earth approach.

The first important test of Bourassa's leadership came in October, 1970, when members of an extremist group of Quebec separatists, the *Front de Libération du Québec,* kidnapped a British diplomat, James Cross, and a provincial Cabinet minister, Pierre Laporte, eventually assassinating the latter. After an agonizing period of uncertainty and danger of anarchy, Bourassa requested the federal government to proclaim the War Measures Act, suspending civil liberties and enabling the forces of law and order to conduct searches and make arrests without warrants. Cross was discovered and his release was negotiated; Laporte's kidnappers were arrested and brought to trial. After teetering on the verge of collapse, the Bourassa Government not only survived but found that some 90 percent of Quebecers, shocked by the appearance of violence in their midst, supported its actions.

The second test came in the following June in connection with the constitutional review begun in January, 1968. Bourassa had inherited this matter with the office of Premier, but took relatively little interest in it, convinced that Quebec's problems could be solved through financial and economic measures rather than through legal forms. His rather half-hearted attitude, which led him to adopt a less categorical stance on behalf of Quebec's autonomy than his predecessors, encouraged the federal and other provincial negotiators to feel that an agreement on significant constitutional changes was possible. At a conference held in Victoria, B.C., in June, 1971, a "Charter" of constitutional changes was agreed upon, or so the other heads of government believed, and it was decided that each Premier should return and consult his Cabinet. Within ten days, they were to inform Prime Minister Trudeau as to whether or not their governments accepted the document and were prepared to submit it to their respective legislatures.

Even before Bourassa returned home, a campaign to reject the Charter was launched in Quebec. Led by separatists, who realized that a constitutional agreement would harm their cause, and by advocates of a "special" or "associate" status for Quebec within Canada, the opposition extended into the provincial Cabinet and the Premier's immediate entourage. Judging discretion the better part of valour, and – we repeat – not considering constitutional reform a top priority, Bourassa informed Trudeau that he could not accept the Charter, at least until the ambiguity concerning certain provisions relating to social security was removed. The other heads of government felt betrayed, and comment was rife in Ottawa that the Quebec Premier was weak, deceitful, and would "have to go." In fact, while he might have been misleading in Victoria, he took the right political decision in Quebec, if one judges on the basis of a politician's ability to remain in power in order to carry out his programme. The mounting campaign against the Charter had increased the traditional apprehension of French Canadians about new arrangements with English Canada, a facet of their preoccupation with survival. In sending a negative reply to Ottawa, Bourassa maintained the unity of his Cabinet, undercut his political opponents, and enhanced his stature as a Quebec leader. What damage he did to Canada as a whole by bringing the constitutional reform process to an impasse remains to be determined; it can be argued, however, that if he had tried to force the Charter through his Cabinet and the legislature, he might have damaged it even more.

A third event is worth recalling in attempting to assess the Bourassa Administration, particularly since it also throws light on the present stage of Quebec's political and social evolution. We stated earlier that the labour movement had played a significant role in preparing the Quiet Revolution. It did so despite the efforts of the Roman Catholic church to keep it in tutelage, and despite the negative attitude of the provincial authorities. During the 1960s, it was able to play an effective role in the modernization process and brought about some notable changes, including winning recognition of the right to strike for provincial public servants. Several labour leaders entered politics; in fact, the troika Trudeau-Marchand-Pelletier, first elected to Parliament in 1965, was formed through participation in the trade union activities. In the late 1960s, the labour movement became increasingly radical in both social and political matters, thus moving closer to the European than the North American model. According to one writer, they became "the most prominent political force in Quebec. Their combined organizational strength and ideological influence have forced Quebec politics into the streets."[2] Labour leaders argued that the Quiet Revolution was a bourgeois phenomenon that profited mainly the middle class; they proposed a more extreme combination of nationalist and social forces to bring about a more genuine revolution.

In 1971, three major unions, the *Confédération des Syndicats Nationaux*, the *Fédération des Travailleurs de Québec*, and the *Corporation des enseignants du Québec*, formed a "Common Front." In October, 1971, they succeeded in organizing a demonstration of 10,000 workers against the owners of Montreal's largest newspaper, *La Presse*. And in March, 1972, they called a general strike in support of provincial employees negotiating with the provincial government. Bourassa and his colleagues bargained with the strike leaders for about a month; then, faced with continuing paralysis of the public service and rising public concern at the danger of anarchy, he had legislation passed forcing a return to work. The three principal Common Front leaders refused to comply and were put in jail. They tried to maintain the struggle from there, but soon found that their support was ebbing, even within their own unions. Their release on bail was negotiated so that they could return to the bargaining table, which they did as chastened men, conscious that they had over-extended themselves. They began serving their one-year sentences in early 1973. Through a combination of resilience, political astuteness and competence in bargaining, the Bourassa Cabinet had survived another crisis.

As he passed the half-way mark of his mandate, Bourassa maintained his economic priorities, but added further dimensions to his programme. Most notably, he placed greater emphasis on the need for Quebec to ensure its "cultural security" or "cultural sovereignty." He also called for decentralization of the federal system, particularly a greater share of tax revenues for the provinces, the maintenance of close relations with other French-speaking peoples, and priority for the French language in Quebec. He let it be known that, in the future, he might challenge the federal government more openly, but he refrained from calling into question the federal system. Not usually given to hyperbole, Bourassa spoke with great enthusiasm of the James Bay power project in northern Quebec, which he described as potentially the largest in the world, and as holding the promise of "the flowering of a new, purely Quebec, civilisation."[3] Clearly he hoped to make it and other projects such as Quebec's first steel plant, opened at Contrecoeur in late 1972, symbols of a modern, self-confident society, and to direct the aspirations and energies of Quebecers into those and other constructive channels. Would the strategy succeed? With Quebec society still in a state of ferment, and the Province facing problems that defied short-range solution, any predictions were bound to be unreliable. Except for Lesage's snap election victory in 1962, no government had been re-elected since 1956. On the other hand, politically Bourassa had demonstrated a remarkable capacity for survival; perhaps he had made that French Canadian theme into a credo for his own political career.

Promise and Constraints

In the years since the advent of the Quiet Revolution, the transformations in almost every phase of life in Quebec have been remarkable, and many of the accomplishments are merely the foundations for still more significant progress. At the same time, there are very real constraints on future developments in certain directions. In order to assess these, we must ask what are the aspirations of the majority of Quebecers. Certainly they go beyond the mere survival of a French-language community in North America; that battle has been won, notwithstanding the fact that some political and intellectual leaders continue to evoke the spectre of "cultural genocide" if their viewpoints are not adopted. They also go beyond cultural *épanouissement* or material prosperity, taken separately, although some persons would plump for one with little regard for the other. Probably the broadest consensus among French-speaking Quebecers can be found for the goal of a society in which they can live and work in the French language without prejudice, and still take full advantage of the material and other benefits of life in North America. If one accepts that perfectly legitimate goal, it becomes easier to evaluate future prospects.

Among the accomplishments of recent years, first place must be given to the reform and development of the Province's political and administrative institutions. The antiquated Legislative Council was abolished, and reforms introduced to give members of the Legislative Assembly a more effective role. (The change in title of the Assembly to "National Assembly" was more symbolic than real). A series of electoral reforms, including the redistribution of seats being carried out at the time of writing,

Quebec Society and Politics

promises to ensure a higher degree of representative democracy. The public service, from the Premier's Office to the smallest regional outposts, was re-organized; and both decision-making and administrative procedures were made more orderly. Few of the present twenty-two government departments, including the Departments of Education, Cultural Affairs, Public Service, Intergovernmental Affairs, and Communications, existed in 1959.

The system of education has probably undergone the most radical changes. Laval University and the University of Montreal have been vastly expanded, and two new universities, the University of Sherbrooke and the University of Quebec, the latter with a network of campuses across the province, were created. The system of church-run classical colleges has been replaced by CEGEPS (Colléges d'Education générale et professionnel) which offer a two-year pre-university programme. In accordance with the recommendations of the Parent Royal Commission, the school curriculum has been radically revised. Technical and scientific training, and programmes in both public and business administration, have been given much greater priority.

French-speaking Quebecers have found much greater career opportunities than ever before. In addition to the provincial public service, where they are predominant, they have won a larger place on the federal scene and in the private sector. French Canadian culture has experienced an unprecedented expansion and enrichment, and has linked up with the broader, world-wide French cultural community.

And yet there remain serious constraints.

First among these is the fact that the French-speaking population is, and is bound to remain, a minuscule proportion of the total population of the continent. Indeed, that proportion is likely to diminish in the future. The "revenge of the cradle" policy is defunct; the present birthrate in Quebec is one of the lowest in Canada, and no public policy of encouraging large families is likely to change that situation sufficiently to have a significant impact. Nor is immigration a substitute, since there are not enough applicants willing to live and work in French in North America. And at any rate, to flood Quebec with immigrants would be at least partially self-defeating, since the distinctive French Canadian culture would be diluted, perhaps beyond recognition.

Second, while Quebec is 2.4 times larger than France, and richly endowed with certain natural resources, it is still limited in its potential for economic growth. Its agricultural base is small; most of its territory is unattractive for settlement; and the climate is severe most of the year. Geographically and economically, it is locked into the rest of the continent, and there is little possibility of circumventing the consequences of that reality by establishing closer relations with other parts of the world.

Socially, Quebec is also closer to the rest of North America than to most other countries, including France, and that situation is likely to become more accentuated. Culturally, closer relations with France and other Francophone countries will be valuable, but Quebec's accomplishments' will probably always suffer in comparison with those of the cultural heartland, France itself. In short, while the possibilities of *épanouissement* are great, limitations exist as well.

It is from this perspective that constitutional relationships between Quebec and the rest of Canada should be examined. In the view of some Quebec analysts, the logical consummation of the Quiet Revolution is complete independence, and nothing short of it will satisfy the aspirations that have been awakened. It is argued, as General de Gaulle did, that once a nation such as French Canadians is awakened to national consciousness, its progress to full sovereignty cannot be stopped. This "inevitability thesis" is current within the Parti Québécois, and specific dates, for instance 1974 and 1978, are mentioned as the year when independence will come to pass. There is a danger in predictions of this nature: their non-fulfilment can result in an adverse reaction. Already Parti Québécois leaders find themselves being accused by young people of having merely replaced one set of myths by another, and of conducting themselves, in their quest for power, like other politicians.

In his volume, *Nos Grandes Options Politiques et Constitutionnelles*, Richard Arès, s.J., outlined what he considers to be the principal constitutional choices facing "the French Canadian community."[4] He identifies them as: (1) Option Canada, "which aims to make Canada into a completely English-language country, and thus to assimilate the francophone community and make Quebec a province like the others: it is the proposal of anglophone nationalism." (2) Option bilingual Canada, which "seeks to rise above the nationalist aims of the two linguistic communities and espouses as an ideal a federal-type political society in which the two languages would be recognized: it is the proposal of Canadian nationalism." This option is reflected in the conclusions of the Royal Commission on Bilingualism and Biculturalism, and identified with the name of Pierre-Elliott Trudeau. (3) Option French Canada, "that of the French Canadian community which, while wishing to survive and *s'épanouir* throughout Canada, wishes above all to maintain Quebec as a base; it is the proposal of French Canadian nationalism." Included within its ambit are frequent demands over the years for recognition of Quebec as a province "different from the others"; the claims of Jean Lesage, Claude Ryan and others for a "special status for Quebec"; and requests, including those of Robert Bourassa, for special consideration. (4) Option Quebec, the aim of which is "the complete sovereignty, the independence of Quebec, following which it will be invited to join in association with whomever it wishes: it is the proposal of Quebec nationalism." Identified essentially with René Lévesque and the Parti Québécois, it includes the notion of "associate states," or two sovereign states within a loose confederation.

Arès' classification is somewhat simplified, but it is a fair statement of the options as perceived from within French-speaking Quebec. The first, Option Canada, is not only a misnomer since "Canada" and English monolingualism are not synonymous; but it also exists more in the minds of French Canadians than of English Canadians, and reflects the two-century-old preoccupation – since the Conquest – with survival. The second option, bilingual Canada, is, like the first, something of a straw man, particularly since Arès interprets it as "rejection of the group identity of French Canadians." He outlines three specific objections to it: that "Quebec might remain the only bilingual province," presumably since bilingualism elsewhere would always be more symbolic than real; that "the campaign in favour of bilingualism could serve as an excuse to keep Quebec on the same level as the other provinces, and to refuse to recognize politically its role as the principal centre of French Canada"; and finally, that its proponents "speak less and less of French Canadians and more and more of French-speaking Canadians, a form of speech that suggests a greater degree of integration into the whole of Canada." (author's translation.[5] These objections reflect the inclination of French Canadians to think in terms of group rather than individual rights, an expression of adversative solidarity. Pierre-Elliott Trudeau is a notable exception, and consequently his views cannot be considered representative of the French Canadian outlook in that regard. The principal criticism that can be levelled against Arès' formulation of the option, bilingual Canada, is its excessive rigidity and his assumption that it constitutes a rejection of the existence of a French Canadian community, society or nation, and of the particular role of Quebec within Canada as the domicile of more than 80 percent of French-speaking Canadians. In fact, that role is recognized politically in many ways. What Trudeau, as the principal spokesman for this option, rejects is a special constitutional status that would weaken the authority of members of Parliament from Quebec compared to those from other provinces and encourage Quebecers to look to Quebec City to meet needs that are nation-wide.

Arès identifies his third option, Option French Canada, with French Canadian nationalism, and it in turn primarily with Quebec. The implications are that French-Canadian group solidarity and identification with all of Canada are incongruent, if not incompatible, notions, and that only in Quebec can the French-Canadian community create its own "cultural, social, and political organization."[6] Arès suggests that this is the majority view in Quebec, and endorses it personally. History lends weight to this argument, since French Canadians have had few guarantees of their distinctive characteristics, either as individuals or as a group, within federal institutions or the institutions of other provinces. But in view of the increased recognition by English Canadians of French Canadian interests, and more pertinently, of the necessity to heed French Canadian desires more in order to meet their own goals (including the goal of national survival), will this situation continue? Who would have predicted a decade ago that the "French fact" would be recognized throughout Canada to the extent that it is today? Arès remains sceptical, particularly since he considers French Canada and Quebec almost synonymous. The essence of the problem, he writes, is that "there exists in Quebec a society, still incomplete, that its members wish to finish building ... Quebec considers itself increasingly as a nearly autonomous society and expects to be recognized as such."[7] In other words, current attempts to enable French Canadians as a group to identify with the rest of Canada are misguided, and at any rate, too late.

The fourth option, Option Quebec, is this last argument carried to its ultimate conclusion: federalism cannot meet the needs of French Canadians; their full *épanouissement* requires them to have their own sovereign state, and only Quebec can play that role.

Are there other options than those which Richard Arès has outlined? Certainly there are variations of each, and perhaps even further distinctive choices. For instance, it is possible that Canada is evolving towards a sort of *quid pro quo* bilingualism, situated somewhere between Option bilingual Canada and Option French Canada. In Quebec, French is becoming the dominant language, just as English is dominant in the other provinces. The re-structured Province of Quebec reflects more and more the characteristics of French Canadians, just as the structures of the other provinces reflect those of their residents. Ottawa is becoming a true bilingual capital. Federal policies, and indeed the federal system itself, are continually being adapted to meet the demands of spokesmen for the French-speaking population. This alternative to integral "coast to coast bilingualism" is not only possible, it is developing before our eyes in response to the continuing interplay of forces. Deeply rooted in reality, it has a degree of credibility that is often lacking in the case of more idealized constructs.

While the future of Quebec society and politics remains obscure in many respects, some certainties can be established. The French language will persist indefinitely in Quebec, and Quebec will remain the stronghold of French culture in North America. The period of isolation is irreversibly over, and French Canada has been integrated into global society. This new situation opens up unparalleled opportunities for the *épanouissement* of the French-speaking population, both as individuals and as a group. As the old barriers disintegrate in the era of instant and pervasive communications, it also presents new problems of survival.

Notes

1. Pierre-Elliott Trudeau, *La Grève de l'Amiante,* Montreal: Editions Cité Libre, p. 90.
2. Daniel Drache, *Quebec – Only a Beginning.* Toronto: New Press, p. xiv.
3. Address to Liberal Party Convention, Montreal: November 9, 1972.
4. Richard Arès, *Nos Grandes Options Politiques et Constitutionnelles.* Montreal: Les Editions Bellarmin, 1972, pp. 8-9.
5. *Ibid.*, p. 43.
6. *Ibid.*, p. 47.
7. *Ibid.*, p. 76.

2
Towards a Self-Determined Consciousness*
by Léon Dion

The Impact of a Changing Society

The fissures in the fabric of modern societies are so numerous and so deep that they defy conventional explanation. It is fallacious to attribute them to the incompetence or bad faith of individuals, or to the transitory shortcomings of organizations. Rather, we are witnessing a fundamental change in the structures of society and in the outlook of its members, a change that marks the end of a social order whose basic tenets were formulated in the nineteenth century. Already, signs of a new order of civilization are increasingly evident. The development around 1950 of the first computers was comparable in its effects to the invention of the printing press five centuries earlier. As did the end of the fifteenth century, so does the second half of the twentieth century mark the beginning of a radical cultural revolution; by demolishing long-accepted dogmas, this revolution is disrupting man's relationships with his fellow-men and with his environment. Today, ideas, organizations, objects, even men themselves, are changing or being replaced so rapidly that there are, so to speak, no longer any focal points of reference. Henceforth, the only possible type of adaptation is to the phenomenon of continuing change.

So violent is the shock of this continuing revolution that to many people it is intolerable. They cannot meet the challenge of change in the nature of accepted knowledge and the mutations of the decision-making process. The initial challenge comes not from machines nor even from organizations, but from people as individuals. Some—doubtless the majority—in a desperate attempt to halt the course of events, take refuge in conservatism or, under the guise of liberalism, become openly reactionary. Others, on the contrary, clamour for change and advocate radical reforms in the pattern of society and in the rules of the game. Caught between these opposing demands, rulers hesitate; they seek a

* This text was originally published in French in the first issue of the *Revue de l'Association canadienne d' éducation de langue française*, under the title, "Pour un Canada français autodéterminé." (Vol. 1, No. 1, December, 1971). Published by permission.

middle ground and, failing to find it, take ambiguous or contradictory positions which can only further envenom the situation. Unable to decipher the distress signals sent out by all those who fear the worst from an uncontrolled change, they become unwitting accomplices both of reaction and of radicalism.

Certainly it is important when considering decisions and plans of action to take account of those who, for one reason or another, wish that the evolution of society would come to a standstill, or, at least, slow down; their motives must be understood and their anxieties allayed. But it is even more important to understand the mood of those who have reason to complain of their treatment by society and of the orientation of society by its rulers. Quite possibly, their aspirations reflect the direction of history. Yet, many of them think of themselves as "dissenters" and are often considered revolutionaries. What in fact do they represent, these diverse groupings of youth, students, intellectuals, minorities, urban and rural poor, who are proliferating in our societies? What are their complaints against the established order of family, school, church, labour unions, industries, media, political parties, the judicial and penal systems, the government? Re-examination of these dissident movements based on a new set of premises, quite different from those generally accepted so far, is a matter of the utmost urgency. Like the new technology, perhaps even more so, these movements are forcing major and inescapable realignments on the organizations of society. Far from being "aberrations" or "systemic malfunctions," they reflect, imperfectly and vaguely perhaps but nevertheless meaningfully, certain features of the world of tomorrow.

The Quebec Revolution and a New Consciousness

Contemporary Quebec, seriously divided as it is by multiple contradictions and shaken, sometimes tragically, by convulsions, provides a perfect example of this drastically changing world. Nowhere else, perhaps, has the new order challenged the old so suddenly and so brutally. Nowhere else, perhaps, is the social framework so inapt to channel this tide of social change. Few societies have experienced such profound changes in so short a space of time as Quebec during the last decade: demographically, in education, in religious outlook and in political life, these changes have taken on the magnitude of a revolution. At a dizzying pace, traditional values have been discarded, the élite dispossessed, and leadership contested. Only yesterday, churches, seemingly impregnable ramparts of a whole civilization, stood proudly in the centre of villages which had been founded in part for religious reasons, or were vital focal points for entire urban neighbourhoods. Today, many of these churches are abandoned and for sale; those that remain active and continue to attract the faithful do so by showing great adaptability.

Breaking the bonds which tied them so securely to a familiar world, Quebecers find themselves suddenly cut off from old beliefs, now obsolete; and, for the first time, they feel the pangs of insecurity. This is the price of existential liberty. Long held in bond by ancient taboos (traditions, prescriptions of all kinds) and hopes for the future (joys of heaven, electoral promises), men and women with no sure sense of direction are brought brutally face-to-face with the present. And yet, for the very reason that they are compelled to build their own life as they go along, they become the creators of their own destiny, under particularly difficult economic and social conditions.

In this way, many of the most underprivileged Quebecers have acquired a new consciousness of themselves and of their destiny. The urban citizens' committees and rural movements like Operation Dignity are made up of individuals who are determined, in spite of their poor material and intellectual resources, to change their present situation and to take their future into their own hands. These movements have so far been judged, often with amazing superficiality, according to criteria which are completely alien to them. It is important to outline the manifestations of this group consciousness and to consider what reforms are necessary to enable it to become an integral part of the broader culture of our society.

I. The Manifestations of the New Collective Consciousness:

(a) Anti-Paternalism and Dissent

Until recently, popular consciousness was determined above all by the paternalistic actions of the rulers and élite. Credulity, servility, dependence—but also confidence, stability, security—were the hallmarks of this consciousness. Isolated "revolts" against the parish priest or the elected representative were merely the reverse of the coin of filial respect, the predominant sentiment of the majority. These short-lived attempts at emancipation were somewhat immature and were understood as such by those in power, who kept them easily within bounds. There are definite signs that this era of paternalism is now behind us. Distressing as they may be, present-day apathy and withdrawal from collective commitment reflect a growing indifference to the old beliefs which formerly stirred the people and to the old stimuli which directed them along paths prescribed by their rulers.

Recently, a small but active minority has become conscious of the new situation through community programmes and a new type of leadership. It is difficult to analyze systematically this new movement towards awareness, for while evidence of it is widespread, it is fragmentary and in continual and rapid evolution. Thus, in the Lower Saint Lawrence and Gaspé areas, there is a considerable difference between BAEQ, a federal-provincial regional development project in the years 1963-66, and Operations "Dignity," a truly popular movement, in 1970-71. In spite of their often ephemeral existence, or even because of it, the existence of "fronts," "citizens' committees," "houses for the unemployed," even terrorist movements, indicates the inadequacy of official structures, the crisis in effective leadership, and ideological realignments among groups as well as individuals. Already, some features of this new Quebec mentality are clearly discernible.

The first basic feature is that the people who acquire the new consciousness reject the old paternalism, which, while offering them security and a certain amount of happiness, denied them justice. They no longer identify with the existing political structures or with those in power. They have cast off illusions such as the transcendental nature of authority, and the assumption that leaders have special innate qualities, which veiled the inadequacies of governments and the weaknesses of men. They are beginning to free themselves from blind, unquestioning faith, and from appeals for solidarity, devices used to make them docile tools of established authority. They are questioning the usefulness of the large interest groups and political parties, which they feel are far removed from reality as they know it. Increasingly, they want to be represented by spokesmen chosen by themselves, and whom they know to be well disposed towards them. Their relationships with their representatives are no longer filial; they demand that the latter reflect their objectives accurately. Authority is becoming personal, and this has two consequences: on the one hand, individuals are increasingly indifferent to religious taboos and partisan struggles, realizing that they pay the heaviest price for them; on the other hand, rulers are becoming more vulnerable. The concept which best reflects this new type of consciousness is that of participation. Although both politicians and intellectuals have scandalously misused this great concept, it will not disappear soon since it has taken root firmly in the most socially-aware segment of the population.

The second basic feature of the new collective consciousness is that it is caught in a vicious circle of rising expectations and mounting frustrations, from which it is difficult to imagine how it can possibly be freed. For some time now, demands for change have been increasing more rapidly than positive response; reforms are inadequate, and consequently, are not even seen as reforms. The insistence with which demands are voiced indicates that the general condition of Quebec society has been deteriorating. Radical dissent against "the system" is no longer limited to the young and to certain categories of intellectuals; it is spreading to poor sections of the cities and to underprivileged areas. And, because it feeds on the misery which prevails there, it promises to be more virulent than among its first adherents.

(b) Man-Centred Rationality

A third feature of the new collective consciousness is the original way in which it defines rationality. In contrast to the abstract concept espoused by scholars and technocrats, it conceives rationality as vibrant and human. Rather than being based on criteria derived from "objective" laws of nature, the output of machines and technology, and the analysis of human behaviour and systems, this "new" rationality is the product of the examination of human motivations and the underlying ideals associated with them. Unlike the case of scientific or technocratic rationality, values according to this standpoint cannot be reduced to a series of data to be taken into account to the extent permissible under "objective" criteria; they are essential elements of rationality itself. For instance, within the framework of the old concept, the value of participation is only one legitimate aspiration to be taken into account as much as possible in developing action programmes based on "objective" criteria; under the new concept, this value is as important a determining factor as the "objective" criteria. In the first case, it is accepted that to lead a decent life, it is sufficient to have a certain level of education, a certain standard of living, etc., while the extent to which individuals are involved in other activities which concern them is not of primary importance; in the second case it is the extent of participation which is the most important factor in determining the quality of an individual's life.

Carried to their logical limits, these two concepts are diametrically opposed. One of the most urgent tasks today is to discover dialectical approaches which would lead to their reconciliation. The proponents of man-centred rationality need to be reminded that science, technology, innovation and, in the last analysis, economic prosperity, are the results of abstract rationality. Conversely, the progress of economics, psychology, and sociology as scientific disciplines makes it increasingly evident that abstract rationality is ill-suited to be the basis for the concrete organization of societies. How many plans, excellent on paper, prove impossible to implement! When used to determine and control human behaviour, abstract rationality is likely to express itself as inhuman manipulation, and engender either revolt or abject apathy. A study of organizations shows that the most difficult problems are caused not by mechanical flaws, but by man's resistance to a rationality imposed from the outside.

(c) Self-Determination and Its Methods of Action

The outstanding characteristic of this new consciousness is that it is motivated by a powerful, albeit not yet clearly perceived, desire for self-determination. Often clumsily, but nonetheless unequivocally, the decision is being taken to shed the status of minor or simple subject which has always been the lot of the majority in Quebec. A people in a state of submission for so long is now lifting up its head and learning to walk straight. Less and less do Quebecers agree to having their behaviour dictated by others. They protest against the unkept promises and hesitation of their leaders. They denounce a situation which reduces them to beggardom. They want to earn their living through work and they want to enjoy the advantages of the twentieth century. They want "things to change," and they want change to start immediately. Fed up with making submissions to a government that ignores their requests or whose responses are unacceptable or come too late, they decide to take the initiative themselves under new leaders, to formulate their own plans, calling on specialists and on the government to translate these plans into specific programmes. In short, they place their reliance on Man as opposed to Bureaucracy. They opt for life. This is the philosophy behind the citizens' committees and the Operations "Dignity."

Perhaps there is no better indication of the nature of self-determined consciousness than the pressure tactics beginning to be used by underprivileged groups to express their demands and to oblige the present leadership to grant them justice. Every age and every society has its own pool of action methods which individuals or organizations can use to meet their particular requirements. The fact that, at a given moment in history, a group uses one means in preference to another is a valuable indication of the state of society at that time. If we are right in saying that our age and our society are characterized by violence, this state of affairs is not essentially due to the outlook of the most powerful groups because although they, today as in the past, will try anything to win, they are on the whole in the privileged position of being able to limit themselves to non-violence. If our age and our society are marked by violence, it is, above all, because underprivileged or unrepresented social groups have resolved to be heard and, if necessary, to use violence to that end! Peasant uprisings, urban guerillas, "creative destruction" by students, terrorism, in many ways recall the peasant uprisings of the fifteenth century. Although they can be extremely effective in the short run, we should not forget that, unless they become organized revolutionary movements, such manifestations will inevitably end in decisive defeats. However, they should convince rulers – as they failed to do in the case of the fifteenth century seigneurs – that radical reforms are essential.

Increasingly, alienated or underprivileged groups understand that politics is a continual test of strength between individuals or groups in their struggle for power. They realize that in liberal societies conflict very often reigns supreme; and they observe that only diffident attempts are made to reduce its causes, while great efforts are made to contain or neutralize their effects. They also become sharply conscious of the blatant inequality of the means available to the different parties in such contests. Their increasingly frequent recourse to violent methods is not a sign of volatile disposition; they would not react so strongly if, like those groups which express moral indignation at their actions, they had the ear of those in power. Their violent leanings reflect the paltriness of the dialogue and the inadequacy of the channels of communications between them and their governors. If they engage in public demonstrations, practise systematic obstruction, even destroy the very tools and resources on which their livelihood depends, it is because they want attention drawn to their situation and their lot in life improved. The weapons of the weak are of necessity destructive. While privileged classes have the choice of many "peaceful" means of action (money, specialized knowledge, information, internal cohesion, bargaining power, blackmail, corruption, etc.), underprivileged classes have the advantage only of their large numbers and the fear that they can generate by skillful handling of this advantage. And who can blame them for playing their only card as best they can? In so doing, are they not obeying the same rules of the game – based on conflict and the rule of strength – which govern the relationships between privileged groups (professionals, businessmen, etc.) and political leaders? Demonstrations and riots are weapons – most often held in reserve – which the underprivileged classes are resolved to use, in the present circumstances, so that they will be taken seriously.

It would be a serious mistake to identify self-determined consciousness

Quebec Society and Politics

with the often violent means which, of necessity, it uses to make itself known. After all, the objectives of the underprivileged are the same as those of the privileged: to gain access to rulers in order to be heard; to attract their attention to problems; to obtain specific action programmes, implemented in the shortest possible time, geared to their own interests; to have some control over the rules governing political action; and, lastly, to take an active part in the decision-making process when their interests are at stake.

Recourse to shock tactics by the underprivileged reveals some fundamental features of their situation; to condemn it out of hand would be deplorably shortsighted. As long as social goals and rules remain unchanged, condemnation is merely quixotic, particularly if confined to the underprivileged and neglected elements of society, while the often scandalous machinations of the affluent are disregarded. It is, in the last analysis, the dissenters who, by persuading their rulers to introduce prompt reforms, inject a measure of progressiveness into liberal régimes, and thus forestall revolutionary confrontations.

II. Conditions of Self-Determination

Self-determined consciousness is undoubtedly the most authentic form of contemporary consciousness. However, even if the rapid advances of democracy favour the full development of this consciousness, there are still many obstacles. To those who have learned to deal with people in accordance with well-tried paternalistic attitudes, it seems strange and intractable; for those in power, it constitutes a disturbing presence. It collides head-on with the familiar beliefs and practices which once guaranteed the permanent character of established institutions. One can understand, then, that faced with these new aspirations, those in power remain deaf, mute or undecided; but the course of events appears irreversible, and grave disturbances must be expected if the structures and conditions of society are not adjusted.

The mechanisms of society – political parties, pressure groups, administrations, parliaments, governments – are quite rightly questioned; yet people, too, should be subject to questioning since it is they who control these mechanisms and who, in the last analysis, have the power to change them if they are inadequate. The people are themselves awakening to self-determined consciousness; also the leaders, and, more precisely, the rulers, since they hold the reins of power and must accept change.

(a) The "Base" and Its Immediate Leaders

Without in any way detracting from aspirations towards self-determined consciousness, it is necessary to recognize clearly the unavoidable constraints on their momentum. It would be an unfortunate delusion for underprivileged groups to imagine that they can on their own develop valid solutions to their many problems, without external assistance. It is true that, in general, they hardly need to be reminded that they are powerless to act alone; they tend rather to under-estimate themselves, and this tendency is one of the causes of their present condition. They recognize their ignorance, and conclude, wrongly, that it is impossible to overcome such a handicap. Fortunately, the government training courses followed by many of them (most often, under the Department of Welfare or the Department of Education), apart from giving them a mass of useful knowledge, also make them aware of their potential and of their limitations. They are aware that specialists are needed to provide the structure of their society. They are not naturally inclined to subversion or revolution; if one day they revolt, it will be because of necessity, and because they have been duped.

To define their aspirations and to give some coherence to their plans, the underprivileged turn to leaders who are "clear-sighted," and have "contacts." These leaders are selected from their own ranks; typically, a parish priest, member of Parliament, solicitor, forestry engineer, president of a professional association, manager of a radio station, etc. Superficially, it would appear that the old élites are being re-installed under a new guise. But nothing could be further from the truth; it is precisely when self-determined consciousness is awakening that the authority of those who in the past held power is most violently attacked. The new leaders are those who can stimulate, encourage, guide and, most often, perform the role of a catalyst. They are the principal agents of the extraordinary changes taking place within the population. They are sought after because of the essential part they play in the development of the human personality and the restructuring of society. They are accepted, but they are refused the right to rule, at least in principle. Their role is that of midwife to the new society being born on our college and university campuses, in the alleys of Saint-Henri and Saint-Roch, and in the woods of Sainte-Paula and Saint-Esprit.

But those who aspire to self-determination are more dependent on the new leaders for choice of objectives and the means to attain them than the leaders are willing to admit. And this presents them with a constant temptation. Their motives are too praiseworthy for the occasional accusations that they are charlatans, demagogues or agitators to be taken seriously. They know their own limits and are the first to appeal for the help of specialists and the cooperation of the authorities. Admittedly, they are not without human weaknesses and their role in the reform movement makes them particularly vulnerable to popular pressures. In their attempt to maintain their reputation, or to pursue the logic of their course of action, they risk exceeding their own competence and unduly exploiting the considerable trust placed in them. They are required, in difficult times, to take upon themselves the responsibility of difficult decisions. It is clear from these demands that self-determined consciousness is only in its infancy; as pride is regained, so will those leaders be rejected who, reverting to old habits, assume the role of benevolent master or father. The new leaders know, as well they should, that if, for one reason or another, they fail in their noble task of contributing to the advancement of the people, they will be the first to feel the anger which will be the outlet for exacerbated frustrations. And yet, it is not they who would bear the main burden of guilt.

(b) Those Most Responsible

Those in authority in all spheres of activity – in government, universities, corporations, labour unions – have a primary responsibility to understand the meaning of the awakening among students, young people, the underprivileged in cities and in underdeveloped areas. They above all attempted for so long, and particularly in the fifties, to dam the flow of new ideas. Then with a sudden about-turn, they encouraged the expression of new aspirations, and in some ways stimulated the current movement towards emancipation. Instead of playing the ostrich or adopting repressive measures, they should now channel this new movement and learn new roles for themselves as ministers, members of Parliament, parish priests, rectors, directors of research institutes, etc.

No one denies, or at least should deny, the need for some form of government. The very complexity of the problems to be solved makes it more than ever necessary to have an organization capable of bringing a variety of qualified persons together, giving them the necessary means to make decisions, and taking action. It has become fashionable to say that the masses should take over political parties and the government to ensure that these institutions reflect their desires and serve their objectives. To the extent that this means that a good government is no longer possible without the people, this argument is completely valid; government programmes can only be successful if they coincide with the views of the groups concerned, which presupposes that these groups have participated in the whole decision-making process from conception of the plan to its implementation. A programme must truly "belong" to the people, not be a bureaucrats' brainwave. This has been very well understood by the Forestry Research Fund of Laval University, directed by André Lafond, which has consistently supported the various phases of Operations "Dignity."

Therein lies the full meaning of participatory democracy. If the rulers refuse to play according to the new rules, the masses will dispense with them and act on their own. Such a situation, the primary responsibility for which would lie with the rulers, would result in the creation of parallel societies, in frustration, chaos, and finally in the extremes of either the most abject apathy or revolution.

(c) The Requisites of Collective Action

So numerous and extensive are the obstacles to social transformations which are created by nature, technology, organizations and by people individually, that their resolution is inconceivable without the help of organizers to co-ordinate available resources, without some kind of systematic and coherent assistance. Despite the astonishing creativity shown by some individuals or small groups of individuals (unfortunately not often enough), the fact remains that a near-monopoly of techno-logical innovation rests with large organizations. And, at least under the present system, most legislative bills and political programmes are drafted by civil servants. Again, a highly integrated system of co-operation between the large private and public organizations is required to determine which factors will bring about the success or failure of a project in a specific sector or region. For example, the creation of stable employment involves many complex operations: devel-opment, management, leadership, marketing, short- and long-term eco-nomic returns, etc.

The path to self-determined consciousness must of necessity go through society as a whole. It involves those in power even more than leaders more immediately concerned. The achievement of self-determination is not the act of a lone champion of an isolated cause, but the fulfilment of one's human potential while remaining an integral part of the great human adventure. Those who have decided to become masters of their own destiny and their immediate leaders both know that their plans will succeed only if those in power assume full responsibility for these plans, so that they cease to be simply the adventures of small, isolated groups and become instead the starting point for vast collective undertakings. Should their expectations not be fulfilled, they and their leaders are determined to proceed alone, whatever the short- or long-term consequences. This constitutes a new fundamental fact which those in authority can no longer ignore with impunity.

Individuals and groups will put little stock in global development programs which fail to take account of their own situation as they perceive it. At the same time, they realize that the coherent and optimal development of a particular area of activity or region must be placed within the context of utilizing the resources and energies of society as a whole. They also realize that, without adequate leadership, the best energies are squandered or, at most, inadequately utilized. The challenge is to ensure that global plans take account of all sectoral and regional considerations; and that everyone, each at his own level and according to his capability, participates in the solution of problems. The piecemeal nature of recent plans for regional development, though sometimes condoned by persons of prestige and organizations of repute and subsidized by the government, emphasizes this problem acutely: how to make the transition from local to regional, and from regional to national consciousness without on the one hand stifling aspirations to self-determination, or on the other encouraging communities to launch into ventures which can only end in failure and frustration. The situation would not have deteriorated to this level if those responsible had taken the right action in time.

The new conditions of collective action raise many important questions. They are all, in one way or another, concerned with the central problem of the re-organization of society, a process which must be sweeping and radical. How is communication to be established between individuals, groups, and authorities in such a way that all required information can freely circulate, and everyone can adequately fulfill his new responsibilities? How can a new orientation be given to intermediary groups (interest groups, political parties, advisory councils, the media) so that society will not eventually grind to a halt? How can the energies of popular movements be channelled towards political action without curbing them or inhibiting the dynamism of the new leaders? How can new life be breathed into governments; how can haughty and arrogant super-bureaucracies and anachronistic hierarchies be abolished without jeopardizing the accomplishment of services essential to the collectivity? In short, how can the essential process of questioning overthrow archaic structures without in so doing destroying society itself? It is certain that, sooner or later, under the implacable momentum of change, the old anchorages will be abandoned. Is it too much to expect of those in power that they will not simply drift like flotsam? If they do,

Towards a Self-Determined Consciousness

37

those who are today clamouring for self-determination will not forgive them.

Self-determined consciousness must be tempered by patience. So many years of retardation cannot be regained in one day. Those in power must prepare the way for a world more accessible and more just. Total justice is a utopia; but it is towards this that mankind, through its manifold tribulations, is tirelessly striving.

3
Historical Background
of Quebec's Challenge to Canadian Unity
by Michel Brunet

Former professor Pierre-Elliott Trudeau, who, thanks to the Ottawa press gallery and the mass media, and by the grace of a majority of the English-speaking electorate, became leader of the federal Liberal Party and Prime Minister of the country, based his 1968 political campaign partly on his self-established claim that there is no Quebec problem in today's Canada. He wished the English Canadian majority to believe that Maurice Duplessis, founder of the Union Nationale party, and his political heirs, helped by a few old-fashioned and narrow-minded French Canadian nationalists whom he had always denounced, were exclusively responsible for the political and social unrest in Quebec since the end of World War II, an unrest which was beginning to make itself felt throughout the whole country in the 1960s. His soothing declarations on an issue that seemed to threaten Canada's unity were received with a sigh of relief by all English-speaking Canadians who were weary of asking themselves, with increasing uneasiness, "What does Quebec want?" and by persons in both French and English Canada who had the habit of indulging in wishful thinking on that subject.

As a political theorist, former Professor Trudeau is free to use a frame of reference that belonged to the Victorian Liberal way of life. But as a political leader called upon to deal with Canada's current problems in the last third of the twentieth century, he should know better. First, he must realize that he would quite possibly never have become leader of a federal party and Prime Minister of Canada if there had not been a Quebec problem. He, himself, is a by-product of this problem, and it will not be solved by denying its existence or pretending that a general and collective submersion in bilingualism "from coast to coast" will drown it. Recent events in Quebec have reminded many thoughtful Canadian citizens that Mr. Trudeau's electoral victory, far from putting an end to Canada's Great Debate of the last decade, has simply further obscured ·the fundamental issues facing the Canadian federation at the beginning of its second century.

The Quebec problem dates from the beginning of European colonization in North America. The French founded Quebec in 1608. One year earlier, the British had established themselves at Jamestown. From the outset, there was a conflict of interests between the English- and French-speaking settlers of the New World; each group pursued opposing collective goals. As early as 1613, the Virginians organized a military raid against the French outposts in Acadia; and in 1628, Quebec was conquered by the British. This first foreign occupation lasted four years. If the Laurentian colony, with a total French population of less than one hundred, had not been handed back to the King of France, there would be no Quebec problem in contemporary Canada.

However, the British had not abandoned the goal of eliminating the French from North America. They were convinced that God had given them a Manifest Destiny on this continent. In 1713, they acquired Acadia, and later deported its French-speaking inhabitants in order to assure the security of Nova Scotia during the French and Indian War. After a long and bitter struggle lasting more than two generations, the leaders of New France, overwhelmed by their old foe, capitulated in 1760. Three years later, the Treaty of Paris recognized that North America belonged to the British. It is hard to say if it was God's decision, but the historian knows that the stronger side had won.

The British American spokesmen who had favoured the conquest of the St. Lawrence Valley, and the imperial leaders who had supported this expansionist policy, fully realized that a majority of the French-speaking and Roman Catholic population, having made a homeland in North America, would choose to remain in the colony. The conquerors had no intention of forcing the *Canadiens* to leave; on the contrary, they knew that their help was needed to develop the resources of the country. However, they were convinced that these new subjects of His Majesty would soon be integrated into the multitude of English-speaking and Protestant settlers, whose arrival they foresaw.

The Royal Proclamation of 1763, and the instructions given to Governor Murray, were based on this assumption that the conquered population would be promptly assimilated. The evolution of this new British colony, it was felt, would be similar to that of New York, first settled by Dutch colonists, and of New Jersey, which had been founded by Swedes. In less than a century, these two distinctive foreign collectivities had melted away. The British conquerors of the St. Lawrence Valley sincerely believed that a similar fate awaited the *Canadiens*.

History, however, rarely repeats itself. The geographical, religious, cultural, and economic conditions in New France were very different from those that the British conquerors had encountered a century earlier in former New Sweden and New Netherlands. The *Canadiens* already formed a collectivity, the members of which were bound together by specific ties of cultural homogeneity. For a century and a half they had lived alone in the St. Lawrence Valley and had dominated the hinterland of North America; from the outset they had waged war against the Iroquois and the British colonists to maintain their separate state. Although finally compelled to bow down before their enemies, they had no intention of renouncing their common goals as a distinctive collectivity on this continent. In proclaiming their loyalty toward the King of Great Britain, they still remained *Canadiens*, animated by a common group consciousness; and, what is more important, they knew that they had the means to express that consciousness.

The colonial administrators and the British government soon realized that the policy proposed for the Province of Quebec by the Royal Proclamation was mere wishful thinking. The factors that had prevented the massive immigration of new settlers during the French colonial period also limited the flow of English-speaking and Protestant colonists that was necessary to bring about the rapid assimilation of the conquered population. Only a few dozen British settlers arrived in the decade following the Conquest. This light immigration, coupled with the agitation in the American colonies, compelled Murray, Carleton, and the British ministers to give some recognition to the fact that the new colony was peopled with *Canadiens*; and incidentally, the *Canadien* leaders were using all their bargaining powers with great skill. The nomination of Bishop Briand in 1766, the consecration of his coadjutor in 1772, and the Quebec Act of 1774, fully demonstrated that the Province of Quebec was not a colony like the other provinces of the British North American Empire.

Most English Canadian historians believe that the decisions then taken by the Imperial government were wrong because they gave birth to French Canadian nationalism – they naturally prefer the expansion of English Canadian nationalism. These historians simply forget that the *Canadiens* already existed as a distinctive collectivity, and they ignore the fact that the measures adopted were absolutely necessary to assure the good administration of the new colony. At any rate, prompt assimilation of the conquered population having been proved impossible for the foreseeable future, the British authorities could only choose among four policies: the deliberate extermination of the *Canadiens*, their deportation, the establishment of a police-state denying any right to the conquered, or some concessions to the *Canadiens* in exchange for the collaboration of their most influential spokesmen in setting up a civil government. Can we blame the British authorities for taking this last course? The most rabid English Canadian nationalist would not dare do so. Accordingly, seventeen years after the Quebec Act, the British government made a fateful decision, the consequences of which are still with us.

The American Independence, and the consequent immigration of Loyalists, altered fundamentally the future of the St. Lawrence Valley and of the remaining British colonies in North America. The projects of the British American expansionists to build a strong nation of their own on this continent were no longer mere dreams. But in order to carry them out, they needed the help of the mother country, and the St. Lawrence Valley had to be made the core of this new British North America. Fortunately for these new nation builders, it was now possible to apply gradually, and with some modifications, the policy outlined in the Royal Proclamation of 1763.

A well-intentioned, but ill-informed and over-worked, Imperial government decided, through the Constitutional Act of 1791, to divide the former Province of Quebec. While the Quebec Act had been a necessity, the creation of Lower Canada was a political mistake, since it gave the *Canadiens* control of a Legislative Assembly on a territory where they were in a majority. This new situation doomed any policy of gradual assimilation to total failure, whereas one would have been feasible if the St. Lawrence Valley had remained united. Through the system of representative government, the *Canadiens* chose new and more responsible leaders, who gave a new impetus to their nationalism, and set more precise nationalist goals. The conviction was strengthened within the conquered population that Lower Canada was its fatherland, and it invited the British Americans who lived there to integrate into the majority group.

The most clear-sighted leaders of British North America soon realized that the error of 1791 should be corrected; but it is always harder to repair a political mistake than to commit one. On the other hand, Louis-Joseph Papineau's lack of political acumen and the Rebellion of 1837-38 proved advantageous to the British Americans. In brief, the nightmare of the English-speaking and Protestant minority of Lower Canada came to an end when Upper Canada and Lower Canada were fused into a single province, United Canada, in 1841.

However, the Union Act repeated the political mistake committed fifty years earlier in introducing the principle of equality of representation between the two sections of United Canada. There were 450,000 inhabitants in former Upper Canada, now called Canada West, and 650,000 in Canada East where most of the French-speaking population lived; but each section was to have forty-two members in the Legislative Assembly. Actually there were some 200,000 English-speaking inhabitants in Canada East; but the British Americans, especially those established amidst the French-speaking and Catholic population of Canada East, were so apprehensive of a Legislative Assembly in which the representatives elected by the *Canadiens* would constitute a majority that they had imposed an undemocratic electoral system. Their hatred and their racism had blinded them to the fact that the total English-speaking and Protestant population of United Canada already out-numbered that of the *Canadiens*. It is true that their numerical superior-ity was still slim, but through political devices such as gerrymandering it would have been easy to limit the representation of the French-speaking voters. Moreover, anyone who had analyzed immigration figures for the preceding twenty-five years could foresee that the scales would soon be permanently weighted in favour of the British Americans.

Through this unequal system of representation, which later became a useful tool in the hands of French Canadian political leaders, and through the establishment of responsible government to which these men contributed, the legislative union of 1841 was transformed into an actual confederation. But its evolution would have been very different if the Union Act of 1840 had set up a representative system based on the total population of all the St. Lawrence Valley.

Another event which had important consequences for the future of Canada was the burning of the Parliament Buildings in 1849 by the British Montrealers. Once more their extremist nationalism misled them. There is no doubt that if the capital of the country had remained in Montreal, Canada's historical evolution during the last four generations would have been different. Ottawa, a provincial and artificial town, could not be, is not and never shall be, a national capital.

The stalemate created in United Canada by racial, religious, and regional conflicts fostered and aggravated by an undemocratic system of representation, the threat of American expansionism, the need to link the St. Lawrence Valley to the Atlantic provinces and to the western part of British North America, and the interests of Great Britain: all these factors convinced political and business leaders in the different British colonies that the time had come to create the Dominion of Canada. Many spokesmen for the British American population favored a legislative union which, they calculated, would best contribute to strengthening the unity of the new country. But the misgivings of the Maritimers and the insistence of French Canadians on protection for their laws, their faith, and their language, led to acceptance of a federal union. One hundred years after the Royal Proclamation and twenty-five years after the Durham Report – two historic documents designed to ensure their complete assimilation – French Canadians were represented as a distinctive collectivity at the bargaining tables in Charlottetown,

Quebec, and London, where contemporary Canada was born.

Since the organization of a Quebec provincial government in July, 1867, French Canadians have gradually become accustomed to self-government and, at the same time, to democracy. To understand this evolution one must remember that they had been deprived of a government of their own since the capitulation of Montreal in 1760 and had never since been free to exercise their democratic right to majority rule in their own territory. They had always been treated as a conquered people and, if not completely assimilated, had nonetheless been obliged to accept the leadership of the British Americans. Even after Confederation, the British Americans had no intention of renouncing their dominant position in Quebec, although the general historical evolution of the St. Lawrence Valley had compelled them to relax somewhat their former hold over the French-speaking population.

Progressively, successive generations of French Canadian leaders over the last century have totally changed their outlook and their frame of reference. They no longer consider themselves as the spokesmen of a minority group whose future in North America depends on the goodwill of English-speaking Canadians – who, incidentally, treat them most of the time just as the British Americans did. They now act as the legitimate representatives of a nationality that can re-negotiate with English Canada the terms on which the union of Canada can be maintained. The new leaders of Quebec have learned that good government in Ottawa by the English Canadian majority is no substitute for self-government in a territory where they have a democratic right to majority rule. Did not English Canada itself come to the same conclusion when its most dynamic leaders compelled the British metropolis and Her Majesty's representatives to grant them responsible government? It was in this process that British Americans became Canadians.

The same process is evident in Quebec. It was inevitable because the French Canadians, living on the shores of the St. Lawrence Valley since the beginning of the seventeenth century, were not completely assimilated into the English Canadian majority; indeed, for more than three centuries they have led a distinctive existence as a collectivity. In fact, there are in Quebec, among the younger generation at least, fewer and fewer French Canadians; the latter are fast disappearing just as the British Americans melted away during the last one hundred years. The French-speaking inhabitants of Quebec are becoming the *Québécois,* and most of the citizens of the Province, whatever their mother tongue, will gradually be integrated into the *Québécois* majority.

The *Québécois* knows that he has a future in North America. He lives at a new pace, in a new mood, and in a new climate. He is opposed to the abuse of power and to entrenched injustice. He already has a sense of having overcome resistance and won victories. He has the will to win. He wants to settle as soon as possible many of the problems which past generations ignored, or did not dare to tackle.

One problem that has practically been solved over the last few years is that of the exact role of the Roman Catholic Church in this new Quebec society. It has been much easier than most observers believed ten years ago to achieve a complete redistribution of power between Church and State. The most difficult task now facing Quebec is to modify radically the pattern of relations between the privileged English-speaking minority and the *Québécois* majority. English-speaking Montrealers and their allies are the only persons in Quebec who still continue to enjoy a special status, and they seem prepared to harden their position in order to preserve their vested interests; they are unable to realize that acquired rights due to historical accident are not necessarily compatible with true democracy. This abnormal and unhealthy situation which has prevailed in Quebec since the British occupation can no longer be supported in these times of decolonization and social democracy.

Strong immediate action is also required to achieve economic expansion and a higher standard of living for the whole population; some effective and bold measures have already been taken and many others will have to follow in the near future. Popular demand for progressive policies in the fields of social security, education, culture, research, natural resources and public investments has compelled the Quebec government to increase its financial resources and to exercise its full jurisdiction. This policy has given birth to the State of Quebec.

Finally, there is the question of Quebec's relations with the federal government and with the other provinces. The *Québécois*, unlike past generations of Canadians, are not interested in fostering bilingualism from Halifax to Vancouver. They believe that it is more realistic to become masters in their own territory than to balkanize the rest of the country by artificially sustaining a few small French-speaking communities in some of the other provinces; these groups are doomed inevitably to assimilation, their empty dreams notwithstanding. The *Québécois* now know that the survival and progress of their distinctive culture have always been, and are now more than ever, identified with the territory of Quebec. They have cast off the illusions of many former French Canadian leaders who, putting their faith in the "revenge of the cradle," believed that the French would one day constitute the majority of the population of Canada. Moreover, they are discovering to their dismay that the numerical superiority of the French-speaking population within

Quebec is being threatened by the assimilation of thousands of immigrants within the Quebec English-speaking minority, and by a decline in the birthrate of the French-speaking population. It is not, therefore, surprising that only two groups in Quebec have given unconditional approval to the recommendations of the federal Commission on Bilingualism and Biculturalism. These are the tradition-minded French-speaking Quebecers who still cherish the out-dated messianic illusion that French Canadians as a collectivity have a future throughout Canada; and the English-speaking Quebecers who dream that only by the development of a bilingual Canada, whatever the cost and consequences of so silly an undertaking, will they be spared the necessity of becoming *Québécois*.

Quebec's challenge to Canadian unity, and the questioning of the leadership of English-speaking Canadians hitherto partially accepted for more than four generations, are no longer simply an internal matter to be discussed only within the frontiers of Canada. In our contemporary world of mass media and instant information, every country lives in a glass house; and its difficulties and problems – especially when it has democratic institutions – cannot long be concealed from international public opinion. Since World War II and the founding of the United Nations, difficulties have arisen for all States or dominant groups controlling the apparatus of government that maintain under their yoke any under-privileged class, coloured minority, colonial population, or conquered national entity. Their politics have been scrutinized, and denounced; they have been adjudged contrary to the Declaration of Human Rights or to the ideals prevalent in this era of decolonization and social democracy. The right to self-respect has modified the old pattern of relations between white and black populations in the United States, South Africa, and Rhodesia; and the right to self-determination has doomed former colonial empires to destruction.

The *Québécois* observed with great interest the process of decolonization in Asia and Africa immediately after World War II. In fact, they have long identified with colonized and dominated peoples. Declarations of loyalty to the monarchy by their official spokesmen notwithstanding – the latter had no choice but to collaborate with their British conquerors – most *Canadiens* applauded when the American colonists rebelled against Great Britain. All the conflicts and wars of national liberation in South America, Greece, Italy, Belgium and Poland during the nineteenth century received the enthusiastic support of most French Canadian political leaders and writers. When English Canada decided in 1899 to support Great Britain in waging the South African War, the *Québécois* sided with the Boers against the British. Their attitude was then considered by the English Canadian majority as a manifestation of backwardness. It was said that they understood nothing about world politics. When World War I broke out, they opposed conscription to defend the British flag and Empire. During the inter-war period, they sympathized with the Irish of Southern Ireland, the Egyptians, the Indians and all the colonial peoples resisting foreign domination. When Canada took part in World War II, French Canadians continued to have the feeling of being pushed around; to them the attitude of the English Canadian majority was that of a benevolent but resolute despot convinced that he knew best what was good for Canada and for Quebec. After the war, they found pleasure in the emancipation of the peoples of Indonesia, the Philippines, Indo-China, India, Tunisia, Morocco, of black Africans and of all other colonial peoples. They discovered, with some amazement, that this time English Canada agreed with them. Who had changed his mind? Not the French Canadians, who for more than ten generations had always been opposed to imperialism.

By then, the *Québécois* were better informed about their situation as a cultural group with a history of survival in the St. Lawrence Valley for three and a half centuries. They were freer to express themselves than former generations who, like all other nationalities or collectivities living under the sway of a dominant group, had developed a "double-thinking" attitude. Accordingly, they discovered that their own case was similar in many respects to that of colonial peoples struggling for independence. When their forefathers had sympathized with down-trodden nationalities, had they not been trying, in a disguised way, to bring to light their own situation? Near the end of the 1950s a few clear-sighted civil servants in the Department of External Affairs began to realize that a delicate situation existed within Canada's own borders. Consequently, whenever the right of dominated peoples to self-determination was discussed in the United Nations after 1956, their interventions became much more prudent. Some out-dated politicians, writers and newspapermen, who could not read the writing on the wall, continued to proclaim that Canada was a heaven on earth, where close and brotherly co-operation existed between the two founding peoples, a unique achievement which was an inspiring example of political wisdom and generous forbearance for all nations in a divided and war-torn world. These empty and boastful declarations only impressed uninformed people, both inside and outside Canada. They often provoked the wrath or hilarity of the new generations of *Québécois*.

The year 1963 marked the explosion of the first F.L.Q. bombs, and since then the Quebec problem has been partially internationalized. Queen Elizabeth's visit to Quebec City in October, 1964; Charles de Gaulle's cry, *Vive le Québec libre* in July, 1967, and his subsequent series of lectures on Canadian federalism and history; the electoral success of the secessionist *Parti Québécois* in April, 1970; and finally the crisis provoked by the F.L.Q.'s kidnappings: all have attracted the attention of the world press. In 1963 and 1964, a handful of young *Québécois* from all classes of society – workers, students, newspapermen, scions of rich and influential families – formed terrorist groups with the aim of arousing public opinion. They achieved their objective of giving publicity to *Québécois* nationalism. Even if these young activists were criticized severely by their fellow-countrymen – primarily questioned was the usefulness of their actions – there is no doubt that a majority of the *Québécois* population were partly in sympathy with them. Realizing that their own freedom of action was very limited, the authorities avoided bestowing the prestige of martyrdom on the young terrorists, who were finally arrested and brought to trial.

Queen Elizabeth's visit in 1964 offered an opportunity for all *Québécois* to let English Canada and the world at large know that their political thinking had changed greatly since the North American tour of King George VI in 1939. Then politicians, the clergy, municipal councils and school children, had been conscripted to acclaim the royal couple. Twenty-five years later the population refused to be mesmerized. When Her Majesty was received there, Quebec City had the appearance of a town occupied by a conqueror; it was a disheartening scene for the royal couple and for all who witnessed it. But it was also very revealing because it symbolized a historic moment, a turning point. Quebec and Ottawa politicians had thoughtlessly implicated the monarchy in an internal, two-century-old crisis marked by the confrontation of two collectivities. It was not a situation that Her Majesty could help; her visit merely served to dramatize it, and accelerated a process that had started a generation earlier. Queen Elizabeth herself fully realized the intricacy of the Canadian political scene; her speech to the Legislature of Quebec reflected great political wisdom in stressing the fact that it was up to the citizens of Canada to solve their own problems and to modify Canada's constitution if it was out-dated.

The invitation to Queen Elizabeth was a political mistake on the part of the Ottawa and Quebec governments. They had misread the new mood of the *Québécois*. They should, for example, have remembered that in 1958 Maurice Cardinal Roy, Archbishop of Quebec, and some French Canadian spokesmen whose thinking was at least one generation behind the times, had been denounced as collaborators, negro-kings, prostitutes and irresponsible individuals when they had proposed the creation of a committee to organize public celebrations to commemorate the second centenary of the British Conquest of New France. The proposal precipitated a general movement of protest, and the project was hurriedly abandoned.

How different had the situation been in 1860 when the first centenary of the British Conquest was celebrated as evidence of a Providential design for the welfare of French Canada!

When President de Gaulle's visit to Quebec during the summer of 1967 was announced, there was a widespread feeling that it would be a spectacular event. The *Québécois* have always admired and loved France; indeed, in the years since the British Conquest and occupation their official spokesmen have often reproached the mother country for having abandoned New France. The clergy of Quebec have long considered that France, after her Great Revolution, betrayed her mission as the "eldest daughter of the Roman Catholic Church"; and they tried to convince the faithful that the Third Republic was a God-less State. But even while they repeated such charges against France and Frenchmen, most of French Canada's traditional élites continued to read French books, newspapers and periodicals, and when they crossed the Atlantic they were eager to visit the homeland of their ancestors. The most modest French Canadian is aware of his family tree, he boasts that his family has lived six to twelve generations in the St. Lawrence Valley, and he is proud of his loyalty to French language and culture. The population as a whole has idealized France, regardless of criticisms by the British conquerors and their French-Canadian collaborators, by the clergy and the traditional élites. *Québécois* have developed a special cult for France, a secret of half-avowed love. The fact that their élites and English Canadians were less enthusiastic towards France was for them an additional reason to be pro-French. That having been said, *Québécois* do have some difficulty in communicating with French immigrants living in Canada, and even distrust them. But the behavior of the *Québécois* toward Frenchmen must not be misjudged; they have so idealized France that they are inevitably somewhat disappointed by the Frenchmen they encounter.

The visit of General de Gaulle fully showed the ambivalent feelings of *Québécois* toward their mother country. That prestigious man represented for them the France of which they have always dreamed; he embodied in their eyes the France of Joan of Arc, of the Catholic Reformation, of Louis XIV, of Napoleon, of Lacordaire, of Pasteur, of Curie and of the atomic age. He was to them the man who had negotiated with Churchill, Roosevelt, and Stalin, and who had defended France's interests when she was prostrate. Called back to power in a time of crisis, he had invited the younger generations to join him in building a new France adapted to the industrial age. In international politics, he had challenged the Anglo-Saxon hegemony of the Atlantic world, and had favoured a policy of détente with China and Russia. Above all, he had displayed statesmanlike understanding toward the former French African colonies claiming their independence, and he had settled the unfortunate Algerian war.

Charles de Gaulle had come to Canada and to Quebec in 1960, but *Québécois* had shown little interest then in his tour; his prestige was not as great, and he was not visiting them, but rather the United States and English Canada. Seven years later, the situation had changed greatly, and the climate was quite different. In July 1967, all *Québécois* were eager to acclaim the great man they admired so much, and to show their deep and abiding affection for France. A honeymoon situation, which had begun with the opening of a Quebec House in Paris in 1961, existed between them and the French leader. Jean Lesage, Liberal Premier of Quebec from 1960 to 1966, and his successor, Daniel Johnson, leader of the Union Nationale party, had each been received by the President of the Fifth Republic as head of a sovereign State. Quebec had signed cultural and mutual-aid agreements with France, agreements which Ottawa had been obliged to recognize as valid. The *Québécois* of 1967 knew that, thanks to de Gaulle, France and Quebec had concluded a true alliance, giving a new dimension to their long struggle to maintain themselves as a distinctive collectivity in the St. Lawrence Valley. When de Gaulle, perfectly aware of the meaning of his gesture, proclaimed "*Vive le Québec libre*," he was simply signalling the high point of the voyage that France and Quebec had begun together in the first half of the seventeenth century. Afterward, the history of Canada and of *Québécois* could no longer be the same. In fact, the situation had already changed before de Gaulle's visit; he simply accelerated an on-going process. De Gaulle did not create the Quebec problem, but his intervention proved that it was much more serious than was thought by those people who indulged in wishful thinking. The French President also drew attention to the historical background of the present situation.

In the Quebec general elections of April 30, 1970, 24 percent of the citizens who went to the polls supported the Parti Québécois, which espouses as its main objective the cause of an independent Republic of Quebec. Counting only French-speaking voters, statistics show that one-third of *Québécois* are ready to proclaim their right to national self-determination. Many revolutionary movements that have changed the course of history did not have as many followers when they first appeared. This result certainly surprised Prime Minister Trudeau, who had thoughtlessly declared a few months earlier that the members of the Parti Québécois merely constituted a "*particule*," a fraction of a faction. Thousands of Canadian citizens began to wonder if they were well-informed on the situation in Québec.

The October Crisis of 1970 brutally demonstrated the weakness of the fabric of Quebec society. The federal authorities, the traditional ruling classes, and the privileged groups committed the fatal error of revealing their state of panic to the *Québécois*; democratic values – the most cherished rights of the citizen, independence of the judiciary, freedom of the press – were trampled upon. The ever-present credibility gap between the French-speaking population of Quebec and its political leaders, who have always favoured a policy of unconditional collaboration with English Canada since the British Conquest, has been dangerously widened. The failure of the Constitutional Conference of Victoria in June, 1971, and the poor economic conditions which now prevail in Quebec, will undoubtedly influence the political thinking of *Québécois*; but, judging by their conduct over the many years since the establishment of a French-speaking collectivity in the St. Lawrence Valley, they will not renounce their own national objectives.

Quebec's revolution – it is useless hiding the fact that there is a revolutionary mood among *Québécois* – requires the rebuilding of the Canadian union. Few *Québécois* doubt that Quebec has to collaborate with English Canada. However, a totally new political equilibrium exists in today's Canada because Quebec, and the French-speaking inhabitants who constitute the majority there, no longer accept the old compromises which were agreed upon by British Americans and French Canadians in the nineteenth century. We are deeply engaged in a long and difficult process from which both a new Quebec and a new Canada will emerge. It is difficult to foresee exactly what form they will take, but there is no doubt they will be very different from the present structures. And they will be the work of the young generations.

4

Quebec and Confederation: Then and Now
by Jean-Charles Bonenfant

In dealing with the subject, Quebec and Confederation, it must be borne in mind that there are many powerful English-speaking people in Quebec and many French Canadians outside Quebec. In most instances, the problems that arise concern French Canadians living in Quebec and their relationship to Confederation, even their place in North America. The subject falls naturally into three parts: French Canadians and the birth of Confederation; the attitude of Quebec to Canadian federalism from 1867 to 1960; and the situation from 1960 to the present.

For a century before Confederation, theoretical projects to unite the British North American colonies in a federal union were common currency among English-speaking political leaders. French Canadians knew few details of such proposals, but since they came for the most part from their political opponents, they equated them often with legislative union. On the other hand, the French-language newspaper, *Le Canadien,* stated on September, 1847, that "they (the French Canadians) confidently anticipate a greater freedom of action in a federation." In June, 1864, federalism ceased to be a subject of academic discussion, and became the main objective of a coalition government led by John A. Macdonald, George Brown and George-Etienne Cartier. The only important group that remained outside the coalition were the French-speaking Liberals of Lower Canada, called the *Rouges*, plus a few English Canadians like Luther Hamilton Holton and Lucius Seth Huntington. A small number of French Canadian and English Canadian Conservatives, including men of stature such as Christopher Dunkin, also remained aloof. Without minimizing the importance of the others, it can be asserted that the only serious opposition to Confederation in the united Canadas was that of the French-speaking Liberals of Lower Canada, led by Antoine-Aimé Dorion.

The opponents of Confederation fought the project for two years, asking repeatedly but in vain for an election on the issue. During the winter of 1865, the Quebec Resolutions, a rough draft of the future constitution, were debated for several weeks in the Parliament of United

Canada in Quebec City. The Legislative Council gave its approval on February 20 by forty-five votes to fifteen, the latter figure including eight Councillors from Lower Canada. Since seven of the eight had been elected rather than being appointed by the Governor-General, they could fairly claim to reflect the views of a large section of Lower Canadian public opinion. In the Legislative Assembly, several divisions were recorded, the most revealing being that of March 10, when the government proposal was approved by ninety-one votes to thirty-three. These figures can be further broken down as follows: in Upper Canada, fifty-four in favour of the measure, eight opposed; in Lower Canada, thirty-seven in favour, twenty-five opposed; among the French Canadians, twenty-six in favour, twenty-two opposed. A resolution to consult the electorate before submitting the project to the Imperial Parliament was rejected eighty-four to thirty-five, the great majority of the latter group being French Canadian members.[1] Thus, it is evident that, even if French Canadian voters could not express their views directly, they indicated through their representatives in Parliament a high degree of opposition to the Confederation plan. On March 14, the Liberal newspaper, *Le Pays*, described the vote as "the most iniquitous act, the most degrading act which parliamentary government has witnessed since the treason of the Irish deputies who sold their country to England for positions, honours, and gold." In contrast, the Conservative newspaper, *La Minerve*, commented on March 11: "The vote in the Canadian legislature marked an important date in the history of Canada. . . . The union of the colonies is the consecration of our political and national existence and the guarantee of our future."

While neither the available statistics nor other sources of information provide conclusive evidence, it seems likely that the majority of French Canadians were favourable to Confederation during the period when it was being formulated, from 1864 to 1867. They already possessed most of the characteristics which, since the principle of nationality had developed, had led people in Europe to dream of independence, and yet they never seriously considered independence as a solution to the political problems they faced. They were, of course, anxious to preserve their group identity. Even though the political system created by the Act of Union of 1840 had been transformed in a manner favourable to them, they recognized that it would have to be altered, since the English-speaking Canadians of Upper Canada could not accept indefinitely their opposition to representation by population. Among the possible alternatives, there was certainly a strong inclination in French Canada towards annexation to the United States, or at least the feeling that annexation was inevitable in the long run, and that it would serve no purpose to resist geographical, economic, and political imperatives. However,

George-Etienne Cartier and the Catholic clergy succeeded in convincing the population of the dangers which annexation would entail for them.

In the years immediately prior to 1867, French Canadians came to accept federalism as inevitable, but did so without having any precise notion of what it implied, either in theoretical or practical terms. Certainly, they would have been incapable of discussing most of the problems it poses to-day; they had no notion of them. They could not imagine, for instance, the potential provincial power in the expression, "Property and Civil Rights," included in Section 92 of the British North America Act, 1867. They could not suspect that this article would be given such importance by the courts. Nor could they perceive all that was hidden in the words "Public Lands, ... Timber and Woods" of paragraph 5 of Section 92, and their relevance in an age of planned economic development.

French Canadians seem to have understood fairly well the powers it was necessary to entrust to the provinces so that Quebec could control its own institutions. Indeed, they were so convinced that the province's jurisdiction would be adequate for that purpose that they gave little thought to ensuring a genuine dual form of representation at the federal level. To understand their attitude, it must be remembered that Confederation was brought about at a time when Canada was still a British colony, and when it was still generally considered that, in principle, the best government was the one which interfered least with the daily life of the people. A hundred years ago, it was not such a serious matter for French Canadians that the federal government was almost completely Anglo-Saxon, since Canada had no international status, and the state intervened little in the economic sector or in areas such as social welfare that affect the individual citizen directly. A more legitimate criticism of the French Canadians of Lower Canada of a century ago is that they failed to understand the precarious situation of the French minorities in Upper Canada and the Maritime provinces. None of these groups was represented at the conference table when Confederation was devised. Also, the fact that the educational rights agreed to were based on religion rather than on language has made their situation more complex and delicate.

Summing up, it can be said that a majority of French Canadians favoured Confederation a hundred years ago because it was the only realistic solution presented to them; and even those who opposed it merely commented that it was premature without offering an alternative. Confederation was achieved because English Canadians had to exist with French Canadians, and the latter could not then become independent. The great majority of nations have been formed, not by

Quebec Society and Politics

people who desired intensely to live together, but rather by people who could not live separately.

How has the situation changed in the subsequent hundred years?

The political history of Canada reveals that Quebec was not the first province to wage constitutional war against the central government. For nearly twenty years after the birth of Confederation, friction between Ottawa and Quebec City was avoided because the Conservative Party was in power in both capitals. However, as a harbinger of things to come, the Quebec Provincial Treasurer, Christopher Dunkin, stated in his first budget speech in 1868 that provincial institutions were as important, if not more important, than federal institutions, and consequently must attract the most trustworthy of politicians. That declaration notwithstanding, the Province of Quebec remained for two decades almost entirely aloof from federal-provincial differences, and gave only modest support to Oliver Mowat, Premier of the Province of Ontario, who is rightly called the "father of provincial autonomy." Outside the Ottawa and Quebec governments, some Quebecers were less reluctant to intervene in the tug-of-war that is inherent in all federal systems. One of these was the young Wilfrid Laurier, who, as a member of the Quebec Legislative Assembly in 1871, launched an attack upon the Conservative régimes in both Quebec and Ottawa, putting forward autonomist views which he was later to maintain in Ottawa. In concluding his speech, Laurier declared:

> It is an historical fact that the federal form was only adopted for the purpose of preserving for Quebec that exceptional and unique position it holds on the American continent. I am jealous to see that this position is preserved intact and I say with the poet: "My cup is not large, but, from my cup, I drink."[2]

Only after Honoré Mercier became Premier of a Liberal government in 1887 did Quebec espouse officially an autonomist position on federal-provincial relations, but since then this position has been maintained with a high degree of consistency.

Mercier's pro-autonomist ideas can be traced to the period of negotiation of Confederation, and they led him to oppose even more vigorously the Conservative government of Sir John A. Macdonald in Ottawa. Soon after taking office he called the first inter-provincial conference in Quebec. The federal government received an invitation to attend, but Macdonald answered sharply that it would be useless to send federal representatives to such a meeting. In order not to displease the Prime Minister of Canada, the governments of British Columbia and Prince

Edward Island also went unrepresented. The resolutions adopted under the influence of Mercier and Mowat at the conference reflect the epitome of provincial autonomy.[3]

The death of Sir John A. Macdonald in 1891, the declining popularity of the Conservative Party, and the arrival in power of Wilfrid Laurier in 1896, mark the end of the first chapter of the history of federal-provincial relations. During that quarter of a century, the legal position of the provinces under the British North America Act, 1867, was made more precise through judicial interpretation and practice. Thanks first to Mowat and then to Mercier, the provinces emerged with increased importance. As good tacticians, these men avoided the pitfalls of insisting on a strict legal interpretation of federalism and of certain ambiguous articles in the constitutional document adopted in 1867. As a result, they were able to widen provincial powers. After 1887 they joined forces to obtain increased subsidies from Ottawa, a struggle only won by their successors in 1907, when the Laurier Administration yielded to their views.

During the first thirty-five years of the twentieth century, the political life of the Province of Quebec was dominated by the Liberal Party under the successive leadership of Lomer Gouin and Alexandre Taschereau, the former holding office from 1905 to 1920, the latter from 1920 to 1935. Both men were imbued with a sense of public order, respectful of the financial powers on which they relied to develop the Province, and were first and foremost good administrators. They shared a deep mistrust of either hurried improvisations or long-range planning, and they opposed any form of adventurousness. And yet Gouin and Taschereau did carry out some astonishing innovations, without always realizing their broader consequences. For instance, they were largely responsible for the transformation of Quebec from a rural to an industrialized society, a step which is at the root of much of the upheaval occurring in the Province to-day. Defensive *vis-à-vis* the world outside Quebec, and fearful of the unknown, they were autonomists in federal-provincial affairs, but they did begin to grasp the importance of the French minorities in other provinces. On the whole, they and their fellow Liberals represented, quite accurately and over a long period, the ideas and feelings of the large majority of the population. The provincial Conservative Party, for its part, found itself weakened because of events at the federal level such as the conscription crisis of 1917, and it never succeeded in becoming a focal point of opposition to the Liberals when opportunities arose.

In the period between the two World Wars, Quebec's leaders adopted a carefully conceived and highly consistent policy in the field of federal-provincial relations. After the relative harmony that marked the years of the Laurier Administration and the first part of the Borden Administration, even transcending the first phase of the 1914-18 war and the imposition of a federal income tax, tension between Ottawa and Quebec re-appeared. The occasion was a federal Order in Council decreeing that provincial bond issues must be approved by the Minister of Finance. The Quebec Cabinet responded with an Order in Council denying the federal government's right to control provincial finances, and declaring that Quebec did not consider itself bound by the decision. This attitude caused considerable concern in Ottawa, where the Minister of Finance, Sir Thomas White, declared that if the Dominion Government did not have the power to control the bond issues of provincial governments, neither did it have the power to control the bond issues of municipalities or of companies operating under a provincial charter. If Quebec's position were accepted, he argued further, the effective powers of the federal authorities in matters of national defence would be seriously restricted. In the end, the regulations under the federal Order in Council were modified to make them more acceptable to Quebec, which thus won its point.[4]

Because of the conscription crisis, the federal government emerged from the war in a weakened state. The provinces, for their part, were beginning a decade of intensive activity. Quebec, for instance, set out to organize a system of public welfare, to develop its hydro-electric resources, and to build a network of roads and bridges. But, notwithstanding its authority and real power, the Government of Quebec remained apprehensive of Ottawa. In a speech delivered in November, 1920, just after succeeding Lomer Gouin as Premier, Alexandre Taschereau denounced the intervention of the federal government in the fields of agriculture, highways, and education, and accused it of reducing the provinces' sources of income.[5] Subsequently, he continued to oppose such encroachments on provincial fields of jurisdiction, albeit somewhat less vehemently after his Liberal friends took power in Ottawa in 1921.

This is the context in which Taschereau's attitude must be assessed with respect to the system of old age pensions created by the federal legislature in 1927. To take advantage of this plan, the provinces were required to pay first half, and later one-quarter, of the cost. Quebec refused to participate, and maintained that the federal law was unconstitutional. It clung to that position even after the Quebec Social Insurance Commission recommended acceptance as a temporary measure, "although it involves dangers of paternalism."[6] The principal criticism of the federal plan by the Commission was that it should have made provision for contributions by potential recipients; hence the warning of "paternalism." Quebec decided only in 1936 to accept the benefits of the federal legislation, having been deprived by then of $25,000,000.00, the amount that the federal government would have paid to the aged of Quebec as its share of the pensions.

There are many other indications of the importance accorded to provincial autonomy by Quebec authorities during this period. For instance, during the federal-provincial conference of 1927, the sixtieth year of Confederation, a conference held to examine the various problems that might arise between the Dominion and the Provinces, Taschereau declared:

> If Canada is to be happy and prosperous, the provinces must be happy and prosperous, and the latter do more for Canada than the federal authorities. The provincial authorities are in closer contact with the people whom they educate, whose roads they build and whose health they care for.

He added that the provinces must strive continually to safeguard their rights, and asked for a more precise delimitation of the taxing powers of the two levels of government.[7]

Two years later, in 1929, the Quebec Legislature adopted a law concerning radio broadcasting, a rather general law empowering the Lieutenant Governor in Council to establish a radio broadcasting station. Another piece of legislation, which was to become law only when promulgated, asserted provincial control over radio broadcasting.[8] At the time, the Quebec Premier had a revealing exchange of letters with the federal Minister of Marine and Fisheries, P.-J.-A. Cardin, concerning the constitutional aspects of radio broadcasting. Eventually the matter was referred to the courts, which declared that the subject fell within the ambit of federal powers.[9]

Undoubtedly, it was the economic depression of the 1930s, and the resulting unemployment, which had the most profound effect on the structure of federal-provincial relations during this period. Some of the poorer provinces found themselves in such a desperate situation that they could not meet their basic responsibilities. The government of Quebec accepted the direct assistance of Ottawa belatedly and with reluctance when some of its municipalities were on the verge of bankruptcy. At the federal-provincial conference of 1935, Premier Taschereau declared candidly: "Our municipalities are at the end of their resources." He insisted that the financial position of the Province was relatively sound, but requested, nonetheless, that it be placed on the same footing as the others. Quebec, he said, must not be called upon to pay more than the others.[10]

Quebec's preoccupation with her autonomy was also reflected in the Taschereau Government's attitude toward Canadian independence from Great Britain. One aspect of the Dominion's gradual evolution to international status as a sovereign state concerned appeals to the Judicial Committee of the Imperial Privy Council. Most French Canadians favoured the retention of the right of appeal, at least in the early 1920s, since they saw in that body a better guarantee of the rights of the provinces than in the Supreme Court of Canada. On this point, Premier Taschereau said in 1921 in Toronto: "In a country possessing as many minority groups as ours, the Privy Council is a safeguard for them."[11] When the Statute of Westminster, 1931, was being drafted in order to give legal form to the sovereignty of the Dominions, Quebec and Ontario made representations to Ottawa to ensure that the new British law would not limit their autonomy. It was on this occasion that the Premier of Ontario, Howard Ferguson, formulated the "compact theory," which claims for the provinces, as the "founding entities" of Canada, the right to be consulted on any changes in the arrangement negotiated in 1867. This argument had already been advanced by French Canadian politicians, and had gained wide acceptance in Quebec, but Premier Ferguson gave it added credence.

Looking back, it is evident that Quebecers, with their traditional autonomist sentiments, were exasperated whenever they felt they were unable to participate in the functioning of the federal system. The formation of the Union government in 1917, and the imposition by it of conscription, are only the most notable of such instances. Quebec's official reaction in this regard reached its peak in 1918 when a motion was presented to the Quebec Legislative Assembly by a Government supporter, J.-N. Francoeur, in these terms:

> This House is of the opinion that the Province of Quebec would be ready to accept the dissolution of the federal pact of 1867, if, in the opinion of the other provinces, Quebec is considered as an obstacle to the union, to the progress and to the development of Canada.[12]

The motion brought about a rather academic debate, and was then dropped without a vote; but almost every speech made on this occasion reflected the strong autonomist feeling that was the dominant and most persistent note in Quebec political life from 1910 to 1935.

Just as Alexandre Taschereau felt freer to express his natural autonomist views when the Conservatives, rather than his fellow Liberals, were
in power in Ottawa, so Maurice Duplessis, when he came to power in
1936 as leader of the Union Nationale, found it easy to express his
Province's traditional outlook with Mackenzie King in office there. He
found a natural ally in Premier Hepburn of Ontario, a Liberal at odds
with the national leader of his party. Duplessis' views on Canadian
federalism were set out concisely in a short document prepared by the
Quebec Government for submission to the Royal Commission on
Dominion-Provincial Relations in 1938.[13] This document reflected the
traditional attitude of Quebec, as indicated by the following extracts:
"Confederation is a pact voluntarily agreed upon and which can be
modified only by the consent of all parties." "It is not from the central
government that the provinces' powers and prerogatives come; it is
rather from the voluntary agreement between provinces that the central
government was born." "The Government . . . does not recognize the
right of the federal government to confer . . . the right of inquiring into
the financial position of the provincial governments (because) . . . each
province in the spheres which are proper to it is an autonomous state,
enjoying all the prerogatives of a sovereign state and in no way subject
to federal authority. . . . To recognize the authority of your Commission
would be to recognize the supremacy of the federal authority in matters
pertaining to the provincial field."

Then war came, Duplessis was defeated, and Adelard Godbout,
leader of the Quebec Liberal Party, came to power. Godbout's opponents have often accused him of having abandoned Quebec's traditional
autonomist attitude. But it is rather difficult to pass judgment on a man
who was governing in exceptional war-time circumstances, when it was
imperative to mobilize all the nation's resources. In the face of serious
outside threats, legal quarrels seemed childish. It should also be borne in
mind that any inclinations Godbout might have had to resist certain
federal policies were mitigated by the fact that the Liberals were also in
power in Ottawa. At any rate, in 1940 Quebec, like the other provinces,
agreed to a constitutional amendment giving the federal government
jurisdiction over unemployment insurance. On the other hand, when
Mackenzie King asked the provinces in January, 1941, to accept the
somewhat centralizing recommendations of the Royal Commission on
Dominion-Provincial Relations, Godbout declared that they required
further study, and remarked that the suggested arrangements implied
serious financial sacrifices for Quebec. In 1943, he joined with the
Leader of the Opposition, Maurice Duplessis, in protesting Ottawa's
decision to delay the decennial redistribution of seats in the House of

Commons until after the war, a delay from which Quebec had most to lose. He even took the unusual step of sending a letter of protest to Prime Minister Mackenzie King, but to no avail.[14]

But the most important decision taken by Adelard Godbout in the field of federal-provincial relations was certainly his acceptance of the war-time tax agreements, which gave the federal government a monopoly of the principal direct taxes in return for subsidies at the 1940 level of provincial income. The Quebec Premier did underline the temporary nature of these agreements by insisting on the inclusion of Article 20, which provided on the expiry of the accord for a reduction of federal taxes on personal and corporate incomes in order to allow Quebec to re-enter those shared tax fields.

Godbout was defeated in 1944, and Maurice Duplessis began his second term of office, marked by frequent and sometimes spectacular clashes with the federal government. Not that he adopted a very different policy from that of certain predecessors, for instance, Mercier and Taschereau; circumstances provided him with more frequent opportunities of taking a strong stand in defence of provincial autonomy, and personal animosities heightened tensions between Ottawa and Quebec City. Generally speaking, the controversy centred around two subjects, taxation and education.

A continuing imbroglio has been created between Ottawa and Quebec because the constitution grants to both the federal government and the provinces the right to collect direct taxes. Difficulties arising out of divided jurisdictions are inherent in any federal system, and the clashes in Canada over tax powers have been merely the most visible manifestations of such difficulties. They did not become apparent in the first years after Confederation because the provinces' activities were relatively limited, and these could be financed to a large extent by federal subsidies. With the increasing state intervention that marks modern society, many fields of provincial jurisdiction took on added importance, and greater financial resources became necessary. At this same juncture of history the federal government found itself obliged to increase its own activities at a rapid rate, first to combat the effects of the economic depression, then to fight World War II, and finally to undertake an extensive development programme. Accordingly, it, too, intervened more in the daily life of the country, particularly in the economic sector, and sought increased revenues. After World War II, Ottawa sought to extend the wartime tax agreements, to maintain a monopoly of personal income, corporation, and inheritance taxes, offering in return increased subsidies. Quebec proved the most reluctant to accept this proposal, creating its own personal income tax in 1954. Quebec taxpayers were then obliged to pay two different taxes on their income, one to the federal, another to the provincial government. The Duplessis administration demanded that Quebecers be allowed to deduct the provincial tax from the federal one. Bitter denunciations were made on both sides, followed by delicate negotiations, at the end of which Quebec emerged largely victorious. Thus was inaugurated the system of both federal and provincial income taxes, which has since become general throughout Canada.

Simultaneously, the field of education gave rise to acute problems between the federal government and the Province of Quebec. In 1951 a federal Royal Commission on the Arts, Letters, and Sciences, better known under the name of its Chairman, Vincent Massey, presented an epoch-making report.[15] The Commissioners drew a distinction which they considered fundamental between formal education and general or out-of-school education, and between culture and what, strictly speaking, is usually called education. On the basis of this distinction, they argued that their investigations encroached in no way upon the rights of the provinces, and that while education as usually understood was the exclusive prerogative of the provinces, the federal government could legitimately take an active interest in cultural matters. Quebec refused to accept this viewpoint. Following its line of argument, the Massey Commission recommended that the federal government assist the universities with direct annual financial grants on a per capita basis according to the population of the different provinces. Ottawa acted on this recommendation. The Duplessis Government accepted the arrangement reluctantly the first year, then asked the Quebec universities to refuse the grants, offering in return some increase in its own subsidies. The situation for Quebec universities was very difficult, and was not alleviated until after the death of Duplessis in 1959, when his successor, Paul Sauvé, reached an agreement with Ottawa.

What can we conclude from this short account of Quebec's attitude to Canadian federalism prior to 1960? First of all, it should be stressed that during most of the period, Quebec was hardly more autonomist than Ontario. Of course, the leaders of a province where French culture is predominant are naturally inclined to express their views in logically structured terms; but let us remember that one of the most famous documents on the compact theory was drawn up by an Ontario Premier.

In order to understand fully the attitude of Quebec, it is necessary to bear in mind that federalism depends on the application of two related principles: the principle of participation and the principle of autonomy. If the first is down-graded, the other assumes greater importance. The political institutions in Ottawa have not always functioned satisfactorily as instruments of federal system, especially for the people of the Province of Quebec. Although representation in the House of Commons is determined on a provincial basis, that body functions in practice as if Canada were a unitary country. Nor does the Canadian Senate reflect the federal reality to the same extent as its American and Swiss counterparts. It is organized on a regional rather than a provincial basis, and its members are too closely tied to political parties to be able to speak impartially for their respective provinces. As for the linguistic situation at the federal level, the practical equality of both languages, and especially of the two cultures, has long since been proved an impossible dream. Even when French is recognized officially, it remains in practice not a working language but a language of translation. Furthermore, administrative concepts, and modes of political thought and action, remain naturally Anglo-Saxon in inspiration. For French Canadians to succeed in the upper echelons of parliamentary and administrative life in Ottawa they have to show exceptional ability, and show it in an environment often culturally foreign to them. These weaknesses in the functioning of the federal system explain why, in the minds of Quebecers, the principle of autonomy seems to have prevailed over the principle of participation. Battles for autonomy by a succession of provincial leaders have merely been a reflection of this state of disequilibrium between the principles.

In a province like Quebec, where race and religion combine with geography and history to produce a distinctive entity, there is naturally a strong inclination to look to the local government as the strongest power base, and this tendency has been accentuated by the difficulties experienced in applying federalism at the national level in Canada. As the State assumes ever-greater importance in the lives of individual citizens, the consequences of this situation are far-reaching. For many years, a deep-rooted instinct led Quebec voters to favour a strong provincial power base, but at the same time to maintain effective representation in Ottawa. Recently, the utility of this presence at the federal level has been increasingly called into question.

The death of Maurice Duplessis marked the beginning of a new act, perhaps the last act of the play. In June, 1960, after a brief interlude under the leadership of Paul Sauvé and then Antonio Barrette, the Union Nationale government was defeated, and Jean Lesage, the leader of the Liberal Party, took office. And so was launched the "Quiet Revolution," marked by major reforms particularly in the fields of education, social welfare, publicly-owned enterprises and the public service in general. These innovations stirred in French Canadians a new sense of enthusiasm and self-confidence; they also greatly strengthened the Province, and engendered a popular demand for a special status within Confederation. In 1966, Jean Lesage was defeated at the polls, but Premier Daniel Johnson, leading a re-invigorated Union Nationale, and his successor Jean-Jacques Bertrand pursued the same objective of reforming and strengthening the Province.

There are three paths open to Quebec today within the federal context: the *status quo*, but with the federal government assuring linguistic duality throughout the country; independence, but with some links with the rest of Canada; and a special status reflecting the "specificity" of Quebec. In my view, the status quo is impossible, since Quebec will no longer be satisfied with being merely one of the ten provinces of Canada, a province like the others. And I am sceptical about the possibilities of political independence. Should it happen, the separatists might soon modify their radical views in the light of realities, and might even find it necessary to rejoin Canada with some form of special status.

As for special status, the third option, the special position of Quebec within the Canadian federal system, existed in fact long before it began to be discussed in theory. It was evident "*in potentia*" in the Quebec Act of 1774. It was recognized in practice in the unofficial federalism which developed under the Union of 1840; and in 1867 it was incorporated, through certain specific provisions, in the British North America Act. Christopher Dunkin, one of the opponents of Confederation, remarked prophetically during the Confederation Debates that these provisions would make Quebec different from the other provinces.[16] A century later, in 1967, T. C. Douglas, leader of the New Democratic Party, declared that in order to resolve the grave problems of the time, the constitution must recognize that Quebec was indeed not a province like the others; and that the distinctive character of Quebec, which none denied, might well lead to special arrangements. The danger with special arrangements is that, if they become numerous enough, they are likely to transform Canada, in the words of Senator Eugene Forsey, into "a simple geographical expression."[17]

On the other hand, we have experienced two crises in recent history as a result of Quebec's determination to follow a distinctive path from that of the other provinces: one in 1954 concerning the introduction of a Quebec income tax, the other in 1965 concerning a special pension plan for Quebec. Neither event shook Canada to the extent that some persons feared; indeed, in retrospect they have lost much of their significance. Thus, one is led to wonder if other arrangements of a similar nature could not be made in order to satisfy the normal aspirations of Quebecers, and to avoid a greater evil. How far it is possible to go without endangering the whole federal system is uncertain; but some steps in this direction would constitute recognition in practical terms of an enduring state of mind in Quebec that transcends political friendships or enmities, and spans the generations from Honoré Mercier to Lomer Gouin, Alexander Taschereau, Maurice Duplessis, Jean Lesage and now Claude Castonguay. The high degree of unanimity that has persisted over the years is convincing evidence that the political problem of Quebec's distinctive attitude towards Confederation is no superficial phenomenon.

It is interesting that some serious English Canadian political scientists have indicated a willingness of late to take some of the risks involved in acknowledging the special Quebec viewpoint. In a brief submitted on January 21, 1971, to the Senate and House of Commons Committee on the Constitution, Professor J. A. Corry accepted the possibility of a republican Quebec within a Canadian monarchical system.[18] This possibility is worth considering. As with other measures designed to meet Quebec's wishes, a republican form of government might be offered to all provinces, with little likelihood that any of the others would accept it. This approach, which I personally support, would recognize Quebec's special status piece-meal, and might well lead to some form of sovereignty. This would not happen precipitately or dangerously, but would rather be the result of a normal evolution. Among possible steps, I even envisage recognition of Quebec's right to self-determination. I hasten to add that acceptance of the principle of self-determination does not imply support for its implementation.

At first glance, my proposal might appear contradictory, since I advocate simultaneously the principle of Quebec's participation in Canadian affairs, and the principle of Quebec sovereignty. It might be argued that I cannot have my cake and eat it, too; but the rules of logic sometimes do not apply to politics. To save a country, it may be necessary to combine all possible solutions, even though they may seem at first glance to be mutually exclusive. Above all, those who deal with this subject must be open-minded; there are not simply the good federalist on the one hand who is always right, and the bad separatist on the other who wants to destroy the country. Nor, I hasten to add, are there simply bad federalists and good separatists. There are, rather, men who, while holding opposite views, are all trying to determine how a few million French-speaking Canadians can find happiness and dignity within Anglo-Saxon America. There may not be an unequivocal answer to the problems of Quebec's relationship with the rest of Canada. Personally, I still have confidence in federalism as a workable formula; but in a renewed federalism, one that admittedly might well lead in the final analysis to the independence of Quebec. As I suggested earlier, separatists might find it more difficult than they anticipated to achieve complete separation; and, moderating their views, they might find it advisable to renew Quebec's relationship with Canada.

A large number of French-speaking Canadians in Quebec wish to endow their state, as they already call it, with very extensive powers; and they are developing the necessary institutions to use them. But they also want to remain Canadians, to participate in the operation of federal institutions. Reconciliation of those two opposite aspirations is not easy; it presupposes a great deal of imagination, flexibility, and even humility on the part of our politicians, a breed of men who normally strive for power and personal prestige. Yet, federalism is not a system that peoples adopt because it is easy to practice, but because it is necessary. And it must be applied justly, intelligently, and systematically. The fact that this has not always been the case in Canada has greatly increased our present difficulties. We have let circumstances, constitutional conventions, the legal pronouncements of an overseas court, even historical prejudices, determine the course of events; we are now suffering the consequences of those attitudes and processes.

It is almost impossible to determine whether it is already too late; but if it is not, we should attempt in the coming years to draft a formal but flexible constitution which would recognize the Canadian duality. This constitution should recognize the special character of Quebec and of any other important area in Canada, even to the point of accepting, subject to certain conditions, the principle of self-determination. I repeat that self-determination does not necessarily mean independence. Legal texts do not have any magical powers; but many people like them, and they give a bad conscience to those who violate them. Through reading the first ten amendments of their constitution, the Bill of Rights, Americans have come to place their trust in them. Words often stimulate reflection and inspire new ideas, even action.

Notes

1. The details are found in *Parliamentary Debates on the Subject of the Confederation.* Quebec, 1865.
2. Quoted in *Report of the Royal Commission of Inquiry on Constitutional Problems,* Vol. 1, Province of Quebec, p. 63, 1956.
3. *Dominion-Provincial and Inter-provincial Conferences from 1887 to 1926.* Ottawa, 1951, p. 50.
4. *The Canadian Annual Review,* 1918, p. 478.
5. *The Canadian Annual Review,* 1920, p. 629.
6. *Quebec Social Insurance Commission: Fifth Report,* Quebec, 1933.

7. Cf. *Proceedings of Dominion-Provincial Conference,* 1927. Official fields of discussion, p. 25.

8. *An Act Respecting Radio Broadcasting in the Province,* 19 Sco. V, Chapter 31.

9. *The Canadian Annual Review,* 1930-31, p. 157.

10. *Proceedings of Dominion-Provincial Conference,* 1935. *Record of Proceedings,* pp. 51-52.

11. *The Canadian Annual Review,* 1921, p. 234.

12. A. Seward and W. E. Playfair, Quebec and Confederation: A Record of the Debate of the Legislative Assembly of Quebec on the Motion proposed by J. N. Francoeur.

13. Quoted in *Report of the Royal Commission of Inquiry on Constitutional Problems,* Vol. 1, Province of Quebec, 1956, pp. 132-33.

14. Cf. *Report of the Royal Commission of Inquiry on Constitutional Problems,* Vol. 1. Province of Quebec, 1956, pp. 157-60.

15. *Report of the Royal Commission on National Development in the Arts, Letters, and Sciences.* Ottawa, Queen's Printer, 1951.

16. *See Le Devoir,* May 15, 1967.

17. Translation from *Le Devoir,* March 16, 1967.

18. *Minutes of Proceedings and Evidence of the Special Joint Committee of the Senate and of the House of Commons on the Constitution of Canada,* Third Session, Twenty-eighth Parliament, issue 36, Jan. 21, 1971.

5

Political Institutions and Quebec Society
by André Larocque

In political science literature, political institutions occupy an important and perhaps exaggerated position. Whole libraries are devoted to scrupulously detailed descriptions of their operations; the long tradition of legal interpretation, out of which modern political science in part developed, has helped to endow the expression "political institutions" with strong connotations of tested wisdom, stability and incontrovertible legitimacy. Many of our university courses are in effect disguised initiations to good citizenship: they teach reverence for, rather than understanding of, the British or American form of parliamentary government. The fact that these two "models" are to be found alongside other European systems in our innumerable studies of comparative institutions may contribute to our knowledge of the nuts and bolts of government in various parts of the world, but it contributes relatively little to a thorough understanding of the basic relationships between a dynamic community and its institutions.

Perhaps the time has come to question whether the political institutions of a country do indeed constitute a formal governmental organization, an authentic set of rules collectively accepted to ensure harmony and prosperity in the community. Could they not be, in fact, a complex but convenient instrument at the service of politicians, an instrument which allows them to exercise unimpeded authority surrounded by a psychological aura of sacrosanctity, ensuring the passive acceptance, if not the willing co-operation of the population?

Quebec is an excellent testing-ground for these and related questions. How genuine and deep are the bonds between Quebec society and its present imposed political institutions? Is Quebec society really attached to these institutions, and to the institutions of a federal Canada? Are there any special implications in the fact that Canada's federal institutions bring two important ethnic groups face to face?[1] Can these long-established institutions act as either accelerator or brake on a society which, in the space of ten years, has experienced sweeping change, a profound re-orientation of its collective consciousness? What are we to think of the argument of politicians,[2] and even of political scientists, who at one and the same time appeal for popular support for existing Canadian institutions and yet, faced with the prospect of major changes, claim that the population is preoccupied with bread-and-butter issues and is completely indifferent to institutional problems?

Quebec is an interesting case study of political institutions. First as a French trading colony, next as a colony of the French Crown, and then as a colony of the British Crown, its institutions were imposed by outside authority on the population. The parliamentary struggles and even the armed confrontations of the nineteenth century revolved for the most part around the claims of the *petite bourgeoisie* to the Catholic religion and to the right to speak the French language within the existing political institutions. From 1867 to 1960, a long succession of Liberal and Conservative governments, supported by the Church hierarchy and based on the rural vote, provided Quebec with ultra-conservative leadership, raising the flag of provincial autonomy for purely electoral purposes, never to establish a truly autonomous government. But in 1954, the historic clash between Prime Minister St. Laurent and Premier Duplessis opened the door to a true political power struggle. The death of Maurice Duplessis in September, 1959, the 100-day Administration of Paul Sauvé, and the inauguration, on June 22, 1960, of the Lesage Administration – the first Quebec Government to have an essentially urban base – created a new situation in which the political institutions of Quebec became of primary importance to a society attempting to translate its new collective consciousness into political power.

Analysis of political institutions in Quebec can be divided into three parts, corresponding to these three historical periods: the period when political institutions were imposed on the population from outside, while local polemicists and analysts discussed whether or not they should be accepted; the period of ineffective government that lasted until the explosion of 1960, a date that marks the establishment of the first truly Quebec institutions; and, finally, the present period, when the whole population is going through a process of self-examination and challenging existing social, economic, and political institutions, including the foremost of those political institutions, the constitution itself.

The Mating of a French Society with British Parliamentary Institutions

This section deals with the confrontation, on both practical and ideological planes, between those persons who recommend, and those who oppose, the continued acceptance of British institutions by Quebecers. Our objective is to identify the main political approaches which underlay basic positions in the past, and which, even more important, are still an unspoken but determining factor as Quebec society faces new choices to-day. Four attitudes corresponding to periods of history are clearly discernible: immediate acceptance of British institutions as an unexpected source of enrichment; passive acceptance of the inevitable; calculated acceptance, accepting or rejecting certain aspects as circumstances dictated; and finally, rejection pure and simple. Besides influencing crucial decisions in the past, each of these attitudes is evident, and has its proponents and adversaries, in the all-important current debate concerning the future of Quebec.

Throughout its history, Quebec has had, broadly speaking, eight sets of political institutions. Created as a commercial colony in 1617, New France was ruled successively by the *Compagnie de Canada,* the *Compagnie de Caen,* and the *Compagnie de Nouvelle France* or *Compagnie des Cent Associés.* The principal governing body in the colony was the *Conseil de la Nouvelle France,* which was made up entirely of appointed members until 1657, when some of the councillors were elected for the first time. The Roman Catholic Church was associated with the political authorities through representation in this Conseil starting in 1648. In 1663, under Louis XIV, Colbert dissolved the *Compagnie des Cent Associés* and New France became a French Crown Colony, ruled by a sovereign council under the chairmanship of the Governor and the Intendant. This system of government lasted until September 13, 1759, when Quebec capitulated to the British troops.

In 1763, following four years of military rule, King George III turned the Province of Quebec into a British Crown Colony. Catholics were excluded by the oath of allegiance from holding public office. In 1774, significantly two months before the Philadelphia Congress, the Quebec Act created an appointed Legislative Council, restored the French Civil Code, and granted religious freedom. The Constitutional Act of 1791 divided the colony into two provinces, Upper Canada (Ontario) and Lower Canada (Quebec), each with a Lieutenant-Governor, a Legislative Council appointed by the King, and an Assembly of fifty elected deputies; this document marked the first step towards a representative government. In 1792, an Executive Council appointed by the King was added to this set of institutions. After 1792, both provinces were the scene of continuous parliamentary struggles for ministerial responsibility under a system of responsible government. A long series of political crises culminated in 1837 in open rebellion, with William Lyon Mackenzie leading the insurrectionary

Quebec Society and Politics

forces in Upper Canada, and Louis Joseph Papineau in Lower Canada. The *guerre des patriotes,* as it came to be known in Lower Canada, was marked by clashes with the British troops, in particular at Saint-Eustache, Saint-Denis, and Saint-Charles-sur-Richelieu. On February 18, 1838, Papineau proclaimed the "Republic of Lower Canada" at Noyan, near the American border; shortly afterwards, the Imperial Government despatched Lord Durham to carry out an investigation into the political situation in the colony.

The Durham Report became the basis of a new constitution, the Act of Union, which took effect on February 18, 1841. The two provinces were united under a single Governor, an Executive Council that was not made responsible to the legislature, a Legislative Council appointed by the King, and a Legislative Assembly. The latter was composed of eighty-four deputies, an equal number from Canada West (formerly Upper Canada) and Canada East (formerly Lower Canada), notwithstanding the fact that their population was 450,000 and 650,000 respectively. The struggle for responsible government continued, with Louis Hyppolite Lafontaine playing the leading role among French-speaking Canadians, Robert Baldwin among English-speaking Canadians; they achieved their objective in 1847. The government of United Canada was marked by a high level of governmental instability, with cabinets succeeding one another in rapid succession. Finally in June, 1864, a coalition government formed under the joint leadership of John A. Macdonald and George-Etienne Cartier was able to survive for an extended period. It called the Charlottetown and Quebec Conferences, respectively, in September and October, 1864; and brought about the British North America Act, adopted by the Imperial Parliament on July 1, 1867. This document, the present federal constitution of Canada, accorded to Quebec and to all the other provinces the political institutions of classic British parliamentary government, and defined provincial powers in Articles 92 and 93.

Thus, under French rule, Quebecers had only a bare introduction to elective institutions. The British, for their part, were very slow to transfer their form of parliamentary government to British North America, and, at most stages, they did so only under the pressure of events; for instance, in the face of Quebecers' sympathy for the American revolutionaries in the 1770s, the paralysis of existing institutions, and the demands of the United Empire Loyalists. Quebec's experience of modern political institutions has been limited to institutions which were alien to its traditions and constituted a break with its past.

We mentioned earlier the four principal attitudes in Quebec towards politics and political institutions. Pierre Charbonneau is probably the most articulate spokesman of those who believe that the implantation of British political institutions was a somewhat miraculous blessing for a people condemned by their traditions to a perpetual authoritarianism. In a very explicit statement, he has defended not only British parliamentary government, but also the British Crown. In his view, New France was condemned to theocracy and authoritarianism; then Great Britain bestowed democratic institutions on the colony.

> We had two choices in 1759: to disappear as a people by being assimilated to the English conqueror or to accept integration with certain preliminary conditions, such as the safeguard of our fundamental rights, that is freedom of language and religion, and this meant in reality being inserted into a governmental system that, even in 1759, was directed towards democracy. For reasons easy to understand, we chose the second solution but we never accepted it more than theoretically and formally. Once that solution had been chosen, we should have adapted ourselves to the political institutions of England and made an all-out effort, beginning by nourished and sustained teaching, to understand their profound significance and to learn their functioning; but our thinkers and leaders had no other pre-occupation than to sabotage those institutions by preaching hatred of their authors and by exposing nationalist theories of anti-democratic inspiration and our politicians had no other ambition but to profit from the liberties and rights offered by those institutions to defend narrow interests and in the end to make sovereign mockery of them.[3]

While this attitude is shared by a decreasing number of Quebecers, it did have strong support in the past, particularly among the French-speaking *bourgeoisie* and church authorities. The latter espoused it in eloquent terms as an alternative to the sort of régime that would have prevailed if New France had remained attached to France after 1760, subject to the "nefarious influences" of the French Revolution, the Commune, religious strife and governments of free-masons! Charbonneau's arguments have more support among English-speaking Canadians. In some "British" and royalist circles, and among so-called left-wing intellectuals, British parliamentary institutions are synonymous with freedom and democracy, while the Quebec community, poorly integrated into this set of institutions, is considered synonymous with backwardness, a rural population clinging to a medieval ideology, a stronghold of obscurantism and political opportunism.

This viewpoint is relatively normal on the part of members of the

Quebec ruling class, since the parliamentary system reinforces their authority; its popularity within the English-speaking population is more surprising. For instance, would-be enlightened persons, such as some members of the Waffle wing of the New Democratic Party, measure Quebec's political maturity according to criteria which, although familiar to them, bear little real relationship to Quebec society.

A second basic attitude identified was that of passive acceptance. In other words, history, reflecting the designs of some higher authority, brought Quebec society and British institutions together and integrated them. This interaction of interest groups or classes, marked by carefully calculated concessions on the part of the British authorities to one group and then to another, is well described in a massive study by Fernand Ouellet.[4]

> In terms of socio-economic history, neither 1760 nor 1763 marks a beginning or a decisive turning-point in the evolution of the Province of Quebec. ...[5]

And again:

> In 1774, every factor drew the clergy and the seigneurs into close cooperation with the government. [For instance] the belief in absolute monarchy by divine right [and] ... the principle of the union of Church and State. ... As for the nobility, it has always considered military service as one of its basic social functions.[6]
>
> The introduction of parliamentary government (1791) did not mean a complete break with the past. It was a compromise between diverging interests and aspirations. ... The strengthening of the bourgeoisie, the Loyalist immigration, and the American threat required a re-assessment of past choices. This is why, although there was no complete break with the past, the necessary reforms were adopted.[7]
>
> The Union government (1840), particularly some of its provisions, was designed to obviate traditional conflicts. The primary considerations were to avoid the recurrence of political anarchy and to prevent French-speaking Canadians from blocking the reforms demanded by the British minority, or more specifically, by the requirements of the Canadian economy and the new Canadian society.[8]

The integration to which Ouellet refers was clearly of a socio-economic character. The evolution of political institutions had no importance except as it reflected the opening of new paths to economic success. The basic preoccupation was with material progress, but for the ruling class alone; and parliamentary government was a sort of chess-board, with the political institutions as pawns, in its quest for influence. Historians such as Ouellet and Alfred Dubuc employ this interpretation of the past in opposition to the traditional nationalistic school of thought. So do some social scientists, such as Hubert Guindon, when they explain the present evolution of Quebec as the emergence of a new middle class, and the constitutional debate as a cover for its drive for political power and prestige.

The third attitude, one of calculated acceptance, is essentially political, with overtones of cynicism. Political institutions are seen as instruments of power; and while British institutions have served first and foremost to enable the British authorities to impose their will, they have more than once lent themselves to the manoeuvres of Quebec leaders. Political institutions are important for every society, but if society is to benefit from them, it must make good use of them rather than vice versa, discarding them if necessary.

In many respects, the most explicit spokesman of this attitude is Pierre-Elliott Trudeau. In a study published in 1962[9] while he was active in the New Democratic Party, he declared:

> The purpose of the Royal Proclamation of 1763 was complete assimilation of the French Canadians.[10]
> .... French Canadians were initiated into the sanctuary of representative government, by the Constitutional Act of 1791, they discovered that it did not mean majority rule through an elected assembly, but rule by the representatives of the conquering minority, nominated to the Executive and Legislative Councils.[11]
> The history of democracy in Lower Canada from 1793 to 1840 was that of one long process of warping.[12]
> ... they (the French Canadians) could hardly be expected to greet as the millennium the advent of representation by population in 1867, which could only mean continued domination, but this time by an English-speaking majority.[13]

Trudeau's analysis leads strangely to a fork in the road of history, as does Pierre Charbonneau's, but then they diverge.

How then were the French Canadians to use the arsenal of democratic "fire-arms" put at their disposal? There were two possibilities: sabotage of the parliamentary works from within by systematic obstruction which, like the Irish strategy at Westminster, might lead to Laurentian Home Rule; or outward acceptance of the parliamentary game, but without any inward allegiance to its underlying moral principles. The latter choice prevailed, no doubt because the years 1830 to 1840 demonstrated that sabotage would lead to suppression by force. Moreover, a show of co-operation would have the added advantage of permitting French Canada to participate in the governing councils of the country as a whole.[14]

.... French Canadians would never settle for anything less than absolute equality of political rights with the English Canadians, a demand which, as I shall show below, was never seriously considered by the Colonial Office before the advent of responsible government, nor by the English-speaking majority since then. In brief, one-third of the nation disagreed with the common good as defined by the other two-thirds. Consequently parliamentary government was unworkable, for, given this situation, there arose a fundamental cleavage between a majority and a minority which could therefore not alternate in power.[15]

This conclusion is important, and has many implications; it appears to explain why the writer decided to "participate in the governmental councils of the country as a whole," including the highest elective office. It also reflects one of the fundamental postulates of the Parti Québécois:[16] institutions must serve the majority; confrontation between a permanent majority and a permanent minority within a set of institutions makes them inoperative. Whether it is evoked to defend federalism or independence, this affirmation is prominent in the present debate, since it encompasses the new concept of harmony between a set of institutions and the society they are designed to serve. The notion of a specific set of institutions designed to meet the requirements of a specific society has inspired a wide range of constitutional proposals, including special status (proposed by Paul Gérin-Lajoie), associate states (proposed by the Saint-Jean Baptiste Societies before opting for total sovereignty for Quebec in 1968), and national independence (the official position of the Parti Québécois, 1970).

National independence is synonymous with the fourth attitude towards British political institutions in a French community: their rejection pure and simple. The option of independence, usually called 'separatism' in English, has always existed in Quebec.[17] At times expressed by isolated intellectuals, at times through armed revolt, the independence movement took the form of a group of intellectuals in the 1930s (André Laurendeau, Jean-Louis Gagnon, etc.), then of a series of political parties: for instance, the *Rassemblement pour l'Independance Nationale* and the *Ralliement National*, both of which participated in the general elections of June 5, 1966, and the Parti Québécois, which participated in the general elections of April 29, 1970. Although the programs of these movements and parties varied widely, they all contained one important element: the conviction that there is a complete lack of harmony between an existing—or emerging—society and the political and other institutions which are—or should be—its framework, its tools, its indispensable aids.[18] This political consciousness of a society as it examines its way of life and its organization is central to our argument. The heritage of the French *régime* is, if anything, a feeling of complete political passiveness, of subjection to God and King. The first British institutions were not chosen, but imposed from outside. Those introduced in the nineteenth century were also imposed, but this time with the self-interested complicity of the local élite rather than through military conquest. In the circumstances, the population as a whole had necessarily a deep-seated feeling of alienation, of being far removed from political matters. For the élite, whose presence was necessary to the British for the maintenance of stability, notably in periods such as the American Revolution, several strategies existed: to accept the *status quo* completely, to adapt themselves as much as possible, to be flexible and shrewd in order to derive maximum benefit from the existing situation, to reject the system intellectually, or, finally, to reject it by force of arms. The people as a whole did remain *Canadien*, indeed the only true *Canadiens*, but this feeling of identity bore no relationship to political power. *Canadien* meant the soil, the parish, acceptance of the protective role of the Catholic Church, and a hard but cohesive existence centred around family life. But political power was completely absent, particularly that subtle and comfortable feeling that results from a community having its own, tailor-made political institutions.

The Awakening of a People
to Political Realty: The Quiet Revolution

Although legally the British North America Act was adopted in London, politics after 1867 were controlled from Ottawa. There are probably less than one hundred Quebecers who could list the Quebec Premiers who held office during the long and dull period between 1867 and 1935. Chauveau, de Boucherville, Joly, Marchand, Parent, Gouin, Taschereau, to name only the major ones, some of them Liberals and some Conservatives, came and went without lustre in the Legislative Assembly. The first thirty years of Confederation, from 1867 to 1897, were years of Conservative rule, except for the temporary hiatus provided by the unusually dynamic Honoré Mercier, and they passed without major problems. Then followed forty years of nominally Liberal, but actually conservative rule, from 1897 to 1936: a period dominated by Alexandre Taschereau, with the support of the rural élite, the religious élite, and the English-speaking financial élite. The relative insignificance of political institutions in Quebec's daily life was reflected in the abstract debates of the intelligentsia, who discussed whether Confederation was based on a compact or a law, or whether the Legislative Assembly was really the type of institution its name implied.

The overthrow of the Liberal Government in 1936 by Maurice Duplessis and the Union Nationale, (an alliance between the Conservative Party and the progressive wing of the Liberal Party, the *Action Libérale Nationale*), resulted in nationalism becoming firmly entrenched in Quebec City. Thus, Quebec countered the report of the federal Royal Commission on Dominion-Provincial Relations, a guide to a centralized federalism, with the report of the provincial Royal Commission on Constitutional Matters, a guide for an autonomous French Catholic Quebec. The Liberal administration, which came to power in 1939 as a consequence of the war situation and lasted until 1944, floundered lamentably on the conscription issue. The fierce opposition of the French-speaking population in Quebec to compulsory military service made it possible for Duplessis to resume power, this time under his true colours, the same ones that had spelled political success for Taschereau. Except for the important confrontation between Louis St. Laurent, Prime Minister of Canada, and Maurice Duplessis, Premier of Quebec, in 1954, as a result of which Quebec was able to enter the vitally important personal income tax field, the long rule of the Union Nationale was characterized by the struggle for the preservation of the linguistic and religious rights of Quebecers.

Maurice Duplessis died in September, 1959, and his natural political heir, Paul Sauvé, took his place. Sauvé adopted the slogan, "Henceforth," raising hopes for change, as yet ill-defined; but he died on January, 1960, after only one hundred days in office. He in turn was succeeded by Antonio Barrette, who found himself with a divided Cabinet and the heavy inheritance of a serious scandal, in which a number of ministers were implicated, relating to the sale by the state of a natural gas network to private interests. He could not withstand the Liberal slogan, "It's time for a change"; and on June 22, 1960, Jean Lesage led to power, for the first time in the history of Quebec, a political party based essentially on the urban vote and supported by an élite composed for the most part of intellectuals.

The years 1960 to 1970 were marked by the construction of a truly modern state. Within the general framework of British parliamentary institutions, which were more or less unquestioned, Quebec adopted its first set of political and administrative institutions, and began to create the first truly Quebec political power. With a rapidly increasing budget, the Lesage Administration established in 1961 a hospital insurance scheme, an Economic Planning Council, a Department of Cultural Affairs, including an Office of the French Language, and an Arts Council. It also set up a Royal Commission to recommend reforms in the school system. The next year, at the instigation of René Lévesque, Minister of Natural Resources, the Government decided to nationalize the eleven electrical power companies in Quebec. This proposal aroused the opposition of business circles, and was the main issue in the election campaign which resulted in the re-election of the Liberals on November 14, 1962, with an increased majority. This outcome took on great symbolic meaning in Quebec political life as the first major economic victory of the population over English-speaking private enterprise. In this same vein, the *Société Générale de Financement*, and the *Bureau d'Aménagement de l'Est du Québec*, the first regional planning organization, were created in 1963. A new labour code was also introduced in 1964, an important innovation in a province widely known for its reactionary views with regard to labour; and, as a very important corollary, the civil servants, whose numbers were rapidly increasing because of the new activities of the state, were permitted to form unions. History will probably record that the most significant action of the Quiet Revolution was the creation in 1964 of the Department of Education, and the consequent transfer of responsibility for education from the church to the state. During the Lesage Administration, Quebec's annual budget grew from 600 million to over two billion dollars; health, education, and welfare replaced roads and agriculture as top priorities, and Quebec was so well launched on the road to becoming a modern state that the process could no longer be stopped.

The surprise defeat of the Liberal Government on June 5, 1966 was interpreted by many as a popular reaction against the Quiet Revolution and as a return to the gloomy conditions that had marked the earlier Union Nationale administration. Under the new Union Nationale leader, Daniel Johnson, such predictions proved highly erroneous. The electoral statistics indicate that, while Johnson was a superb electoral strategist, public opinion – which makes and unmakes revolutions – gave less support than in 1962 to the Union Nationale. Its share of the vote dropped from 42.1 percent to 40.9 percent while the Liberal share fell from 56.4 percent to 47.2 percent. Thus, the Union Nationale did not defeat the Liberal administration by taking away from it a slice of the popular vote; the outcome was rather the result of the nuisance effect of the two separatist parties, the *Ralliement National* and, even more, the *Rassemblement pour l'Indépendance Nationale*. Together, they garnered 8 percent of the popular vote, and brought about the defeat of Liberal candidates in a number of constituencies. Yet these two parties, particularly the RIN, were dedicated to speeding up the Quiet Revolution, not to stopping it. Their goal was not to retard the construction of a national state in Quebec, but, on the contrary, to develop it as an independent national entity.

In fact, the new Union Nationale administration continued the Quiet Revolution, and did so with greater zeal than the Liberals had shown at the end of their period in office. The Department of Education remained intact, and continued to receive top budgetary priority; between 1967 and 1970, 34 General and Vocational Colleges (CEGEPs) were created, replacing the church-owned classical colleges. In 1970 a state university, the *Université du Québec*, was founded, with campuses throughout the Province, and also the *Ecole Nationale d'Administration Publique* in Quebec City. In other fields, *Radio-Québec*, the Department of Inter-governmental Affairs, and the Department of Public Service, were all established in 1967; and the Department of Financial Institutions, Companies and Co-operatives and the Department of Immigration in 1968. Daniel Johnson crossed swords on several occasions with Pierre-Elliott Trudeau at federal-provincial conferences; he also published an explosive manifesto, *Equality or Independence*. He died in late 1968, and was succeeded by Jean-Jacques Bertrand.

Towards the end of its term, the Union Nationale administration created the Department of Communications and the Office of Planning and Development. Then, prior to its major defeat on April 20, 1970, it had the Legislature pass the controversial Bill 63, recognizing the right of English- and French-speaking parents to decide the language of education of their children. This legislation ignored the fact that the French-speaking population of Montreal lives under the constant threat of becoming a minority because of its decreasing birth-rate, the influx of immigrants, and its inferior economic status. Following a stormy public debate on this Bill, what will probably prove to have been the last Union Nationale administration called general elections for April 29, 1970. The results were devastating: the Union Nationale's proportion of the popular vote fell from 40.9 percent to 19.8 percent, and its number of seats from 58 to 17. Another page of Quebec's history had been turned.

In discussing this important chapter of Quebec's political history, some reference must be made to the development of relations with the outside world and, first and foremost, with the 30-odd states and the 160 million people that make up the French-speaking world.[19] This was not the first time that Quebec had tried to make its presence felt on the international scene as a distinct entity, but only in the 1960s did it take steps of sufficient significance to create problems for the federal government. Following the election of the Liberals in 1960, Quebec began to develop a true foreign policy. In 1961, Paul Gérin-Lajoie, one of the most influential ministers of the Lesage Government, declared that Quebec alone was empowered to conduct international relations, including the signing of international agreements, in fields allocated to provincial sovereignty under the British North America Act. Premier Lesage was received as head of the Quebec state in Paris, general delegations were opened abroad, a general agreement for cooperation between France and Quebec was signed, and an interministerial Franco-Quebec Committee was established. In April, 1967, a Department of Inter-Governmental Affairs was created; the law defined its functions as "overseeing all relations between the Government of Quebec, its departments and agencies, and other governments or agencies, in accordance with Quebec's rights and interests."

It is in this context that the visit to Quebec in July, 1967 of General Charles de Gaulle, President of the French Republic, must be understood. His famous cry, *"Vive le Québec libre!"* in response to wildly popular acclaim, echoed around the world, and gave many countries their first indication of the changes that had taken place within Quebec. As a result of de Gaulle's cry for freedom Ottawa adopted a more intransigent attitude on the subject of Quebec's initiatives abroad. Tough negotiations took place concerning the role of Quebec in a proposed association of French-speaking countries. In the end, an understanding was reached: Canada alone was empowered to sign the international convention establishing the *Agence de coopération culturelle et technique*, the organization consisting of thirty-three French-speaking states; Quebec was authorized to participate fully in the Agency, but with prior agreement from the Canadian federal authorities. While Canada alone was recognized as a signatory power, the very creation of the Agency was a step forward for Quebec, and Jean-Marc Léger, a militant separatist, became its first Secretary-General.

The decade 1960-70 was marked by feverish development in the Province of Quebec, which became, in common parlance, the State of Quebec. The verbal battle for provincial autonomy gave way to the construction of a modern state. The government built up a competent public service which, in turn, organized itself in trade unions. Whereas economic matters had previously been left to others, the state began to acquire the tools of economic action through such measures as systematic planning, utilization of public savings according to governmental priorities, and development of the powerful network of *caisses populaires*, or savings banks, which serve 67 percent of the adult French-speaking population of Quebec. In a country where religious practices and family structures resulted in a social philosophy essentially different from that of English Canada and the United States, detailed studies were made in areas of vital interest, such as the report on social welfare by the Boucher Commission, and the splendid and monumental report on health services by the Castonguay-Nepveu Commission. These two documents led to the creation in 1970 of the Department of Social Affairs. Notwithstanding the fact that the control of the Church had been so entrenched, particularly in matters of education, that in the past no one had thought of attacking it seriously, a complete system of public education, from kindergarten to university, was set up in the space of ten years. As a counterweight to federal instruments of popular education such as the Canadian Broadcasting Corporation, the Canada Council, and the National Library, Quebec created *Radio-Québec*, the Quebec Arts Council, and the Quebec National Library. Isolated and xenophobic for so long, Quebec began to develop contacts with the outside world, and, particularly, with the French-speaking world. In short, through an intense effort to re-structure society, Quebec changed in ten years from a province to a state.

The Quest for Harmony Between a People and Its Institutions.

The awakening of the dynamic national consciousness of a people must begin with the awakening of its group consciousness. It is probably an over-simplification to assert, as is frequently done, that an omnipresent Church produces a passive attitude towards human misery, holding out hopes of celestial rewards for earthly trials. But certainly senior public servants, labour organizers, and leaders of popular movements are now very concerned with the day-to-day problems of Quebecers, and are trying to devise a set of institutions to deal with them efficiently.

New indicators of economic, social, cultural and other facets of life in Quebec are becoming available on almost a daily basis. A list of the ten richest cities per capita in Canada, published in a report of the federal Department of Revenue on September 20, 1971, did not include a single city from Quebec; Montreal and Quebec City ranked twenty-fourth and thirty-fourth respectively. According to a "conservative estimate" of the

Quebec Department of Social Affairs released on November 28, 1971, 200,000 Quebecers of 18 years or younger were disabled and present provisions to assist them were inadequate. A study made by the *Associations co-opératives d'économie familiale* revealed in 1970 that Quebec consumers owed about one billion dollars to finance companies. The net profits of these companies reached 72,800,000 dollars in that year, and 29,000,000 dollars were paid in dividends to shareholders, most of whom were American. The Castonguay-Nepveu Commission learned in 1971 that one out of five Quebecers lives in a family with insufficient income, representing a total short-fall of 500,000,000 dollars. The newspaper *Québec-Presse* found that though Quebecers' savings amount to 11.3 billion dollars, they control only 23 percent of this amount. Finally, the 1971 Canadian census showed that the French language is losing ground throughout Canada; 26.9 percent of the population reported French as their maternal language, compared to 28.1 percent ten years earlier; the proportion of English-speaking Canadians increased from 58.5 to 60.2 percent. The decrease in the proportion of French-speaking persons is even more marked in Montreal, where they now constitute only 58 percent of the population. This trend towards a minority situation for French-speaking persons in the Montreal area highlights the whole question of the survival of French culture in Quebec.

The mass of information being showered on Quebecers, of which we have given only a representative sample, spurs them to think in terms of institutional reforms. Professor Léon Dion has perhaps described better than anyone else the present state of Quebec society in transition:

> Contemporary Quebec, seriously divided as it is by multiple contradictions and shaken, sometimes tragically, by convulsions, provides a perfect example of this drastically changing world. Nowhere else, perhaps, has the new order challenged the old so suddenly and so brutally. Nowhere else, perhaps, is the social framework so inapt to channel this tide of social change. Few societies have experienced such profound changes in so short a space of time as Quebec during the last decade; demographically, in education, in religious outlook and in political life, these changes have taken on the magnitude of a revolution. At a dizzying pace, traditional values have been discarded, the élite dispossessed, and leadership contested . . . In this way, many of the most underprivileged Quebecers have acquired a new consciousness of themselves and of their destiny. The urban citizens' committees and rural movements like Operation Dignity are made up of individuals who are determined, in spite of their poor material and intel-

lectual resources, to change their present situation and to take their future into their own hands.[20]

Among the manifestations of this new consciousness that is shaking Quebec and redefining its institutions are the popular movements, the labour unions, and the political parties.

The growth of popular movements in the past decade has indeed been spectacular but they have lacked any semblance of unity. Citizens' committees, increasingly well organized and politically influential, have taken roots in the cities. The revolt of the population of the Lower St. Lawrence and the Gaspé against the ineptitude of both federal and provincial governments has resulted in the creation of the two movements, Operation Dignity I, and Operation Dignity II. The *Associations co-opératives d'économie familiale* are setting an example of efficiency in eight regions, and taking the lead in establishing networks of sales co-operatives throughout both rural and urban Quebec. When the government agency the *Société générale d'exploitation forestière,* decided to turn over its lumber mills at Mont Laurier to a private firm, the workers launched a united protest and demanded to take over the operation themselves. In the Abitibi region, the population of the village of Cadillac blocked the national highway for several days to force the government not to close a local mine. The tenants of Quebec, for their part, have taken steps to form a national federation. And the *Caisses populaires Desjardins* are planning a mass meeting in May, 1973, a highly significant step in view of the fact that 67 per cent of the French-speaking adult population, or the mass of persons with small-scale savings, are members of this movement.

The present significance of these popular movements is difficult to assess accurately since they are evolving rapidly in response to a wide range of impulses, and they are anything but uniform in character. Organized in a federation, they would constitute an enormous force. That stage of development is probably still remote, but all the evidence suggests a marked increase in the power of the people through these means.

The Quebec labour movement, too, has brought about a number of changes in the attitudes and behaviour of the population. While they represent only one-third of the work force, their significance is much greater. In addition to their traditional union activities, the three principal organizations, the *Confédération des syndicats nationaux,* the *Fédération des Travailleurs du Québec.* and the *Corporation des enseignants du Québec,* have been involved for several years in the political education of their members, and increasingly have undertaken direct political activity. This "Europeanization" of the Quebec labour movement is disliked by the Canadian Labour Congress, with which the *Fédération des Travailleurs du Québec* is affiliated, but the attitude of the C.L.C. can be turned to advantage by the F.T.Q. in its ideological struggle. It has refused automatic support to the New Democratic Party, for instance, whereas the C.L.C. is committed to support it by its constitution.

In his report to the Canadian Labour Congress in May, 1972, Jean Gérin-Lajoie, President of the Quebec section of the United Steel Workers of America, one of the most important affiliates of the F.T.Q. declared that, in the present context, the Parti Québécois best represents the aspirations and needs of the workers of Quebec. The fact that the seven constituencies won by the Parti Québécois in April, 1970 are in the blue-collar sections of Montreal shows that Gérin-Lajoie's view is shared by a large proportion of the union membership. In fact, the largest majorities were won in Montréal-Maisonneuve, the constituency where labour is best organized, and in Saguenay, a stronghold of the *Conféderation des syndicats nationaux*. The F.T.Q. has published a lengthy manifesto which has been submitted to its general assembly, and has led to its association, still tacit rather than formal, with the Parti Québécois. The C.S.N. has published a somewhat similar, but more ideological manifesto, which was submitted to the membership in June, 1972. The *Corporation des enseignants du Québec* is moving in the same direction.

The establishment of "common fronts" composed of the three labour organizations and other movements, most frequently the Parti Québécois and the *Mouvement national québécois* (formerly the *Société Saint-Jean-Baptiste*) had resulted in certain concerted actions, as in the struggles against Bill 63 concerning language rights and against the application of the War Measures Act. The labour unions are determined to lead the challenge to Quebec's traditional institutions. Thus far, they have distributed information, sought to define their ideological positions, and engaged in certain direct confrontations with the authorities that have led to the imprisonment of three of their leaders. Their activities are clearly in the direction of a socialist society and an independent Quebec. One can well imagine the tremendous impact of the unification of these labour organizations into a single, wholly Quebec union with some 600,000 members. This would be the logical step after the experience of "common fronts."

The political party system in Quebec is also in a period of transformation, and even confusion. No longer can a party, once elected, count on a long period in office; changes in the party in power are frequent and often surprising. Since April, 1970, the traditional two-party system has been replaced by a four- or even five-party system. The Union Nationale, all-powerful in the years after World War II, has declined to the point of being threatened with extinction. Fifty-five percent of the Quebec electorate (65 percent of the French-speaking electorate) is represented in the National Assembly by three opposition parties dedicated to radical reform of the existing political institutions. The *Ralliement des Créditistes* stands for self-determination of the Canadian provinces, and a true confederation. *Unité Québec*, formerly the Union Nationale, favours a republican form of government for Quebec, and equality between Quebec and the rest of Canada within a confederation. The Parti Québécois proposes full sovereignty for Quebec, a common market with the rest of Canada, and a separate currency for Quebec if the rest of Canada refuses to agree to a common currency.

With 72 seats out of 108 in the National Assembly, the Liberal Party appears to be in a strong position, but, in fact, it has the support of only 45 percent of the electorate, including the 20 percent comprised of English-speaking voters. Elected on a platform of creation of 100,000 new jobs in 1970-71 and a final attempt to prove that Canadian federalism is a paying proposition, it has failed at least partially on both counts. The most favourable statistics indicate that only 55,000 new jobs were created in 1970-71. But more important, "paying" federalism has come to a dead end. No real progress has been made in transferring powers from Ottawa to Quebec, a fact reflected dramatically in Quebec's categorical "non" at the end of the Victoria Conference. The election-inspired budget of the federal Minister of Finance, John Turner, in 1972, which was prepared without prior consultation with Quebec, has thwarted Quebec's plan to establish an integrated social policy, probably the only reform that might have reduced current social unrest. This incident resulted in the resignation, since suspended, of two Ministers in the Quebec Government, Claude Castonguay and Jean-Paul L'Allier; violent denunciations by two others, Jean Cournoyer and Normand Toupin; and a stiffer attitude by Premier Bourassa himself. Claude Castonguay, the dominant figure in the Bourassa Cabinet, has already declared that "political pressures building up in Quebec necessitate a re-definition of the federal system in the near future."[21]

In short, the only party standing for the preservation of existing institutions is prey to serious internal problems. An English-language newspaper, the *Montreal Star*, has summed up the delicate situation of the Government of Quebec:

When he took power in 1970, Premier Bourassa believed that by down-grading federal-provincial conflicts he would be able to restore a greater degree of stability to Quebec politics and at the same time do away with some of the political factors which tended to scare off investors. The idea was that a more business-like government could deal effectively with the sources of disquiet in Quebec. Premier Bourassa also believed that a conciliatory attitude towards the government of Prime Minister Pierre Trudeau would result in constitutional and fiscal gains for the provincial government. . . . On none of these things has Bourassa been vindicated. Unrest in the province has mounted to the point where it now threatens public order. Civil disobedience on the part of the labour movement is undermining the authority of the government. With respect to the federal government, Quebec did get some financial relief but it happened to be delivered in a variety of special programs which hampered the administration rather than assisted it. . . . But one thing is sure: it is that members of the Bourassa cabinet are having a hard and unsympathetic look at the uncompromising attitudes of Prime Minister Trudeau. Quebec ministers are unanimous now in believing that Ottawa's unyielding attitudes on taxation and constitutional problems are directly responsible for the provincial government's difficulties in meeting the tense situation which prevails in Quebec.[22]

Until recently, the evolution of Quebec's political institutions has been long and relatively calm; now it has become explosive. The key to understanding this new situation lies in the fact that Quebec has always had political institutions, but not of its own choosing. The Quiet Revolution marked the first step towards correction of this situation, but because of the rapid rate of change, the measures adopted at that time were soon outmoded. To-day, Quebec has a government elected by a minority of the population, holding power thanks to the English-speaking voters; the majority is thus prevented from gaining access to economic and political power. True power is not granted, it is taken. In every corner of Quebec, sometimes by forceful means, sometimes with too much ideological enthusiasm and too few specific tools, new centres of power are being formed. The cultural consciousness of French-speaking Canadians has been transformed into the political consciousness of the Quebec nation. This new consciousness reflects a new mentality that Léon Dion has attempted to analyze:

The first basic feature is that the people who acquire the new consciousness reject the old paternalism, which, while offering them security and a certain amount of happiness, denied them justice. . . .

Quebec Society and Politics

The second basic feature of the new collective consciousness is that it is caught in a vicious circle of rising expectations and mounting frustrations, from which it is difficult to imagine how it can possibly be freed. . . .

A third feature of the new collective consciousness is the original way in which it defines rationality. In contrast to the abstract concept espoused by scholars and technocrats, it conceives rationality as vibrant and human . . . In the first case, it is accepted that to lead a decent life, it is sufficient to have a certain level of education, a certain standard of living, etc., while the extent to which individuals are involved in other activities which concern them is not of primary importance; in the second case it is the extent of participation which is the most important factor in determining the quality of an individual's life. . . .

The outstanding characteristic of this new consciousness is that it is motivated by a powerful, albeit not yet clearly perceived, desire for self-determination. . . . Fed up with making submissions to a government that ignores their requests or whose responses are unacceptable or come too late, they decide to take the initiative themselves under new leaders, to formulate their own plans, calling on specialists and on the government to translate these plans into specific programs. In short, they place their reliance on Man as opposed to Bureaucracy. They opt for life. This is the philosophy behind the citizens' committees and the Operations "Dignity."[23]

Will this new mentality triumph and lead to a new set of institutions marked by a greater degree of decentralization and greater popular participation? Prime Minister Trudeau's attitude may change, or he may be replaced by Robert Stanfield, and the federal government may make enough concessions to satisfy the demands of Quebecers. We do not believe that concessions, however large, would satisfy their basic requirement, which is not merely to obtain specific things, but simply to be themselves. The traditional powers may prove obstinate, and call upon an authoritarian leader to put down the social unrest; he would come from one of the traditional parties representing the financial powers which yesterday spawned Duplessis and Taschereau. He would not be elected by the citizens' committees, and so Quebec, and all of Canada, would miss a chance for a genuine popular revolution. The feeling would persist in English Canada that Quebecers still have a penchant for dictatorship, but they are really victims of dictators who owe their power to English Canadian financial groups.

On the other hand, the broad majority of Quebecers may seize the opportunity to use the Parti Québécois as a catalyzing agent, a common meeting-place, a spearhead to put forward their demands effectively. And having won their political sovereignty, they may create a set of institutions in their own image. There could result a society of Latin culture and therefore articulated, socially based on the family and with special concern for children and the aged, economically based on a cooperative creed, and politically on a vast network of communities, each practising participation as a first principle. To-day, the institutions of Quebec are British, élitist, capitalist, and oppressive. If present trends continue, tomorrow they will be French, popularly-based, and inspired by the principles of co-operation and participation.

Quebec Society and Politics

Notes

1. In his classic work, *Federal Government*, K. C. Wheare emphasizes the significance, for Canadian federalism, of a socially and culturally compact French-speaking minority.
2. See, for example, the speech of Gérard Pelletier, Secretary of State for Canada, at Holy Blossom Temple, Toronto, November 28, 1971.
3. Pierre Charbonneau, "La Couronne, essai sur les Canadiens français et la démocratie, in Les Ecrits du Canada français," VIII. Montreal, 1961, pp. 20-53.
4. Fernand Ouellet, *Histoire économique et sociale du Québec, 1760-1850*, Montreal: Les Editions Fides, 1966.
5. *Ibid.*, p. 1.
6. *Ibid.*, p. 118.
7. *Ibid.*, pp. 147-148.
8. *Ibid.*, p. 530.
9. Pierre Elliott Trudeau, "Some Obstacles to Democracy in Quebec," in *Federalism and the French Canadians*. Toronto: Macmillan of Canada, 1968, pp. 103-123.
10. *Ibid.*, p. 115.
11. *Ibid.*, p. 116.
12. *Ibid.*, p. 116.
13. *Ibid.*, p. 117.
14. *Ibid.*, p. 106.
15. *Ibid.*, p. 115.
16. René Lévesque, *An Option for Quebec*. Toronto: McClelland & Stewart, 1968.
17. Maurice Séguin, *L'idée d'indépéndance au Québec, génèse et historique*. Trois-Rivières: Les Editions Le Boréal Express, 1968.
18. See André Larocque, *Défis au Parti Québécois*. Montreal: Les Editions du Jour, 1971.
19. For an excellent chronological review, see: Jean Hamelin, "Quebec and the Outside World, 1867-1967," *Québec Yearbook 1968-69*, (49th Issue). Quebec, Department of Industry and Commerce, 1968.
20. Chapter II, above, pp. 27-8.
21. *The Gazette*, Montreal, Feb. 15, 1972.
22. Article by Dominique Clift, "Nasty Old Ottawa," *Montreal Star*, May 13, 1972.
23. Chapter II, above, pp. 29-31.

6
The Quebec Public Service
by André Gélinas

The Socio-Economic Setting and the Role of the State

Quebecers, more than 80 percent of whom are French-speaking, form a distinct society. Their history, customs, behaviour, culture and even economic status[1] make them different from other Canadians. Of course, they share certain concerns with the latter and, in North America as elsewhere, they must face the challenge of modern life. To infer from these similarities that there exists an increasing desire on the part of Quebecers for further integration with their neighbours would be, however, presumptuous. On the contrary, for at least twenty years there appears to have been a growing collective urge for self-determination, and the provincial state of Quebec has been the pole of attraction for these aspirations.

If it is agreed that a modern state is not only a purveyor of services, but also an instrument of the collective will through which priorities are established and choices made, then it must also be agreed that a given society must have greater control over the collective decisions affecting it, even though it shares certain technical needs with others. Specifically, this means that Quebec, as the only Canadian state with a French-speaking majority, should add to its regular duties the special task of protecting and developing this community. Many political figures have made statements to this effect and they are fully logical in the present context; the challenge is to draw the proper inferences from this situation in practical terms.

In this connection, the decision of the late Premier Duplessis to levy a provincial income tax was probably the most significant step taken during the 1950s. Among measures adopted in the 1960s, the creation of the Departments of Intergovernmental Affairs and Cultural Affairs, and the negotiation of certain international and interprovincial agreements, deserve special mention. In the present decade, however, this development has slowed down considerably, if not stopped completely, as new vertical arrangements are being made with the federal government.

The present spectrum of political approaches to Quebec's future ranges from one extreme to the other, from complete independence to be followed by some new form of association, to "profitable" federalism which in present circumstances appears to mean exchanging acknowledged constitutional powers for increased financial aid from Ottawa. Between these two extreme positions are various compromise and middle-of-the-road arrangements, which lost much of their support during the last provincial elections. This is particularly true of the approach taken by the Union Nationale party, which is somewhat comparable to that of the Social Credit party.

One thing is certain: there is little evidence today of preoccupation with national goals in the Quebec public service. For example, the Government recently gave parents complete freedom of choice of schools for their children; in the Montreal area, this has meant an increase in the enrolment of recent immigrants in English schools. The irony of this situation is that it is a case of a minority being more liberal than a majority, since in the other provinces teaching French-speaking children in French is still considered a special privilege. Another incongruity is the tragic weakness of the *Office de la Langue Française*, apparently because of a feeling that laws are not passed with regard to an official language, although it is a normal thing to do all over the world. Meanwhile, the proportion of French-speaking executives in Canadian or "international" firms, and in the federal public service, is far below the proportion of French-speaking citizens in the total population of Canada. It is a delusion to think that a federal government, in which the French-speaking element must necessarily remain a minority, can take more effective action with regard to language rights than the government of Quebec, when even the latter has difficulty in applying the usual majority rule.

That having been said, it must be acknowledged that the role of the state cannot be assessed exclusively according to cultural terms, however fundamental they may be. Still older nations find themselves confronted with awakening nationalism or, more precisely, with a new collective consciousness as a counter-movement to world-wide trends towards cultural homogeneity.

The Quebec state, like so many others, is a purveyor of services; and in this respect, it has developed similarly to practically all western countries. Ian Gow and Guy Bouthillier of the University of Montreal have shown that, as early as the end of the 19th century, the Quebec state played a significant role in the establishment of the economic infrastructure, in, for instance, the fields of agriculture, forestry and mining, transportation and, of course, public safety. With the advent of industrialization and greater specialization in the 20th century, it assumed another and more discrete role through safety and welfare measures, as arbiter between individuals and as guarantor of their personal safety and their property. One administration led by Maurice Duplessis, which espoused the traditional liberal ideology, created a set of administrative mechanisms that strengthened the auxiliary role of the Quebec state while affirming the primacy of private enterprise as the principal agent of economic development. Notably, this strategy grew out of a concern with balancing the budget in order to maintain a certain freedom of action relative to various pressure groups, in particular the financial community.

This narrow concept of fiscal policy, and the hard line adopted by the Duplessis Administration against the unions, gave rise to frequent critical debates among members of the Quebec intelligentsia. In their discussions of various aspects of Quebec life, they probably exaggerated the lag in the development of adequate educational facilities, which was really only serious at the secondary level. In the economic sector, the Duplessis Administration certainly did encourage industrial progress. But it must be borne in mind in that regard that federal policies are paramount in the selection of industrial location; as a result Quebec still faces the problem today that industry is concentrated in the neighbouring Province of Ontario.

During the 1960s, the Government of Quebec was able to use its almost untapped financial credit to create several public corporations. The state was thus given a new and positive role as a developmental agent. It is still too early for us to be able to assess the impact of this step. On the other hand, massive investments during the same period in education and social welfare, representing today more than half of the four billion dollars of state expenditures, leave very little space for an autonomous industrial strategy. Quebec, like Canada as a whole, also has to contend with a very advanced state of internationalization. Among the other inhibiting factors are Quebec's rather limited powers to regulate economic and technical matters and the under-representation of French-speaking persons in the management of Canadian and foreign firms operating in the Province.

The Constitutional Framework

Our purpose here is not to outline the history of the Canadian federal system. Even today, historians do not agree on the nature of the principal constitutional document, and discussions continue over questions such as whether it is a contract between two peoples or simply a peremptory law of the British Parliament. At any rate, we do not yet have a method of amending the Canadian constitution, and, if we did, it would only isolate Quebec in a minority position. Some lawyers have observed rightly that the federal system oscillated[2] between periods of centralization and decentralization in the nineteenth, and the first half of the twentieth century. But Quebec remains the real centrifugal force within the system and, were it not for Quebec and her society, the different levels of government would have been integrated in very large measure long ago.

Some federal government departments are operating today in the same sectors as provincial departments. For example, Ottawa recently followed the example of the American government in creating a Department of Urban Affairs. True, the central government's intervention in this sector is limited for the moment to financial assistance, but this assistance is very generous because of its "unlimited spending power." Since regulations gradually follow financial assistance, the provincial government will find eventually that, in its day-to-day operations, it has become subordinate to federal standards. This is the inevitable fate of joint programmes, of which the development of the Lower St. Lawrence and Gaspé areas is probably the best example. This programme has resulted in duplication not only of studies and objectives, but also of administrative structures and specific projects. Morton Grodzins' comparison of contemporary federal systems with marble, rather than layer cakes, is certainly accurate; for the public administrator, the absence of a clear-cut division of responsibilities implied by that analogy can only make his own efforts unproductive, and lead to conflicts that are costly for the ordinary citizen.

In the near future the Canadian provinces will surely come under pressure from both the federal government and the municipalities as they seek to expand their activities; the American states are already facing similar pressures. In view of its special situation, Quebec will not likely be able to agree to its government's being reduced to the status of a mere regional administration.

Administrative Structures

Although the history of Quebec's administrative institutions has yet to be written, they appear to have followed a pattern of development similar to those in other Western countries. This observation is based on an examination of formal structures and not of specific programmes, which undoubtedly vary from country to country and are certainly not synchronized. One of the short-comings of current comparative analysis is the failure to identify the "outputs" of public administration according to a uniform schematic model.

At the end of the nineteenth century, Quebec's public service was made up of a small number of departments dealing with subjects pertaining to natural resources and transportation. Their activities were limited normally to inspections and supervisory functions with a view to standardizing certain operations and arbitrating conflicts between individuals. A number of autonomous agencies already existed, similar to the *offices* that have long existed in France. Later, an attempt was made to integrate them more closely into departments responsible to the Legislative Assembly. But with the creation of public corporations and administrative commissions or boards in the 1940s and 1950s, the process of decentralization was resumed; and this trend was accelerated in the 1960s, with the result that there are today about one hundred autonomous agencies of various kinds: consultative bodies (councils), judicial bodies (administrative tribunals), economic and technical regulatory agencies (*régies*), commercial, industrial, and financial management agencies (corporations), and state management agencies (*offices*). At the same time, organizations were also established to ensure centralized control of the provincial administration, for instance, the Treasury Board and the Civil Service Department and centralized internal services, for instance, government procurement, and air transport services. As was to be expected, conflict between these centralizing and decentralizing trends was inevitable, and in 1971 a committee on administrative reform was created by the Cabinet to study the whole question of functional decentralization. Since this committee has not yet reported, we can only assume that its recommendations will reflect an awareness of the dangers of the present administrative fragmentation, and will suggest a halt to the proliferation of autonomous agencies, which occasionally owe their existence more to political expediency and short-term or local considerations than to the requirements of administrative efficiency.

This committee has also been studying the distribution of authority among the various governmental services. Under the present system, the Cabinet has to pronounce on a host of small subjects that could easily be delegated to a department, and it is left with insufficient time to examine basic questions and establish comprehensive guidelines. The consolidation of Quebec's 1500 municipalities into more workable units, especially in the urban areas, is another matter of urgency; beginnings have been made in the three urban centres öf Hull, Montreal and Quebec City. Ideally, this policy of municipal consolidation should have been combined with a policy of regional development, so that the inevitable political bargaining among local elected officials, and between local officials and the provincial government, would have been kept in proper perspective. At any rate, the growing problems confronting the municipalities cannot easily be met until new fiscal arrangements are negotiated between the federal and provincial levels of government. The progressive take-over of local responsibilities by the two higher levels of government will create great difficulties for the municipalities, and make them the target of continual criticism on the grounds that they are failing to meet the needs of various groups.

The Administrative Process

While changes in administrative structures are usually brought about rapidly enough, the same is not true of changes in the administrative process, and even less of changes in well-established policies.

We noted earlier the creation in the 1960s of a number of agencies designed to ensure centralized control of the provincial administration, and of internal governmental services. However, with the exception of the Public Service Department and, more recently, the Treasury Board, these agencies have no clearly defined legal authority and have failed to bring about the degree of standardization on which centralization depends. Their usefulness could well come into question if no attempt is made to estimate their cost to the client agencies that are supposed to benefit from them, and to make them operate in an orderly manner.

Modification of the present planning and regional development programmes is also imperative. These terms are still anathema to certain politicians. There is a curious paradox in the fact that the present Government, which has tried to project an image of administrative efficiency, hesitates to authorize the creation of machinery to facilitate political decisions and make regional development projects more coherent. Recently the Government of Ontario, taking advantage, it is true, of Quebec's experience, was able to have considerable influence in determining the location of its international airport.

The P.P.B.S., or Planning, Programming and Budgetary System, which has already had its rise and decline in the United States, has found new admirers in both the federal Government and Government of Quebec. In fact, it represents the most important innovation of the last few years. This does not mean that the reform of the system of budgetary management has been completed; several years of testing will be necessary before all its implications can be assessed. Certainly, success cannot yet be claimed, although implementation of the new system may be facilitated by several factors, for instance, by the fact that Quebec's system of government is similar to the British one, by the prevailing conditions of austerity, and by the more modest size of the governmental organization compared to that of some other countries.

The Public Service

The history of the public service in Quebec can be divided into four stages, which we will describe in what are sometimes considered synonymous terms, but each of which has a very specific meaning. These are: civilian employees, civil servants, bureaucrats, and technocrats.

Civilian Employees – In the nineteenth century, this expression referred to employees of the state who were not in the armed forces. It reflected the fact that the tasks of ensuring public security, in the strict sense of the term, were just beginning to include some civilian roles. Naturally, there was no feeling of solidarity among these persons. As everywhere else in North America, ministers and other important politicians could set the terms of access to government employment. The first association of civilian employees was created as late as 1921, and even then its primary purpose was to promote recreational activities among its members. There still exists a "civilian employees" tennis club in Quebec City.

Civil Servants – The concept of civil servant really took shape with the creation in 1944 of the Civil Service Commission to centralize recruitment. However, the Commission was not given a very significant role until 1959, when, for the first time, specific steps were taken to ensure recruitment and promotion on the basis of merit through its establishment of a recruitment and promotion board. A law passed in 1960 recognized that civil servants had certain rights, and not merely obligations as before. Scientific personnel management was introduced with the adoption of a new system of job classification. The era of patronage in the Civil Service was declared to have ended.

Bureaucrats – Subsequently, one reform followed another in rapid succession. Instead of consolidating the legal status of civil servants, as was done in most European countries and in the United States, the decision was taken in 1965 to subject a large proportion of them to a system of collective bargaining similar to the one in effect in the private sector. Civil servants in professional categories are now authorized to form their own unions, and have held costly strikes. The public service is becoming bureaucratic, although the over-all pattern is admittedly different from that of French, British and American administrations. The 24-hour general strike, in 1972, of the 210,000 employees of the public and parapublic sectors, the largest strike in Canada's history, indicates the possible consequences of such a system. Observers signalled that the inevitable result of the common front presented by the leadership of the trade unions (C.S.N.-F.T.Q.-C.E.Q.) would be to challenge the whole economic policy of the state at the bargaining table and to bring about an even greater politicization of the negotiating process. In my view, the entire economic system is hardly likely to be modified through this process, but unfortunately some union members appear to be convinced that it can be, and this can only make the negotiations still more acrimonious. The highly centralized decision-making power within the common front gives the leaders almost absolute control over member unions, a situation which is tolerable in a context of consultations, but not of negotiations.[3]

Technocrats – Just as the majority of public servants were becoming bureaucrats, a counter-balancing phenomenon appeared: the technocrats, or super-bureaucrats. Recruited at the beginning of the 1960s by the government that initiated the Quiet Revolution, these top civil servants not only manage day-to-day business, but also give political advice. They have made such an important contribution to the modernization of the state of Quebec that the recent departure of several of them caused much surprise. During the last few years, there have been attempts to replace these highly qualified analysts with straight administrators borrowed from the so-called "business world." Unfortunately, the ignorance of the latter concerning the way a state functions may be as great as their desire to reform it at any cost. The suggestion has been made that appointments to these senior posts should be on a contractual basis for a specified period; however, this procedure would not ensure the continuity that is essential in any organization, a consideration that is duly recognized even in private business. Applied discriminately, this policy would clearly be extremely controversial as the American experience has shown. Those who advocate it apparently forget that the top-level management of autonomous government agencies is already on a contractual basis in that they are appointed for fixed terms. It is not at all self-evident that this policy should be applied to departments where a long experience in the public service is most needed.

In summary, the public service in Quebec is obviously going through a difficult period. The progressive and dynamic attitude which was its hallmark at the beginning of the 1960s is gradually fading. Every society needs collective and individual successes that reflect well upon the community. The private sector, particularly the large corporations, has remained aloof from the community, and has always seemed to identify with reactionary causes opposed to its progress. A harmonious balance of forces within Quebec requires a different strategy on their part.

Notes

1. See: *Report of the Royal Commission on Bilingualism and Biculturalism*, Volumes 3 and 4.
2. A recent study by Claude Morin, former Deputy-Minister of the Department of Inter-governmental Relations, has demonstrated that oscillations were mistaken for periods when the central government's expansion simply marked time.
3. The very recent history confirms this proposition. The excessive concentration of power has resulted not only in the practical disruption of the Department of the Civil Service (this agency was responsible for the government side), but also in the disaffiliation of members and unions of the C.S.N. (the leader of the labor side).

7
The Provincial Party System in Quebec*
by Vincent Lemieux

In 1967, one hundred years after the birth of Confederation, René Lévesque, formerly a Liberal Cabinet minister, resigned from his party to form a movement which was to shake Quebec's party system to its depths; the following year, he became the founding President of the Parti Québécois. Daniel Johnson, Premier of Quebec and head of the Union Nationale party, died suddenly, in September, 1968. And in 1969, the *Ralliement Créditiste* decided to enter the provincial arena. These events marked the change from a two-party to a multi-party political system. The provincial elections of April, 1970, confirmed this new situation; each of the four parties received at least 10 percent of votes cast. The Liberal Party won 45 percent of votes cast and 72 seats, the Parti Québécois 24 percent and 7 seats, the Union Nationale 20 percent and 17 seats, and the *Ralliement Créditiste* 11 percent and 12 seats.

Until the beginning of the 1960s, the political party system in Quebec was relatively simple: an autonomy-conscious, or Quebec-oriented, party faced a more pro-federalist, or more Canadian, one. The Liberal Party was in the first category until the late 1930s, then switched into the second category as the Quebec wing of the Conservative Party reorganized under the banner of the Union Nationale, and pre-empted the "Quebec first" position. Another characteristic of the party system during the period was that the governmental party, whichever one was in power, drew its support mainly from the rural areas while the opposition party was stronger in the cities, particularly Montreal. What has become known as the Quiet Revolution, launched around 1960, put an end to this relatively uncomplicated situation. In its negotiations with Ottawa, the Liberal Government under Jean Lesage, in power from 1960 to 1966, became as autonomy-conscious as the Union Nationale.

---

* This chapter is a slightly modified version of a study which appeared in J. L. Migué (ed.), *Le Québec d'Aujourd'hui*, Montreal, HMH, 1971, under the title, "Les Partis et leurs Contradictions." Reprinted with permission.

Furthermore, the Liberals continued, after taking office, to receive more support from the urban than the rural areas, a situation explained in large part by the fact that the rural population had declined from 60 percent of the whole in 1901 to 44 percent in 1931, and 26 percent in 1961. Another cleavage in the electorate was equally significant: the Liberal Party became the party of the better-educated, including the English-speaking voters, while the less-educated gave their allegiance to the Union Nationale. This division reflected the fact that the former identified more readily with the Quiet Revolution.

The results of the 1970 elections reveal that the new parties, the Parti Québécois and the *Ralliement Créditiste*, divided along similar lines. The Parti Québécois became largely a party of well-educated persons bent on pursuing the Quiet Revolution until it led to the independence of Quebec, and then to a completely modern society. The *Ralliement Créditiste* appeared as the party of the less-educated who were opposed to the course the Quiet Revolution was taking. The Liberal Party, for its part, enjoys more than ever the support of the English-speaking population and both it and the Union Nationale, which was called the *Unité Québec* from 1971 to early 1973, accept, more or less, the changes implied in the concept of the Quiet Revolution. On another level of comparison, these two parties, and the *Ralliement Créditiste*, remain federalist in orientation, as opposed to the Parti Québécois which has as its principal goal the independence of Quebec.

The objective of this chapter, which covers the period from 1944 to the present, is to analyze the contradictions which have arisen – or may conceivably arise – between the positions adopted by the Quebec parties and their electoral successes, or more generally, their impact on Quebec society.[1] Drawing on certain theories of organization, we consider parties as collective agents that mobilize or allocate, both inside and outside their structure, resources that are factors of political power. For reasons of convenience, these resources are divided into four categories: jural, material, symbolic, and informational. By jural resources, we imply all the rights and prerogatives, and not merely the strictly legal ones, at the disposal of such an agent. The electoral support given to a victorious candidate, or to a party, has a jural character since it confers upon the candidate the right to represent his constituency, and upon the party the right to govern. This is an institution-based right, but other rights are not necessarily related to institutions – for instance, the many links between members of the same family, the same circle of friends, the same parish, or the same party.

The notion of material resources is easily understood, but it should be noted that from the point of view of political analysis, they do not confer power as automatically as jural resources. If we define power as the possession and effective control of political weapons or stakes[2] – possession of one's own and control over those of others being understood – material resources only ensure control when they are accompanied by prestige, or used as rewards or punishment. In such an instance, prestige is an example of what we call symbolic resources. It provides the means of control, but not necessarily the means to possess or dominate. A person can have prestige in relation to another without even being aware of it, and thus without being able to allocate the political stakes according to his own preferences; on the other hand, an agent is always aware that he has certain rights, even when these rights are not accompanied by prestige.

Finally, informational resources – or, simply, knowledge – make up our fourth category. Not themselves a direct means of possession or control, they feed the other means and enable the conversion of certain material or symbolic resources into the equivalent of rights. In a representative system of government, they are operative on the upper levels of political activity where "ideologies" and "utopias" are discussed.[3] This is the level on which political systems, with their distribution of political stakes, and the resources which make them possible, are contested or supported.

Starting with these concepts, we will outline the more or less contradictory relationship between the positions adopted by the parties and their impact, electoral or other, upon Quebec society during three periods: from the end of World War II to the end of the 1950s; the 1960s; and the foreseeable future.

The Uncomplicated Years, 1944-60

During this first period, the relations of the Union Nationale with the voters produced electoral results reflecting the principal objective of this party, which was simply to remain in power by holding an adequate number of seats. The party operated on the premise that the government should reflect the prevalent social system, not transform it; hence the minimum of state undertakings and controls, as reflected in the small budgets and short parliamentary sessions. The Union Nationale presented, in a way, a true image of Quebec society with its solid majorities, election after election, based on traditional rights and prerogatives; and sustained, despite increasing industrialization and urbanization, by economic prosperity and inferior school and information systems. Studies carried out on the local level have shown that during this period the power of the Union Nationale was in direct proportion to the strength of the bonds of kinship, and the cohesiveness of parish life.[4]

Less passively, the Union Nationale managed in four distinct ways to perpetuate a type of society favourable to its re-election. First, it took steps to assure those groups that comprised the major elements of the society that the conditions which enabled them to maintain their controlling influence would be perpetuated. The electoral map was allowed to remain unchanged, even though it favoured the rural over the urban areas – the former being, of course, the bastions of the traditional groups. The electoral laws were amended, but in such a way as to benefit the governing party. Constraints were placed on the labour unions, the major popular movement contesting the current distribution of material and other resources. On the other hand, care was taken not to infringe upon the privileges of the Church, which, together with the family and the local communities, determined the rights and obligations which held the society together.

Secondly, the Union Nationale used political patronage to ensure loyalty to its own organization, adopting for this purpose the very personal pattern of social relations that was prevalent in Quebec families and parishes. The system of patronage had the added effect of placing material resources in the hands of certain local units of the party, and of the less privileged segments of society. Since the objects of patronage were so visible and existed in individual units (bridges, roads, schools, pensions, etc.), the rewards of loyalty to the party were clearly evident. Thus the system appeared to maintain existing party support and even to extend it into more recalcitrant segments of society; by offering political favours as rewards or withholding them as punishment, patronage was made into a control mechanism to win people over to the governing party.

Thirdly, by the way they manipulated the predominant elements of Quebec society, the leader of the party, Maurice Duplessis, and members of the legislature operating at the constituency level succeeded in establishing a symbolic identification between these elements and the government which gave the system its legitimacy. Of the three types of authority identified by Weber,[5] only a certain charismatic authority could legitimize this form of government. The traditions of the parliamentary system belonged to the conquerors, not to French Canadians; and its democratic rationale, involving the interplay of government and opposition, could not be superimposed on a society with a social organization that rejected the very principle of conflict. There remained the identification of the population with political "chiefs" who had the ability – not to say the charisma – to enable the society to see itself in their image.

Quebec Society and Politics

Finally, the creed of provincial autonomy provided the educated classes supporting the Union Nationale with an elementary set of concepts that enabled them to argue in favour of both the régime in Quebec and, to borrow an expression from Paul Mus, its "adversative solidarity,"[6] vis-à-vis Ottawa. In the name of this provincial autonomy, elements that contributed to federal unity in Canada were discounted, and with them the Liberal Party, which enjoyed their political support. In the circumstances, this party inevitably had to identify itself, in distinction to the Union Nationale, as the party of the minority groups, or the party that aimed to destroy certain traditional rights guaranteed by the Union Nationale. The Union Nationale was thus cast in the role of the party working to prevent the fragmentation of Quebec society; by the same token, it strove to keep the base of Liberal support from expanding. In fact, the most solid Liberal support came from the English-speaking citizens, the more urban and developed areas, the university community, and to a certain extent, labour union leaders.

If the Union Nationale put itself forward as the party of the majority groups in Quebec, and of unity against the federal Liberal Party, the latter represented French Canadians at the federal level in opposition to the Conservative Party which, particularly since 1917, had lost almost all identification with them. Thus, it was possible to vote Union Nationale to defend the autonomy of Quebec against federal centralization, and simultaneously to vote Liberal to protect French Canadians against English Canadians. The popular support received by the Union Nationale had constitutional overtones, while that received by the federal Liberal Party was of an ethnic character; but the two could co-exist easily as long as federalism itself was not called into question.

It took a real electoral sweep in 1958 and the replacement of the French Canadian Louis St. Laurent as federal Liberal leader by the English Canadian Lester Pearson, for Quebec to give fifty out of seventy-five seats to the Conservative Party; and this radical shift in the voting pattern was achieved only with the effective intervention of the power structure of the Union Nationale. This foray into federal politics by the Union Nationale proved dysfunctional and contradictory in view of its provincial objectives. With the election of the Conservative Party to power in Ottawa, the Union Nationale lost the "adversative solidarity" at the federal level which both united it and placed it in opposition to the Liberals; it could no longer accuse the provincial Liberal Party of being in league with the centralizers in Ottawa. Moreover, following the death of Maurice Duplessis in 1959, and of his successor, Paul Sauvé, six months later, Antonio Barrette became party leader, and his lack of charisma was in striking contrast to the dynamic personality of the new Liberal leader, Jean Lesage. In other words, the factor of charismatic leadership became a Liberal asset.

But the most important factor contributing to the defeat of the Union Nationale in 1960 was the set of contradictions that arose between the practice of patronage and its electoral consequences. As long as the patronage system was not tinged with corruption or obvious graft in favour of the principal Union Nationale personalities, it had certain positive effects that have already been noted. The "natural gas scandal" of the late 1950s, cleverly exploited by the Liberals, tarnished the image of a party that reproduced on a larger scale and in the political arena those personal relationships that marked the family, the local community, and the parish. The father who spends his paycheck on drink rather than feeding his children is an unworthy father. The parish priest who builds an oversized rectory with the offerings of the faithful comes under criticism. More precisely in the terms of our analysis, the patronage of the Union Nationale degenerated to the point where it allocated too many material resources to certain ministers and "friends of the régime," reducing the prestige of the Union Nationale and the feeling of obligation of the voters towards it. Along with the other factors previously mentioned, this situation led to the party's electoral defeat. In our field research we were often told: "Duplessis was a good man, but in the end, there was too much corruption in his entourage...."

Transformations during the 1960s

Since the victory of the Liberals in June, 1960, relations between the dominant party and Quebec society have been changing. The challenge is no longer to perpetuate and reflect a static society with fixed majority groups and traditional scales of values, but to reform certain facets of it through governmental action. The Salvas Commission, which investigated the "natural gas scandal," and the fight against patronage, were aimed at breaking down the political mechanism that made politicians into paternal figures enjoying bonds with the voters similar to those found within the family and other communities where traditional feelings of solidarity were maintained. Reform of the public service and certain other legislative steps served the same purpose by greatly restricting the favours and jobs available for distribution through patronage. Modernization of the labour code and the authorization of collective bargaining in the public service have increased the jural as well as the material resources of the trade unions. Finally, changes in the electoral laws between 1962 and 1966 placed the two major parties on a more equal basis at election time. It will be noted that these measures did not suppress traditional groups, but made it difficult for them to be represented to the same degree as previously in the party system, or to obstruct the rights of other groups.

The Liberal Government was even more innovative concerning material and informational resources than jural or symbolic ones. By establishing certain structures to promote economic development, by taking the first steps in the direction of regional development, and by giving priority to the construction of super-highways to the detriment of the network of rural roads, the Liberals offered the voters more collective benefits than the disparate rewards distributed by the Union Nationale. In another sector, they undertook through sweeping educational reforms to increase the informational resources available to the young people of the Province. Finally, with regard to constitutional matters, the Liberal Government adopted positions very different from those of the Union Nationale. Rather than calling for protection of Quebec's autonomy against the centralizing policies of the federal government, it set out to make the state of Quebec a self-sustaining unit for the development of Quebec society, and demanded that Ottawa grant it all the rights and the means necessary to accomplish its objectives.

In the general elections of 1962 a strong majority of the voters of Quebec approved the first phase of this programme, influenced certainly by the collective but very visible benefits such as hospital insurance, increased pensions, and allowances to the parents of schoolchildren that had been made available without a significant increase in taxes. The Liberal Party did, however, suffer a setback in some ten rural constituencies near Quebec City, all very old and relatively static communities that had maintained their traditional social structure more than most. They had also been hit hard in the previous two or three years by an economic recession that the provincial government had done little to counteract. In the federal elections of 1962, which had preceded the provincial elections by several months, the Social Credit Party had made considerable gains in these same areas. It had also made inroads in the more urban parts of Quebec outside of Montreal, where, in addition to feeling the effects of economic stagnation, the population was becoming aware that it possessed few of the jural and material resources that were gradually replacing the traditional values in both the public and private sectors. Liberal reforms were more readily accepted in these areas than in more rural ones to the degree that they held the promise of new forms of solidarity and equality.

The Liberal plan for the reform of Quebec society was highly complex. The central theme was a collective increase in jural, material, symbolic and informational resources, but there was no clear indication of how they were to be distributed. The Liberals' operational structure reflected this complexity. In the first place, the party's electoral organization, which was still highly traditional, was largely independent of its "governmental" organization. Within the latter, the members of the legislature, and particularly the ministers, gradually took their distance from the Liberal Federation, the purpose of which was to take cognizance of and formulate popular demands as a guide to party action. The conceptions held by the different party agents of the political process covered the entire gamut of possibilities. There were the election organizers who played the game of politics for patronage, or simply for the pleasure of winning; the local personalities who sought through their party affiliation to enhance their personal prestige; the lawyers and financial brokers who displayed their talents within the party without conviction; the aspiring candidates who hoped to become members of the legislature and gain access to the jural, symbolic, material, or even informational resources that went with such posts. But there were also those who were less motivated by personal goals than by an interest in the operation of the system as a whole. Some of the latter advocated a considerable increase in all resources without concerning themselves with their distribution; others were more preoccupied with the equal distribution of these resources, or at least of those controlled by the governments in Ottawa and Quebec City. As we shall see later, the views of the members of this last sub-group on constitutional questions were also highly diversified.

The Contradictions in the Liberal Party

In our view the defeat of the Liberals in 1966 can be attributed to the fact that they accomplished a large number of things but in hodge-podge fashion, without any indication of the relative, or even the distinctive, significance of each one. Nor did they pay sufficient attention to the task of distributing the resources they stimulated. The nuisance effects of third parties (particularly the *Rassemblement pour l'Indépendance Nationale*) and the timidity displayed by the Liberals in redrawing the electoral map, contributed to turning a reduction in electoral support into a defeat. The 1966 elections provide another illustration of a party with a relationship to the voters that was not reflected in the voting pattern because it tried to accomplish too many things, some of which had unforeseen negative results, or which detracted from the more positive achievements.

Take, for example, certain aspects of the educational reform programme. The reorganization of secondary schooling in large districts made necessary the busing of students, and occasionally the children had to make such long trips that they could not return home for lunch. Some parents viewed this situation as a direct threat to familial and local unity. They were unable to understand why each local community could not continue to provide secondary education and thus preserve the existing ties among young people. The absence of their children at noon, and the fatigue resulting from the long bus rides, were seen as dangers to family solidarity. Finally, the religious unity of the parish was also felt to be endangered by these trips, during which, it was said, the young people indulged in all sorts of exchanges of views, and boys and girls were thrown together. Even worse, religious unity seemed threatened by the purposeful reduction of church influence; the Liberals were accused of aiming to remove the crucifixes from the schools. In the rural regions particularly, these perceptions in terms of the jural resources which bound the pupils to the family, the community, and the parish, cancelled out the positive effects of the reforms – free education (material resources) and better education (informational resources). The negative effects of this situation on Liberal fortunes were made worse by the fact that the electoral organization of the party lacked the informational resources necessary to publicize the positive aspects of the innovations. For many voters, educational reform, like other measures carried out by the Liberals, was the work of technocrats who conceived their wide-ranging plans on some elevated and abstract level of operation without taking into account the aspirations of the population as a whole.

On the economic front, the Liberals alienated a good number of both unionized and non-unionized workers. Their policy of increased government intervention in the life of the Province, and their efforts to modernize the public sector, did enable organized labour to obtain a larger share of economic resources. But it is a well-known fact that modernization stimulates appetites which demand satisfaction, even if the satisfaction is achieved at the expense of elements of the population lacking the organization to make similar demands. In the public service, the schools, and the hospitals, tensions and strikes marked negotiations between the government and labour unions; meanwhile, farmers were reduced to organizing marches on Quebec, while non-unionized workers, the unemployed, and the retired had practically no means at all of applying pressure on the government. From an electoral point of view, the Liberals' effort at modernization thus led to the contradictory situation of alienating both those whom that policy was intended to benefit, and those who saw their position worsened by this redistribution of material resources.

The constitutional position of the party also reflected a certain ambiguity between the federalist viewpoint which was still expressed officially, and the actual practice in negotiations, which in some ways seemed oriented towards achieving a special status for Quebec. Officials acted as if Quebec could wrest practically all power and resources from Ottawa, and yet remain within Confederation. As the official Opposition, the Union Nationale was able simply to outbid the Government by making still more exaggerated demands on Ottawa, and the *Rassemblement pour l'Indépendance Nationale* exposed this ambiguity by demanding the complete independence of Quebec. To voters familiar with the technical questions involved, these opposition programmes were more attractive than the more laboured policies of the Liberal Party. This equivocal Liberal position was clarified somewhat in late 1967, following the party's defeat, by the departure of René Lévesque and those who shared his views, and its return under the leadership of Robert Bourassa to a clear-cut federalist position.

.

The Contradictions of the Union Nationale

After being returned to office in 1966, the Union Nationale tried on the one hand to re-establish the relations with the voters that had characterized the Duplessis régime; but, on the other hand, it proved hesitant, not knowing how to deal with a society that had undergone such sweeping changes. At the end of four years it, too, succumbed to the numerous contradictions inherent in its policies, contradictions that its political organization, which had engaged few public relations specialists since 1960, was powerless either to recognize or to rectify. Notwithstanding these organizational handicaps, the Union Nationale tried at first to ensure the loyalty of the voters through the old practice of patronage; but the only kind that was still possible – that for architects, engineers, salesmen, lawyers, and members of the highest or lowest echelons of the civil service – was not as profitable in electoral terms as the "small" patronage of earlier times. Moreover, it is likely that this activity, limited by the new conditions of society, produced more discontented than loyal voters; the local organizations of the Liberal Party had already encountered this problem in 1966.

Many of the measures implemented by the Union Nationale government between 1966 and 1970 had either been prepared by the preceding government or were conceived by technocrats in the public service. Examples are the creation, the *Collèges d'enseignement général et professionnel* (CEGEPs), and the metropolitan administrations in Montreal and Quebec; and the highly controversial Bill 62 and Bill 63 concerning language rights in the school system. All these measures had the same shortcomings that had hurt the Liberals: they could not be distinguished easily from one another, and the advantages of each were not immediately apparent; they appeared to constitute a threat to certain resources – the French language, for example, which had a high priority among certain elements of the population – and they were prepared and applied in a highly technocratic manner.

With regard to the socio-economic problems facing Quebec, the Union Nationale adopted generally a wait-and-see attitude, asserting that they were being studied or setting up commissions to gain time. This posture resulted in an image of inefficiency and lack of ideas to resolve current problems. One Minister, Marcel Masse, performed well in his negotiations with the newly-unionized public service employees; but the Union Nationale did not succeed any more than the Liberals had done in winning over either the unionized or the non-unionized sectors of the lower classes. On the constitutional question, the party returned after the death of Daniel Johnson to a position somewhat similar to that taken by Duplessis. A self-styled federalist, Premier Jean-Jacques Bertrand spent more time in accusing Ottawa of centralization than in devising means of assuring the autonomy of Quebec. This do-nothing stance was replaced during the election campaign of 1970 by a four-year time limit for re-structuring Canadian federalism; but it had already alienated many voters, who preferred the Parti Québécois' clearly separatist platform or the equally clear federalist position of the Liberal Party. By the end of the 1960s, the contradictions had multiplied between the relations that governmental parties had attempted to establish with the voters, and the latter's assessment of those parties. Actions or policies designed to ensure re-election, and even the more or less coherent projects conceived for the benefit of Quebec society, had the opposite effect in electoral terms than was intended; but neither the Liberal nor the Union Nationale Administration was able to resolve these contradictions.

The Gray Dawn of the 1970s

If we examine the solidarities* existing today in Quebec society, that is, the rights and obligations which bind different sub-groups of social agents, it is apparent that along with the traditional ones related to the family, local communities, and parishes, and the French Canadian ethnic group itself, others have developed recently which are based on

Table 1:

Declared Incomes in Quebec for the Fiscal Years 1960 and 1968

Occupation	1960 Average Income ($)	1960 Index relative to the average	1968 Average Income ($)	1968 Index relative to the average total	Increase in position on index from 1960 to 1968 (1960 = 100)
Liberal Professions	11,208.	269	18,748.	332	167
Salesmen	5,825.	140	7,703.	136	132
Owners of Businesses	5,545.	133	6,427.	114	116
Farmers	4,473.	107	4,092.	72	91
Employees of Businesses	3,944.	95	5,482.	97	139
Provincial Employees	3,795.	91	6,331.	112	167
Teachers and Professors	3,608.	87	6,106.	108	169
Pensioners	3,400.	82	3,757.	67	110
Employees of Institutions	2,645.	63	4,441.	79	168
Cumulative Average	4,168.	100	5,649.	100	136

Source: 1970 Edition, *Taxation Statistics, Analyzing the Returns of Individuals for the 1968 Taxation Year and Miscellaneous Statistics.* Department of National Revenue, Taxation shared qualities such as age, profession, region, and the "nation."

Age-based solidarities are especially evident among the educated youth of Quebec. Because of the rapid increase in educational opportunities since the beginning of the 1960s, the generation gap in Quebec reflects perhaps a broader cultural cleavage than anywhere else in the Western world. Statistically, the difference is very great between the amount and quality of information received by the young and that received by their parents. This phenomenon falls in the category of informational resources, which will be discussed later. The increase in professional solidarities, concomitant with the decline in traditional ones, was clearly stimulated by the growth of trade unionism and the extension of government activity into new sectors of Quebec life. In order to defend their interests or take advantage of this growth in the public sector, members of the professions most affected had to organize more effectively and strive for greater unity within their respective groups. The medical profession is only the most recent example of the strengthening, more or less under pressure, of professional solidarities. Somewhat haltingly, regional solidarities have also developed in opposition to the many local interests that have curtailed them in the past. Here, too, government action, either direct or indirect, has sometimes acted as a catalyst: for example, regional development schemes such as the BAEQ in the Lower St. Lawrence and Gaspé areas, TEVEQ in the Saguenay-Lac, Saint-Jean area; and the new metropolitan structures in Montreal and Quebec. Finally, the increase in support for political independence, first within voluntary associations or weak parties, then in more cohesive form in the Parti Québécois, gave rise to a new solidarity encompassing all of Quebec, in opposition to the existing Canadian or French Canadian solidarities.

Aggregate resources have certainly increased in Quebec society, but the pattern of distribution has resulted in income disparities that are often greater than at the beginning of the 1960s. The following table shows the declared incomes for certain categories of occupations during the fiscal years 1960 and 1968.[7]

This table reveals that the gap in absolute terms between the average income of the liberal professions and that of the other occupational categories widened from 1960 to 1968. On the other hand, the situation of provincial employees, teachers, and professors improved substantially

---

* "The fact or quality, on the part of communities, etc., of being perfectly united or at one in some respect, especially in interests, sympathies, or aspirations." *The Shorter Oxford English Dictionary*, Third Edition.

in relative terms. This is true also of the institutional employees, even though their average income is still well below the provincial average. The relative situation of salesmen and business employees hardly changed at all, while three categories of occupations clearly regressed: owners of businesses, who, however, still remained above the average; farmers, who dropped from a relative index of 107 to 72; and pensioners, who fell from 82 to 67. Note that farmers were the only group that experienced a decrease in average income in real terms. Note, too, the similarity in the gains made by members of the liberal professions (167), teachers and professors (169), employees of institutions (168), and provincial employees (167). These are clearly the four categories of occupations that have profited most from the Quiet Revolution, while the owners of businesses, farmers and pensioners have suffered from it, the relative increase in their incomes being very inferior to the provincial average of 136. In this context, it should also be borne in mind that the unemployment rate in Quebec, which had decreased progressively from 1961 (9.2%) to 1966 (4.7%) has since increased to 6.5% in 1968 and even higher in 1969 and 1970.

We observed earlier that the rapid increase in educational facilities has widened the gap in levels of instruction between the younger elements of the population (particularly those under twenty-five) and the older ones. But these same young people have only limited access to other political resources, whether material, jural or symbolic, and, in any event, they lack the skills and experience to make use of them. As a result, for many young students, the informational resource, "utopia," as defined by Mannheim, serves as a substitute for the resources they lack. Remember, the purpose of a utopia is to challenge existing social systems. More specifically for the purpose of our analysis, it challenges the institutions, the practices, and the norms which govern the distribution of influence and other resources in Quebec. In the hands of a generation which, as we have said, is more united – against the others – than ever before, and which has set out to convert its elders (particularly parents) to its point of view, this weapon has certainly weakened the legitimacy of the traditional social system.

As elsewhere, the proliferation of tele-relations has modified the political impact of informational resources in Quebec. While this phenomenon has been much discussed, its specific effects remain unclear; but there is one aspect that seems to relate directly to our research. As Georges Lavau[8] has noted, tele-relations have given a more specific image to politics, portraying it as part of daily life. In this way, they have torn away some of the myths surrounding politicians, who in the past were only seen or read about during electoral campaigns, when they were making speeches and participating in other activities that were not part of every-day life. The information disseminated through television is so abundant and varied that it can hardly be encompassed within traditional concepts of politics; at the same time it tends to discourage new "utopias." Neither traditional ideologies nor utopias stand up to scientific scrutiny, but scientific knowledge, too, is often ineffective in that it is not integrated into a coherent whole including all sectors of society and the men who activate them.

In the preceding pages, we have scarcely touched on the subject of symbolic resources. These are without doubt the most difficult to identify and measure. Yet, if prestige is defined as the capacity of a person to create positive expectations in others from his actions, it can be argued that political prestige has diminished in the last ten years. The increase in the number of solidarities, and the proliferation of tele-relations, along with other factors, constitute a threat to existing forms of prestige. The political prestige of Jean Lesage lasted only six or seven years, that of Jean-Jacques Bertrand even less. To the degree that a politician's prestige depends on specific acts, and on the positive reaction or expectations they elicit, his involvement in many, and often mutually contradictory, activities is bound to detract from that prestige.

The Legitimacy of the Governmental System

This weakening of prestige appears all the more serious since, as suggested earlier, the legitimacy of Quebec's system of government has been apparently based largely on charisma. As the prestige of the political leaders has declined, so the legitimacy of the system has been disintegrating in the eyes of ever larger segments of the population. At any rate, it is dangerous to base a supposedly democratic system on a form of legitimacy that is more charismatic than rational-legal, to use once again the categories established by Max Weber. Given the present situation in Quebec, it seems to us that two principal qualities, if incorporated in a renovated system, could assure it of the rational-legal legitimacy that it lacks to such a tragic degree: transparency on the level of interplay of political forces, and equivalence as a specific operational postulate.

By *transparency* of the governmental system, we mean reduction of the distorting effects and narrowing of the distance that separates the governors from the governed. Within the governmental system, the electoral system can be distinguished from the legislative system, or in terms of roles, the selection of governors from the selection of governmental measures. Electoral laws must be reformed in order to assure equal opportunity, both among parties and among voters. The electoral map must be re-drawn so that each vote has approximately the same weight. The electoral system itself must be changed so that parties obtain a proportion of seats corresponding more closely to their proportion of total votes. The parties themselves must become more transparent with regard to their real sources of support. This is not the place to examine the technical aspects of these reforms, but to state categorically that if the electoral system does not take on this transparency and provide an assurance of fairness to all voters and parties, then more and more people will espouse other means of choosing – or getting rid of – their government leaders. The legislative system also needs to have restored that transparency it lost long ago through the subtle games that are played in what an American author once called "the house without windows" (Parliament). Again, without elaborating on the necessary reforms, we suggest, for instance, that the Cabinet and certain legislative committees become itinerant; like commissions of inquiry, they could meet outside the capital and solicit information and opinions through direct contact with the citizens on poverty, regional development, education, leisure, and other topics. In this way, they could demonstrate to a degree not possible in the present circumstances of parliamentary life that elected representatives are transparent before the fellow citizens they represent.

It is also our view that a basic postulate of the governmental system is the principle of equivalence, which must be continually evoked in contradistinction to the rule of prevalence, or priority to the dominant elements of society, in the distribution of jural, economic, symbolic, and informational resources. The brief outline we have presented indicates clearly that, in the present distribution of resources in Quebec, certain groups and certain sectors prevail over others; a study by regions would reveal even more significant disparities. The rationale of the governmental system is to pursue policies that, from a normative point of view, result in the greatest degree of equivalence, or equality of distribution, of the total resources at the disposal of political agents. The allocation of political power, which is the object of political analysis, is related to the control of all jural, material, symbolic, and informational resources, and not of just one or two of them. Hence the necessity of distinguishing equivalence from equalization, which refers to equal, or more or less equal, allocation of one category of resources. The distinction made earlier between the ownership and control of the four types of resources now becomes more precise. To provide a political agent with information does not ensure him equivalence of power with another who has jural resources at his disposal that are effective in a particular situation. After all, information is only an indirect attribute of ownership and control, while a right is a direct prerogative.

This basic logic underpinning the principle of equivalence which, we argue, should characterize the governmental system, cannot be assured unless the government makes a continuous effort to dissociate itself from the social systems within the state that it must keep in harmony, and makes conscious choices between what are often contradictory options. The two principal contradictions concern the increase in the quantity of resources and the assurance of equivalence in their distribution, and the pursuit of equivalence and the increase in disparity of resources between the governors and the governed. If the increase in total resources is not regulated by the governmental system, there is a risk that it will be accompanied by growing disparity among political agents; on the other hand, if the governmental system pushes too hard for equivalence the growth in resources could suffer. A possible strategy could involve playing the different "prevalences," or privileged groups, against one another, since equivalence, we repeat, does not necessarily mean an equal distribution of each of the resources. More rights could be given to those who have fewer material resources; those who have less prestige could receive more information. As for the contradiction between a far-reaching intervention by the governmental system and the growing disparity between governors and governed, that can also be resolved by a conscious and deliberate strategy based on the objective search for equivalence, but not by interventionism for its own sake or even by a simplistic form of equalization. The state would thus play the role of stabilizer; it would make its influence felt forcefully at times, and less forcefully at others, as the requirements of equivalence varied from situation to situation, or sector to sector.

The Shortcomings of the Parties

None of the four principal provincial parties in Quebec, in our view, has espoused this conception of the governmental system with sufficient coherence and relevance. Their greatest weakness lies certainly in the area of legislative reform, where their proposals have been limited to an imported presidential form of government, or to superficial modifications in the working of the parliamentary system. It is not clear how these changes could give the legislative system a greater transparency. In the area of electoral reform more specific suggestions have been made. The Parti Québécois, for instance, has put forward a coherent and comprehensive plan with perhaps only one weakness: the technical aspects of the mixed electoral system, partly based on simple majorities in each constituency, partly on proportional representation, might well have been examined in greater depth to assess their ramifications.[9] One can also ask whether such a formula would not be so complicated that it would reduce the transparency of the electoral system rather than increase it. The Liberal Party, for its part, has not been able to overcome its internal divisions sufficiently to formulate a proposal of its own, while the Union Nationale and the *Ralliement Créditiste* have shown little interest in reforming the electoral system.

There is even less willingness within the four parties to apply the principle of equivalence. The reticence of Union Nationale in this regard is so flagrant that it has become a serious obstacle to the continuing existence of that party. Torn between its nostalgia for a form of society in which the governmental system reflected the traditional, outdated equivalences, and recognition of the necessity to develop new equivalences appropriate to a set of conditions irrevocably different from the Quebec of Maurice Duplessis, the Union Nationale must soon choose between the past and the future. The rather passive role of the governmental system to which it clings hinders it from seeing government activity as a factor to be invoked in varying degrees as the pursuit of equivalence dictates. The *Ralliement Créditiste* at least has a clear position in this regard; its objective is a general increase in material resources (through monetary policies) to be brought about in a way that would add to the resources of the poor without taking away from the rich. Informational resources do not count for much in its plan; the party sees in educational reform a threat to the traditional solidarities and forms of prestige that it cherishes. The *Ralliement Créditiste* programme is based on the unlikely possibility of reconstructing the society of ten or twenty years ago, with additional allocations of material resources to ensure a higher degree of equivalence. While this party has a rather clear understanding of the principle of equivalence which must be reflected in a governmental system, it can be criticized mainly for deluding itself and others concerning the possibility of achieving a high level of equivalence in Quebec in the next few years. Unless, of course, traumatic events, such as the kidnappings that occurred in late 1970 cause the majority of voters to turn, in need of reassurance and stability, to a quest for a lost order. . . .

Except for the early 1960s, the Liberal Party has aimed for a general increase in all resources, or at least an increase in those that have been neglected, rather than concentrating on assuring a high level of equivalence in their distribution. It has also sought to extend the scope of governmental activities, but has shown insufficient concern for the growing distance between governors and governed that results from such a policy. Under Robert Bourassa, efficiency is a fundamental preoccupation of the Liberals; efficiency *per se* as applied to any undertaking, however, and the particular demands of a governmental system are not taken sufficiently into account. To regain a more appropriate perspective, the Liberals must return to the priorities governing their actions at the beginning of the 1960s; they must assure a high level of equivalence through a balancing of prevalence or privileges, rather than pursuing growth for its own sake and taking corrective action to reduce the most glaring disparities. But they must first demonstrate, by party reform and particularly reform of party financing, that they are free to take action against certain prevalences or privileged sectors of society on which they are dependent either to win elections or for other purposes.

Finally, the Parti Québécois has given first priority among its objectives to strengthening the state, first through political independence, then by allocating to it a dynamic role with regard to all resources. The program of the Parti Québécois aims to do everything, an aim which is not a policy. There is also a danger that the governmental system envisaged by the Parti Québécois would be still more cumbersome than that of the Liberal Party, and that its technocratic character would be even more of an obstacle to the re-election of those in power. Thus the options of the Parti Québécois should be better defined, particularly in view of the possibility that political independence would place the resources of Quebec, at least for a certain period, in the control of persons favorable to independence. Nothing in the present program offers the assurance that the governmental system, in the hands of the Parti Québécois, would reduce the prevalences or assure a better balance among them, or that it would not lead to the interposition of new prevalences between the omnipresent bureaucracy and the population.

Parties lack most at the moment a coherent position with regard to the logic, or the specific requirements, of a governmental system, a position developed through rigorous analysis of the political forces at work and based on a strategy for increasing the measure of equivalence. Meeting this need has a higher priority than the Parti Québécois' goal of independence *per se*, the Liberals' efficiency-oriented state, the Union Nationale's comfortably familiar régime, or the *Ralliement Créditiste's* concepts based on a new monetary theory. In this urgent undertaking, social considerations must take precedence over national ones, whether Quebec- or Ottawa-based. And it is necessary to keep clearly in mind the essentially complex nature of the situation in order to avoid espousing too exclusively nationalist or nationalizing solutions in the quest for those forms of equivalence that characterize rational political societies.

Notes

1. For more details on the provincial party system in Quebec, see our study, "Heaven is Blue and Hell is Red," in M. Robin (ed.), *Provincial Party Politics*. Scarborough: Prentice-Hall of Canada, 1972.
2. In this regard, see V. Lemieux, "Le Jeu de la communication politique," *Canadian Political Science Review*, September, 1970, pp. 359-375.
3. This famous distinction was made by K. Mannheim in *Idéologie et Utopie*. Paris: Librairie Marcel Rivière, 1956.
4. On this subject, see our book, *Parenté et Politique*. Quebec: Presses de l'Université Laval, 1971.
5. Max Weber, *The Theory of Social and Economic Organization*. New York: Oxford University Press, 1947, p. 328.
6. Paul Mus used this expression in his course at the Collège de France.
7. We have chosen the year 1960 as a starting point because it marks the beginning of the Quiet Revolution. As for the year 1968, it is the last one for which we have current data. In interpreting the data, it is, of course, necessary to take into account the fact that 1960 and 1968 were years of economic recession: the unemployment rate was 9.1% in 1960 and 6.5% in 1968. It should also be noted that the following categories of occupations, of less significance for us, have been omitted from the table, so as not to overload it: federal, municipal, and unclassified employees; fishermen; investors; property owners; as well as non-classified occupations. The final total, however, includes the categories which do not appear in the table.
8. See his study, "Les aspects socio-culturels de la dépolitisation," in G. Vedel and others, *La Dépolitisation*. Paris: A. Colin, 1962, pp. 167-207.
9. These questions have been examined in the study, *Le Système électoral québécois, Réforme ou réformette?* published by the *Société Nationale des Québécois du centre du Québec* (1970). Because of technical considerations, the authors proposed a different formula from that of the Parti Québécois, calling for the election of half the deputies by majority vote, the other half (and not a third) by proportional representation.

8

The Ongoing Political Realignments in Quebec[1]
by Maurice Pinard

The 1970 Quebec provincial elections provide an example of a surprisingly sudden and extensive political realignment.[2] While not unique in Canada (comparable swings occurred in Alberta in 1921 and 1935), this phenomenon is rare in the electoral politics of Western nations.[3] In 1970, Quebec's traditional two-party system was superseded by a multi-party system as two new parties obtained significant proportions of the popular vote. The extent of this realignment emerges clearly from a simple comparison of the results of the 1966 and 1970 elections, as seen in the first two columns of Table 1.

From one election to the next, the Union Nationale, a major party in Quebec provincial politics since the mid-thirties and governing party for most of this time (1936-39, 1944-60, and 1966-70), lost half its support, dropping from 41 percent of the votes in 1966 to 20 percent in 1970. Conversely, the strength of the independentist** Partie Québécois and the right-wing *Ralliement Créditiste* – both new parties running for the first time in 1970 – was substantially greater than that of their counterparts in 1966; they gained respectively 23 percent and 11 percent of the votes as opposed to 6 percent and 3 percent. Furthermore, no seats were won in 1966 by either the *Rassemblement pour l'Indépendance Nationale* or by the *Ralliement National*. In 1966 the two traditional parties captured 88 percent of votes cast – in itself a low mark for recent decades – but in 1970, the percentage suddenly dropped to only two-thirds of the electorate (65 percent), an unprecedented low for elections when the two main parties have contested all or nearly all seats.[4] This overall realignment, however, disguises what appear to be in fact two quite separate realignments, one in the Montreal area, the other affecting the rest of the province.

---

* Editor's note: In this chapter we ignore the fact that the Union Nationale was called *Unité Québec* for a brief period ending January, 1973.

** An expression accepted increasingly in both French and English in Quebec to describe a person or group that favours the independence of Quebec.

Table 1
The Results of the 1966 and 1970 Provincial Elections in Quebec

	Province-Wide		Montreal Only*		Outside of Montreal	
	1966	1970	1966	1970	1966	1970
	% of Votes					
Liberal Party	47	45	53	57	45	39
Union Nationale	41	20	30	10	46	25
R.I.N. ('66) – Parti Québécois ('70)	6	23	9	30	4	20
R.N. ('66) – Ralliement Créditiste ('70)	3	11	1	2	4	16
Others	3	1	6	1	2	+
	Number of Seats					
Liberal Party	50	72	19	21	31	51
Union Nationale	56	17	6	-	50	17
R.I.N. ('66) – P.Q. ('70)	-	7	-	6	-	1
R.N. ('66) – R.C. ('70)	-	12	-	-	-	12
Others	2	-	2	-	-	-

+ Less than 1 per cent

* Includes the 27 electoral districts of Montreal Island (25) and Ile Jésus (2). (Note that this is different from the Montreal metropolitan area, to be considered in Table 2 below).

The Realignment in Montreal

The Montreal realignment was quite drastic, and may have definitely shaped its political map for the foreseeable future. In the brief period between one election and another, this area has shifted from one basically two-party system of Liberals and the Union Nationale to another two-party system of Liberals and the Parti Québécois. In 1966, the two main parties together polled 83 percent of votes (Liberals 53 percent, Union Nationale 30 percent); in 1970, two parties again together polled as much as 86 percent of the votes (Liberals 57 percent, Parti Québécois 30 percent).[5] (See the Montreal panel of Table 1.) In both elections, the third and fourth contenders in Montreal won only marginal positions, together polling only 10 percent of votes in 1966, and 12 percent in 1970. The Union Nationale is now a marginal party in Montreal; if it fails to keep the 10 per cent support it won in 1970, and if the *Ralliement Créditiste* does not attract its supporters, the movement to a new two-party system in this area would be accentuated.

It is difficult to say how durable this realignment in Montreal will be. It certainly seems unlikely that Unité Québec could make a strong come-back there in the very near future. That the *Ralliement Créditiste* could suddenly and radically strengthen its position is also unlikely, though some gains are not impossible. This is indicated at least by the success of Social Credit in this area in the recent 1972 federal elections. Albeit without the Parti Québécois as a challenger, the *Créditistes* succeeded for the first time in running second to the Liberals in Montreal. Nevertheless, it seems that the new two-party system of Liberals and Parti Québécois will continue in the near future.

Long-term developments are, however, difficult to forecast. For one thing, the existence of a strong relationship between social cleavages and party systems[6] suggests the possibility of a three-party system in Montreal. The presence of a permanent class cleavage and the saliency at the present time of the "national" question especially among the more privileged, produce three different groups, and each could have its own party. There could, for instance, be a party of the underprivileged (*e.g.*, the *Ralliement Créditiste* or Union Nationale); a party of privileged separatists (the Parti Québécois); and a party of privileged federalists (the Liberals).

At present, the Parti Québécois has succeeded in becoming the representative of the first two groups and it is not unlikely that it will continue to do so. After all, the Union Nationale did just that for many years. But the latter had in its favour its milder position on nationalism;

the Parti Québécois may in future be hindered by its more extreme and more costly option. Rejection of the separatist option by the underprivileged could conceivably in the long run open the way to a third party, perhaps under the guise of a more "modern" Ralliement Créditiste or even a rejuvenated Union Nationale.

It is equally difficult to forecast the relative electoral strengths of the Liberals and the Parti Québécois in Montreal. The indications are, in mid-1972, that the Liberal Party continues to hold its dominant position, while the Parti Québécois is not making substantial gains. In fact, an August, 1972, poll of the Montreal metropolitan area showed that Liberals, Parti Québécois and *Ralliement Créditiste* remained fairly stable, at best making rather minor gains, compared with their actual support in 1970. The Liberals were 6 percent ahead of their 1970 showing, the Parti Québécois 3 percent, and the *Ralliement Créditiste* 2 percent. Gains were made largely at the expense of Union Nationale, which lost 8 percent (see Table 2). Clearly, this poll gives little support to the belief that the Parti Québécois has been making significant advances in Montreal. The situation at mid-term looks like a stalemate: the Liberals and the Parti Québécois are in exactly the same position, relative to each other, as in 1970, with electoral support remaining in a 1.9 to 1.0 ratio.

In terms of seats, the overall results of the poll suggest that an August 1972 election could have produced a distribution similar to that of 1970. However, a change in the relative concentration of vote intentions for the two main parties could very much affect this. According to the poll, 48 percent of the French-speaking electorate in the Montreal region intended to vote for the Liberals, 44 percent for the Parti Québécois. The figures for the non-French-speaking electorate are 85 percent and 10 percent respectively.[7] These figures cannot be compared with actual results in 1970, which are not available by language groups. Nor are the 1972 vote intentions given separately for eastern and western parts of Montreal, which would have given a better idea of potential gains or losses in terms of seats for each party.

Certainly there are no signs that the Parti Québécois will capture any seats in the western, English-speaking section of Montreal. Even the Union Nationale in its heyday failed to do so, despite its more moderate nationalism. But in the French-speaking eastern section, slight shifts in the relative position of the Parti Québécois and the Liberals in terms of votes could mean large shifts in terms of seats. A slight decline in the Parti Québécois vote could leave the party with no representation at all, particularly in a two-party contest. It is significant that in 1970 the Parti Québécois captured its few seats in downtown Montreal with a propor-

Table 2

Actual 1970 Vote and 1972 Vote Intention
in the Montreal Metropolitan Area

	Actual Vote in Montreal, 1970* %	Vote Intention in Montreal, 1972* %
Liberal Party	56	62
Parti Quêbécois	29	32
Union Nationale (Unité Québec)	11	3
Ralliement Créditiste	2	4
Other parties	1	–
100% =	(1,175,202)	(270)

* Based on the actual results of the April, 1970 election in the Montreal metropolitan area, *i.e.* in the 27 electoral districts of Montreal Island and Ile Jésus, plus Chambly, Taillon, and part of Napierville-Laprairie, Châteauguay, Verchères, Vaudreuil-Soulanges, Deux-Montagnes, Terrebonne and L'Assomption.

** Recomputed from the weighted results of a CROP poll of August 1972 in the Montreal metropolitan area and published in *La Presse*, August 15, 1971. (Those who did not give a vote intention – 36% – are assumed to be distributed among parties in the same proportions as those who gave one; with those undecided, the total N is 406).

tion of votes no greater on the average than its share in other French districts. But in downtown Montreal the Union Nationale remained strong, thus diminishing the Liberal share of votes and enabling the Parti Québécois to emerge first; the reverse was true in the other French ridings. In other words, the Liberals won where a two-party system was approximated since the Parti Québécois vote was relatively constant. Note, however, that as the incumbent party, the Liberals may be in a less favourable position next time.

At the other extreme, the Parti Québécois could reach a situation of clear dominance in French Montreal with a relatively slight increase in its vote, capturing all or practically all seats, as the Union Nationale did, for instance, in 1948 and 1956. But even this situation would leave the Parti Québécois with little more than fifteen seats out of a total of 108.

Again, uncertainty about the net impact of two strong forces working in opposite directions makes predictions unreliable: on the one hand, economic grievances (particularly if there is no rapid improvement in that area) turn voters away from the Liberals; on the other, separatism, opposed even by the large majority of the French-speaking electorate for the last ten years,[8] alienates voters from the Parti Québécois.

The Ongoing Political Realignments in Quebec   123

Realignment in the Province Outside Montreal

If the new two-party system in the Montreal area seems to have been stabilized, at least for the time being, the same cannot be said of the rest of the province. The previous Liberal and Union Nationale two-party system outside Montreal may have been broken, but the new situation created by the 1970 election certainly cannot be described as another two-party system. True, as in Montreal, the situation has changed from that of 1966, when Liberals and Union Nationale together obtained 91 percent of the votes; in 1970 together they received the support of only about two-thirds, or 64 percent, of the electorate (see Table 1, right-hand panel). But whereas in Montreal the Liberals captured almost all of this combined vote (57 percent), outside Montreal this vote was split more evenly (Liberals 39 percent, Union Nationale 25 percent). Again, whereas in Montreal almost all of the remaining third of the electorate voted for the Parti Québécois, outside Montreal the same proportion was more closely divided between the Parti Québécois (20 percent) and the *Ralliement Créditiste* (16 per cent). Thus, outside of Montreal there has emerged a four-party system rather than a three-party or a new two-party system (compare the last two panels of Table 1).

This new four-party system outside Montreal raises some interesting questions. Is it a temporary phenomenon only, due perhaps to some lag, and soon to follow Montreal into a new two-party system? If it does follow Montreal, will the parties be the same? Or does it follow some dynamics of its own, with a different party configuration and the assurance of some stability?

Again, the theory predicting a relationship between cleavages and party systems could, in some respects, lead to the conclusion that this new party system outside Montreal would in all likelihood be less stable than that of Montreal. In rural Quebec there are possibly now more parties than there are cleavages. If there are only two cleavages – primarily the class cleavage, which separates the more privileged from the less privileged and secondarily the ideological cleavage on the "national" question which seriously cross-cuts only the more privileged group – then it would seem that at the most three parties would be necessary. These would be the Liberals for the privileged federalists, the Parti Québécois for the privileged separatists, and the *Ralliement Créditiste* or Union Nationale for the less privileged. Naturally, because of the historical circumstances of their development, party systems are not necessarily the perfect mirror images of existing social cleavages; for instance, the *Ralliement Créditiste* and the Union Nationale could represent the same group, but in different regions of rural Quebec. However, in the current context the Union Nationale might very well be superseded by the *Ralliement Créditiste*.

If it is assumed for a moment that, at least in the near future, the likely outcome is a three- rather than a four-party system – and the results given below (Table 3) of a poll conducted outside Montreal in April, 1972, point in this direction – then how stable would this three-party system be compared to the two-party system of Montreal? The theory implies, as we have seen, that such a system is the more con-

Table 3
Actual 1970 Vote and 1972 Vote Intention
Outside the Montreal Metropolitan Area

	Actual Vote Outside Montreal, 1970* %	Vote Intention, 1972** %
Liberal Party	38	33
Union Nationale (Unité Québec)	26	12
Parti Québécois	19	21
Ralliement Créditiste	17	30
Other parties	+	3
100% =	(1,697,768)	(360)

+ Less than 1 percent.

* Official results for Quebec, excluding the ridings and parts of ridings comprising the Montreal metropolitan area, i.e., the 27 ridings in the Island of Montreal and Ile Jésus, Chambly, Taillon, and part of Napierville-Laprairie, Châteauguay, Verchères, Vaudreuil-Soulanges, Deux-Montagnes, Terrebonne and L'Assomption. These results differ somewhat from those published at the time of the poll, because then only the ridings in the Island of Montreal and Ile Jésus were excluded. In the present calculation, the vote percentage for the Liberal Party and the Parti Québécois is reduced by 1%, while that for the Union Nationale and the *Ralliement Créditiste* is increased by 1%.

** Results obtained from two questions: the first, asking voting intentions "tomorrow," was followed by a second asking those who said they did not know, which party they would be inclined to support. On the first question, no less than 46.5% were undecided; after the second question, this percentage fell to 30.6%. It is interesting to note that this technique, while increasing the percentage of those expressing an intention, alters the results only marginally; in fact, omitting the second question, the percentages in the second column would have been: Liberal Party, 34%; *Unité Québec*, 11%; Parti Québécois, 20%; *Ralliement Créditiste*, 32%; other parties, 3% (N = 270). See also footnote 12 to the text.

gruent, particularly if the cleavage on the national question remains salient. We might therefore discover that, contrary to previous trends and to the now established pattern in Montreal, the less privileged and the privileged nationalists will continue to be represented by separate parties, rather than by the same party.

On the other hand, in the past, two parties have been sufficient to represent these two social groups, albeit under conditions when the salience of the national question was generally lower. It could therefore be envisioned that just such a party system, or something close to it, could reappear. If it is assumed that the Liberals could not easily be evicted from their position as one of the parties, then the second slot would have to be filled by either the Parti Québécois or the *Ralliement Créditiste*. The Parti Québécois would, one assumes, have the advantage of its strength in Montreal, its dynamic organization, its charismatic leadership and, possibly, its positive stance towards the problems of the less privileged – though in Quebec, as elsewhere, leftist politics has not in the past been a guarantee of working-class support.[9] But the Parti Québécois would probably suffer from its radical image and from the fact that the separatist option still appeals to only a limited number of voters. The *Ralliement Créditiste*, on the other hand, would have the advantage of being closer to the large number of less privileged because of its more conservative ideology, its populist stance on economic questions and its moderate stance on nationalist questions. In reality, its orientations are very similar to those of the Union Nationale, and no one can dispute that such positions have been politically rewarding in rural Quebec.

This speculation cannot, of course, lead to definitive conclusions. On the other hand, a poll conducted outside the Montreal metropolitan area in April 1972 makes it possible to estimate what would have been the results of an election held at that time.[10] Whereas the Montreal poll presented in Table 2 showed that the situation there appeared relatively stable (except for the further decline of the Union Nationale), outside Montreal the situation appears much more fluctuating.[11] Table 3 presents the results of the 1970 election, together with the results of the 1972 poll.

The most striking feature to emerge is the position of the *Ralliement Créditiste*. Though beset by internal conflict and split into two factions at the time of the poll,[12] the results indicate that it was making substantial gains outside of Montreal, while the Parti Québécois, the other new party, was virtually standing still. In fact, the poll indicates that outside Montreal the *Ralliement Créditiste* would have moved from fourth place, with 17 percent, to second place, with 30 percent of votes (28 percent if the probable non-francophone alignment is taken into account).[13] It would thus have replaced the Union Nationale, which in turn would have fallen from second to fourth place (from 26 percent to 12 percent of the votes). The Liberal Party would have lost about 5 percent of its votes (2 percent after correction)[14] while the Parti Québécois would scarcely have changed, going from 19 percent to 21 percent of the votes (20 percent after correction). This is to say that if an election had been held in April, 1972, the *Ralliement Créditiste* would have won as many if not more seats than the Union Nationale won in 1970 (when the Ralliement Créditiste had 13, the Union Nationale 17). Although it is difficult to transcribe the results of such a poll into seats, and although it is not known how the Parti Québécois would have fared in Montreal, it is not inconceivable that the *Ralliement Créditiste* could have replaced the Union Nationale as the official opposition in Quebec.

All in all, it would appear that its internal crisis did not too seriously affect the advance of the Ralliement Créditiste in the province outside Montreal; in any event, any losses provoked by the split are more than offset by the gains realized since the 1970 elections. This substantial advance warrants a more detailed analysis.

Limited Information on the Conflict

In considering the reasons for this advance, the first factor – though probably not the most important – is the relative lack of repercussion of the internal conflict on the population. People were asked towards the beginning of the interview:

> There have recently been disagreements within the *Ralliement Créditiste*, and the party is divided into two groups, that of Mr. Camil Samson and that of Mr. Armand Bois. Are you very aware, quite aware, hardly aware, or not at all aware of what has happened within the *Ralliement Créditiste?*

The response was 26 percent for the first two categories combined, and for the last two, 45 percent and 29 percent respectively (N=577). This shows that very few electors had any significant awareness of the conflict. Even the *Créditiste* voters, who should have felt more affected by these events, were not very much better informed: in their case, the response was 28 percent (for the first two categories combined), 59 and 13 percent respectively for the others (N=108). That is to say, hardly more than one in four *Créditiste* voters declared themselves very or quite aware of the events. This is not so surprising when it is realized that *Créditiste* voters have less formal education and are thus in general very likely to be less well-informed politically. On the other hand, it could be expected that the better-informed *Créditistes* would be the most partisan. In fact, our results indicate that the *Ralliement Créditiste* kept 96 percent of its better-informed 1970 voters, while it kept only 84 percent of the less well-informed (N = 19 and 48 respectively).

In short, it is evident that the crisis did not make too many inroads into the *Créditiste* ranks: either they were hardly aware of the conflict, or if they were, they were too partisan to defect.

Strength of the Party on the Federal Level

A second factor in the *Créditiste* advance. – and this is an important factor – lies in the superior power, at least until recently, of Social Credit on the federal level. Whereas in its first breakthrough in 1962 Mr. Caouette's federal party mobilised 36 percent of the electorate in the 54 ridings outside Montreal, Mr. Samson's provincial party gathered only 16 percent of the vote in the same area (that is, excluding only the Island of Montreal and Ile Jésus) in its first advance in 1970. Mr. Caouette's party lost ground after the 1962 and 1963 elections, but in 1968 it still collected 26 percent of the vote outside Montreal.[15] That is about 10 percent more than the provincial party won in 1970. The same proportion (26 percent) of those interviewed in the 1972 poll declared their intention of voting Social Credit "if a federal election were held tomorrow."[16] The percentage of persons intending to vote *Créditiste* at the provincial level (28 percent, including the non-francophones) seems to indicate that, carried along by the success of the federal party, the *Ralliement Créditiste* would have reached provincially the same level of support as the Social Credit federally.

The evidence supports this analysis. Consideration of those who intend to vote Social Credit federally reveals that, in 1970, only 57 percent of them voted *Créditiste* provincially, but that now 83 percent of them intend to vote for the *Ralliement Créditiste* (N = 84 and 93 respectively). Thus a closer identification between the two groups is being established, with a similar allegiance on the two levels of government. This is the classic phenomenon of voting the straight ticket, which also occurs in general with the other parties, but is very significant at the moment in the case of the *Ralliement Créditiste*. The gains thus realized are being made at the expense of the two traditional provincial parties, especially the Union Nationale.

Among those who intend to vote Social Credit federally, 80 percent of the 1970 Union Nationale electors and 58 percent of the Liberals now intend to vote *Créditiste* provincially (N = 13 and 14 respectively).

Decline of the Union Nationale

The third factor contributing to the present expansion of the *Créditistes* outside Montreal is the rapid and marked decline of the party which until recently dominated the Quebec political scene. The Union Nationale has continously lost ground since 1956. From its peak of 51.6 percent of votes in 1956, it fell successively to 46.7 percent in 1960, 42.1 percent in 1962, 40.8 percent in 1966 and precipitately to 19.6 percent in 1970. According to our poll, the decline continues, at least outside Montreal. As shown in Table 3, the Union Nationale would now have only 12 percent of the vote outside Montreal, compared with 26 percent in 1970. In fact, results show that among those who said they had voted Union Nationale in 1970, only about half (53 percent) would remain faithful while a quarter (26 percent) would cross to the *Ralliement Créditiste*, 12 percent to the Parti Québécois and 9 percent to the Liberals (N=51). It is difficult to foretell whether in an electoral campaign this party can reawaken old partisan loyalties and regain some of its past strength; the task will certainly not be easy. The Union Nationale has finally declined to the level of support of the federal Progressive Conservative Party although it would be difficult to say which one, of late, has been carrying the other along. In the last federal elections (in 1968) in the region under study the Progressive Conservative Party obtained 25 percent of the vote, while in 1970 the Union Nationale was almost equal with 26 percent; now both are at 12 percent. Among those who intend to vote Progressive Conservative federally, the Union Nationale has kept a large measure of its support, with 80 percent of its 1970 votes (N=20). But among voters favouring the Liberals federally, the Union Nationale has kept only 31 percent of its 1970 votes (N=9), and it has kept a mere 14 percent of its 1970 votes (N=13) among those intending to vote Social Credit federally. Of these, as has been seen in the preceding section, 80 percent intend to support the *Ralliement Créditiste* provincially.

It should not be too surprising that outside Montreal the *Ralliement Créditiste* should be the main beneficiary of Union Nationale defections; in 1962 the federal Social Credit party also attracted many Conservative and Union Nationale voters.[17] Moreover, the *Ralliement Créditiste* and the Union Nationale now have several common traits. Both are predominantly rural. The *Ralliement Créditiste* represents the lower socio-economic strata of society, as did the Union Nationale previously, and this situation is becoming more marked. Moreover, the Union Nationale had gradually become the party of the elderly[18] while the *Ralliement Créditiste* started off as the party of youth;[19] but the negative correlation between age and *Créditiste* vote intention has diminished. Indeed, if only these two variables are considered, there is no relationship between age and *Créditiste* vote intention; and with the level of education constant, there is less of a negative correlation than in the past.

Moreover, we know that in 1962 the poor resisted the appeal of Social Credit on the federal level, even though at that time they were provincially the strongest supporters of the Union Nationale.[20] Now we see that, as previously with the Union Nationale, the *Créditistes* find their strongest support among the economically underprivileged. Indeed, it is within this income group that the *Ralliement Créditiste* has made its biggest gains since 1970: it increased its support by 20 percent among those earning less than $4,000 per annum, while its support among those earning between $4,000 and $6,000 per annum, or more than $6,000, increased only 5 percent or less. The *Créditiste* vote intention in these three income groups, from the lowest to the highest, is now 50 percent, 32 percent, and 15 percent respectively (N= 100, 109 and 123); this represents a very strong negative relationship.[21]

The similarity between the *Ralliement Créditiste* and the Union Nationale is also manifested on another level. In the early 1960s, there was no correlation between traditionalism or conservatism and support for Social Credit, even if at that time there was a positive correlation between traditionalism and Union Nationale support,[22] particularly in the middle class. But our analysis shows that such a correlation does now exist as far as voting for the *Ralliement Créditiste* is concerned. Those who feel that the pace of change in Quebec is too fast or who disapprove of trade unions are more favourable to the *Ralliement Créditiste* than others, even with education constant.[23] This is another point in common between the *Ralliement Créditiste* and the Union Nationale. The new relationship between conservatism and the Créditiste vote is due to at least three factors. First, there is the fact that the Créditistes, by inheriting the Union Nationale vote, have also inherited its characteristics. Secondly, Social Credit is no longer a new phenomenon causing hesitation among the conservatives or eliciting non-ideological support. Thirdly, the emergence of the Parti Québécois as a second political movement, a very different one ideologically, gives the electorate a clear choice.

Quebec Society and Politics

Bad Economic Conditions and Grievances against the Government

Serious economic grievances, particularly in rural areas, contributed decisively to *Créditiste* success in 1962. Our results indicate that this is still important. The political factors already mentioned are conducive conditions which are activated by economic or other grievances. It is noteworthy that, of the people questioned in our poll, three out of ten (29 percent) said that they or members of their family had at some time been unemployed during the past two years. Also, while 63 percent described their financial position over the past year as very good or quite good, 23 percent described it as neither good nor bad, and 14 percent as quite bad or very bad (N=577).

An elector's financial situation has a strong impact on his vote intention, as is demonstrated in Table 4. Poor financial situations increase the

Table 4
Vote Intention According to Economic Situation
and Dissatisfaction with the Government

Financial Situation

	Very Good %	Quite Good %	Neither Good Nor Bad %	Quite Bad %	Very Bad %
Liberal Party	53	39	23	19	36
Unité Québec	9	12	15	11	7
Parti Québécois	24	19	20	30	13
Ralliement Créditiste	14	26	37	38	44
Other parties	0	3	5	3	0
Number =	(26)	(180)	(92)	(46)	(14)

Satisfaction with the Government

	Very Satisfied %	Quite Satisfied %	More or Less Satisfied %	Not Satisfied %
Liberal Party	48	63	25	7
Unité Québec	16	9	14	13
Parti Québécois	16	9	21	38
Ralliement Créditiste	20	19	34	39
Other parties	0	0	6	2
Number =	(19)	(101)	(147)	(86)

likelihood of a *Créditiste* vote and weaken that of a vote for the party in power. This relationship is less evident – and is certainly less marked – for the Union Nationale and the Parti Québécois. Because of these economic grievances – and certainly others – dissatisfaction with the present government is increasing. The second section of Table 4 shows the effect of this dissatisfaction on vote intention. The results are largely similar to those just reported.

To sum up, the recent upsurge of the *Ralliement Créditiste* to second place outside Montreal is explained by the lack of awareness of the movement's internal conflict and by the fact that those who were aware were unaffected by it; by the influence of the stronger Social Credit Party at the federal level; by the decline of the Union Nationale to the benefit of the *Ralliement Créditiste*, its natural heir; and by serious economic grievances and the consequent dissatisfaction with the present government.

Why Not the Parti Québécois?

This analysis has revealed some of the reasons for the recent increase in *Créditiste* support outside Montreal. Put differently, the question becomes: Why did this new support for the *Ralliement Créditiste* not go, at least in part, to the Parti Québécois? Did these two parties not experience approximately the same growth in strength in 1970, with 17 percent and 19 percent of votes respectively? (See Table 3.)

While their growth was, on the whole, about equal outside Montreal, their respective strength varied greatly from one region to another. The Parti Québécois made its greatest gains in the periphery of Montreal, in the city of Quebec, in the Saguenay-Lac St. Jean, North Shore and Lower St. Lawrence areas. The *Ralliement Créditiste* made most progress in areas that had been Social Credit federal strongholds since 1962: the North West (Abitibi), the Eastern Townships, the Bois-Francs and the Quebec area. Where Social Credit was already strong, the Parti Québécois did not fare too well. The first occupant is not easily dislodged, as has already been observed elsewhere.[24]

But despite these inequalities, the strength of the Parti Québécois was more evenly distributed than that of the *Ralliement Créditiste*. While both won 40 percent of the votes in their most successful areas (North Shore and North West respectively), the Parti Québécois' portion did not fall below 11 percent (in the North West) while that of the *Ralliement Créditiste* fell as low as 3 percent (on the North Shore). In fact, the Parti Québécois won between 10 and 20 percent of the votes in six of the nine regions that were analyzed; the *Ralliement Créditiste* reached this level in only three regions. [25]

Although it is difficult to be precise because of the smallness of the sample in some regions, it would seem that the *Ralliement Créditiste*, while making some overall gains, is extending its zone of influence and making its electoral power base more uniform; the Parti Québécois, on the other hand, already more evenly established throughout the different regions of the Province, does not appear to be making further gains outside Montreal. The Parti Québécois succeeded earlier than the *Ralliement Créditiste* in establishing a uniform base, we suggest, because it was perceived earlier as a serious alternative to the traditional parties; this could be the result of the more stimulating character of its leaders and its platform,[26] the greater attention given to the party by the media, and the higher level of information of its supporters. In contrast, people in certain regions may have believed less strongly in the *Ralliement Créditiste* until it had shown itself capable of electing members to the Quebec Assembly. More generally, the Parti Québécois' inability to make at least as much progress as the *Ralliement Créditiste* outside Montreal is due partly to the difference in socio-economic characteristics, attitudes and motivations of Parti Québécois supporters and voters now leaning towards the *Ralliement Créditiste*. The Parti Québécois' greatest strength comes from the more educated, the upper middle class and the more highly paid. It has strong support among youth, although surprisingly this correlation on the basis of age tends to disappear when the level of education is held constant. In other words, the level of education of youth sharply affects their attitude towards the Parti Québécois.[27] As for political leanings, the Parti Québécois draws its support most readily from the less conservative elements of society and above all from those who favour independence (although 23 percent of Parti Québécois supporters are against independence and 13 percent are undecided – N= 75). Because of these factors, the *Ralliement Créditiste* is much more apt to inherit the old Union Nationale vote, and to attract persons who are presently inclined to switch parties. Actually, the Parti Québécois could hope to make more gains from the Liberals than from the Union Nationale because their supporters are more alike, especially in terms of socio-economic status.

Of course, one must not forget the similarity between the attitudes of the Parti Québécois and the Union Nationale on the "national question."[28] But apparently this factor no longer favours the Parti Québécois to the same extent as previously; the party's extremist position on independence limits the number of possible recruits,[29] and, at any rate, it has already attracted about as many Union Nationale supporters as it can. Indeed, there is strong evidence that the proportion of voters favouring separatism remains small. In response to the question:

> Personally, are you for or against the separation of Quebec from the rest of Canada?

only 15 percent of French-speaking voters living outside Montreal declared themselves in favour, 65 percent opposed, and 19 percent were undecided.[30] Thus, there are many more people against than there are for independence. Furthermore, the many polls taken over the past ten years indicate that the proportion of people favouring independence has scarcely increased at all during this period. [31]

Thus the independentist option of the Parti Québécois, cornerstone of its platform, seems likely to remain a serious handicap in its efforts to attract additional voters. Indeed, our data indicate that the 1970 Union Nationale voters, now the main source of *Créditiste* gains, were closer to the other parties than to the Parti Québécois on this question. While only 18 percent of Parti Québécois supporters opposed separation, no less than 64 percent of the Union Nationale voters were opposed; the latter were thus closer to the Liberals and the *Ralliement Créditiste* who each registered 75 percent opposed.[32] We therefore suggest that the Parti Québécois' independentist option is a further contributing factor towards the levelling off of its support outside Montreal. If we distinguish the "decided" (those giving a vote intention to the first question) and the "inclined" (those doing so to the second question – see note of Table 3), it is interesting to note that among those who were decided to vote for the Parti Québécois, 76 percent were in favour of independence and only 13 percent against (N = 54). But among those who were only inclined to vote for the Parti Québécois, only 34 percent favoured independence and no less than 50 percent were opposed (N = 21). A negative attitude toward separation seems to render one hesitant to support the Parti Québécois.

Furthermore, our analysis reveals that among those favouring independence, change in political preference (*i.e.*, from one party to another, from undecided to support for a party, etc.) occurs more frequently towards the Parti Québécois than towards the Ralliement Créditiste or another party (19 against 5 and 7 respectively). But the reverse is true of those opposed to independence; here the change is towards the *Ralliement Créditiste* or the other parties rather than towards the Parti Québécois (36 and 36 against 15 respectively). But the pool of people opposed to independence is much larger than that of people in favour, another factor that militates against the Parti Québécois. If this analysis is correct, it means that the Parti Québécois, whose *raison d'être* is its independentist option, would be much more successful if it abandoned this option. And that is a tremendous electoral paradox.

Summary

Some basic realignments took place in Quebec as a result of the 1970 elections. But the realignment in Montreal was quite different from that outside the city, reflecting more clearly than ever the traditionally different reactions of these two parts of Quebec. Montreal moved from a two-party system comprised of the Liberals and the Union Nationale to a two-party system composed of the Liberals and the Parti Québécois. The rest of the province moved from a two-party system to a four-party system, adding the *Ralliement Créditiste* and Parti Québécois to the traditional Liberals and Union Nationale.

It is not easy to assess the durability – or transience – of these realignments. It seems possible that the Montreal realignment will remain stable in the short run, but the realignment outside Montreal may not yet have run its course. In mid-1972, on the basis of firmer evidence from recent polls, we ascertained that the Liberals continue to dominate in both areas, gaining a few percentage points in Montreal and losing a few outside that city. Conversely, the Union Nationale has now fallen to fourth place in both areas, losing more than half of its already low level of support.

Of the two new parties, the *Ralliement Créditiste* has made heavy gains outside Montreal and moved from fourth to second place, but it has remained very weak in Montreal, about equal to the Union Nationale. Finally – and surprisingly to many observers – the Parti Québécois is, basically, standing still in both areas, gaining just a few percentage points in each case. As in 1970, it is in second place in Montreal, and in third place outside Montreal. If the Parti Québécois were to fail to gain seats outside Montreal, the *Ralliement Créditiste* could very well be the official opposition in the next National Assembly.

Notes

1. I am indebted to Richard Hamilton for his comments on an earlier draft of this paper.

2. On the notion of political realignments and their nature, see for instance V. O. Key, Jr., "A Theory of Critical Elections" in Nelson W. Polsby *et al.*, eds., *Politics and Social Life: An Introduction to Political Behavior.* Boston: Houghton Mifflin Co., 1963, pp. 465-475. For the case of Quebec, see Vincent Lemieux, Marcel Gilbert and André Blais, *Une élection de réalignement: l'élection générale du 29 avril 1970 au Québec.* Montreal: Editions du Jour, 1970.

3. That such realignments should be more likely to occur in smaller political units (states, provinces, etc.) than at the national level should not be too surprising. This is related to the greater homogeneity of the former and the ensuing widespread nature of the underlying factors of such realignments.

4. The 1935 figure was lower, but in that election the Conservatives had made an alliance with the *Action Libérale Nationale* and ran only 33 candidates (Howard A. Scarrow, *Canada Votes.* New Orleans: The Hauser Press, 1962, p. 208).

5. More precisely, the Liberals with 56.6% and the P.Q. with 29.5%; hence the total of 86 and not 87%.

6. See for instance S. M. Lipset, *The First New Nation: The United States in Historical and Comparative Perspective.* New York: Basic Books, 1963, chap. 9.

7. Recomputed from the CROP poll published in *La Presse* (see footnote ** to Table 2).

8. During the last ten years, through various polls and surveys, the question of separatism has been submitted practically every year to the Quebec electorate, or at least to its French-speaking constituents. The proportion favourable to separatism, in all of French-speaking Quebec, has always been below 20%, and, in fact, around 15%. The proportion against separatism in the same group has always been around 70% (the others being undecided). If one were to try to discern a trend in these data, one would have to conclude that *both* the proportion of people favourable *and* the proportion of people unfavourable to separatism increased over time; the only decline was among the undecided.

9. See our "Working-Class Politics: An Interpretation of the Quebec Case," *Canadian Review of Sociology and Anthropology,* vol. 7, 1970, pp. 87-109.

10. The data came from a poll carried out under the responsibility of the *Société de recherches en communications* (SORECOM) and ordered by *Inter-Vidéo*, producer of the TV program, *"Droit de Regard"* for the *Radio-Canada* network. The questionnaire and the analysis of the results were done by the writer. The poll was conducted by telephone between the 6th and 10th of April, 1972, with 577 French-speaking people 18 years and over residing in the province of Quebec, outside the Montreal metropolitan area. The sample is a random one, respondents having been chosen from telephone directories, and is representative of this electorate (except for the small minority of people who do not have a telephone). Starting with an initial list of 801 eligible telephone numbers, a total of

577 interviews were completed, thus giving a rate of 72%. The non-completed interviews (28%) are distributed in the following way:

No answer after 3 calls	6%
Absence of selected person after 3 calls	6%
Declined to take part in interview	14%
Sick, too old, etc.	3%

All results presented here are weighted in order to get a correct representation of the population living in each of the nine regions of the province included within the sample.

11. From here on, the text follows closely the third part of our paper "*La scission du Ralliement Créditiste et ses conséquences électorales*," to be published in a collection of essays on Quebec political parties under the editorship of Réjean Pelletier.

12. The party became involved in a leadership struggle in February, 1972, which led to the formation of an additional Social Credit Party. The split was, however, of short duration, the two groups becoming reconciled in August, 1972. For details on the conflict as well as an analysis of public reactions to it, see our "*La scisson du Ralliement Créditiste.*"

13. It should be mentioned here that questions concerning vote intention were presented towards the end of the questionnaire, coming after (among others) eleven other questions concerning the *Ralliement Créditiste*, two concerning the Union Nationale, and two concerning the other parties. It is possible that some of those interviewed considered that the poll was being made on behalf of the *Ralliement Créditiste* and that they thus gave a false vote intention for the *Ralliement Créditiste,* or that those intending to vote for *the Ralliement Créditiste* revealed their intention more freely than the others. But in our opinion this would explain only a very small minority of *Créditiste* gains registered in the poll. It should also be noted that only francophones were interviewed, so that if anglophones and others had been included the percentages of vote intention could have varied a little. If, on the basis of three polls analyzed by Lemieux and his colleagues (*Une élection de réalignement.* Montreal: Editions du Jour, 1970, page 60), it is assumed that 6 percent of non-francophones would have voted for the *Ralliement Créditiste*, 8 percent for the Parti Québécois, 12 percent for Unité Québec, and 71 percent for the Liberals, and if it is assumed that 7 percent of the electorate concerned is non-fracophone, the percentages in column 2 of Table 3 would read: Liberals, 36%; Unité Québec, 12%; Parti Québécois, 20%; *Ralliement Créditiste*, 28%; other parties, 3% (N= 387, estimated).

14. That our evaluation of the Liberal vote outside Montreal is quite valid is demonstrated by the result showing that 32% of those responding declared themselves "very" or "quite" satisfied with the present Quebec provincial government (N = 554). It is known from the work of the Social Research Group at the beginning of the 60s, that this is an excellent indicator of the electoral strength of the party in power. See Le Groupe de Recherche Sociale, *Les préférences politiques des électeurs québécois en 1962*, Montreal [mimeo], 1964. And it has since been validated several times; see, for example, Lemieux *et al.*, op. cit.

15. This excludes the 24 ridings on the Island of Montreal and Ile Jésus, as well as Vaudreuil, Chambly, Longueuil and Laprairie.

16. The others were divided as follows: Liberals, 51%; Progressive Conservatives, 12%; N.D.P., 5%; *Bloc Québécois*, 5%; other parties, 1% (N = 353).

17. See *The Rise of a Third Party*, chapters 2 and 5, and particularly Tables 2.3 and 5.3.

18. See our study, "Classes sociales et comportement électoral," in *Quatre élections provinciales au Québec, 1956-1966*, published under the direction of Vincent Lemieux, Les Presses de l'Université Laval, 1969, pp. 166 ff; and *Une élection de réalignment, ibid.*, pp. 60-62.

19. See *The Rise of a Third Party*, chapter 9.

20. See *Classes sociales . . .* , ibid. p. 150.

21. This, incidentally, confirms the hypothesis that the poor will eventually join a political movement when it has become a viable alternative; see *The Rise of a Third Party*, chapter 8.

22. *Ibid.*, chapter 12, and *Classes sociales . . .* , pp. 153-156.

23. Thus, for example, the proportions of Créditiste vote intention are 35%, 21% and 19% among those who felt, respectively, that things had changed a little too fast, just fast enough, and not fast enough. The corresponding percentages for the Parti Québécois are 18%, 22% and 51% (N = 232, 75, and 31); this reveals a strong negative relationship between resistance to change and support for the Parti Québécois.

24. See on this subject, Richard F. Hamilton, *Affluence and the French Worker in the Fourth Republic*. Princeton University Press, 1967, pp. 284-286. See also our arguments in *The Rise of a Third Party*, pp. 94 ff.

25. The standard deviations of the vote proportions for each of these new parties in the nine regions are 9.3% for the Parti Québécois and of 12.5% for the *Ralliement Créditiste*; this well indicates the greater uniformity of the Parti Québécois vote.

26. See *Une élection de réalignement*, chapter 7.

27. Among those with nine or fewer years of schooling, the youngest (34 or under) opt for the Parti Québécois in a proportion of 15%; this proportion falls only to 9% among the 35-49 year-olds and to 8% among the more elderly (N = 51, 58 and 91, respectively). Among those with more than ten years' schooling, the corresponding proportions are 36%, 34%, and 34% respectively (N = 109, 29, 21).

28. See for example, *Une élection de réalignement*, pp. 88 ff.

29. *Ibid.*, p. 142.

30. About 1% gave no answer (N = 577). If it is assumed that all non-francophones would have been unfavourable or undecided, the proportion favourable to independence for the whole of the electorate outside Montreal becomes 14% (N = 620, estimated).

31. For example, the same question in 1963 gave a percentage of 11% favouring independence among francophones living outside Montreal, against 16% in Montreal (N=587 and 400). *Le Magazine Maclean*, November 1963, p. 24.

32. The proportion of those favourable to separation, in each of these parties, were respectively, 57%, 17%, 12%, and 7%; the others were undecided (N = 52, 72, 180 and 78).

9
The Quebec Economy: A General Assessment
by André Raynauld

The purpose of this review of the economy of the Province of Quebec is to provide a perspective on the dissatisfaction of French Canadians, and on the general unrest in Quebec. It focuses on the disparity in economic opportunity between French Canadians and other ethnic groups. The subject is divided into three parts. First, short-term indicators of recent economic activity are reviewed, and comparisons made with those in other provinces. Medium-term prospects until about the year 1975 are then examined, providing a useful framework to draw attention in a systematic way to the major structural problems in Quebec. The last part deals with income distribution and control of industry under the heading of social background.

Recent Economic Performance

Short-term variations in economic activity are usually similar in direction, if not in magnitude, in all of the regions of Canada. The recession that lasted from 1958 through 1961 was followed by a period of economic recovery that reached a peak in 1966. In more recent years an uneasy and delicate balance has been struck between inflation and unemployment, with unemployment increasing gradually and inflationary forces receding. This pattern was evident in Quebec as well as in the rest of the country. But while the trends in the different regions were in the same direction, their rate of movement varied. The effect of leads and lags also differs from region to region, and as a rule these differences are very significant for analyses that go beyond the large national aggregates and averages.

Personal income per capita increased more rapidly in Quebec than in Ontario between 1961 and 1969, maintaining a relatively strong aggregate demand. This was reflected in Quebec's gross national product, which increased in 1969 at a rate close to Ontario's. Prices, on the other hand, increased less rapidly in Quebec than in Ontario or in Canada as

Table 1
Labour Force, Employment and Unemployment (1966-1970, Québec, Ontario, Canada)

Year	Labour Force			Employed			Unemployed		
	'000	Variation '000	Rate per 1,000 pop.	'000	Variation '000	Rate per 1,000 pop.	'000	Variation '000	Rate of Unemployment
Québec									
1966	2,116	94	366	2,015	104	349	100	− 9	4.7
1967	2,196	80	374	2,080	64	354	116	15	5.3
1968	2,227	31	376	2,082	2	351	145	29	6.5
1969	2,290	63	383	2,132	50	356	158	13	6.9
1970	2,327	37	387	2,114	12	357	183	25	7.9
Ontario									
1966	2,719	105	391	2,651	103	381	69	3	2.5
1967	2,834	115	396	2,745	94	384	89	20	3.1
1968	2,934	100	402	2,830	85	387	104	15	3.5
1969	3,032	98	407	2,836	106	394	95	− 9	3.1
1970	3,130	98	410	2,995	60	392	134	39	4.3
Canada									
1966	7,420	279	371	7,152	290	357	267	−13	3.6
1967	7,694	274	377	7,379	227	362	315	48	4.1
1968	7,919	225	382	7,537	158	363	382	67	4.8
1969	8,162	243	388	7,780	243	369	382	−	4.7
1970	8,374	212	392	7,879	99	369	495	113	5.9

Source: *The Labour Force* Statistics Canada (Ottawa: Information Canada), (Cat. 71-001).

a whole, so Quebec's increases in gross national product reflected real increases in volume of production. According to consumer price indexes, the annual rate of increase in Montreal in 1968 and 1969 was a full percentage point lower than the Canadian average, with similar differences between Montreal and Toronto. But gross national product and prices are the only two bright spots in the general economic picture in Quebec in the recent past.

In examining the figure relating to employment, we find a clear downward trend after 1968 in the rate of increase in Quebec, but not in Ontario. The annual rate of increase in total employment from 1968 to 1970 was 1.5 percent or 23,000 new jobs annually in Quebec; 3.0 percent or 84,000 new jobs annually in Ontario; and 2.4 percent or 166,000 new jobs annually in all of Canada (see Table 1). Although the rate of population increase in Quebec has fallen to an all-time low – it was 1 percent between 1967 and 1970 – the measured increases in the labour force have remained substantial: 1967, 3.8 percent; 1968, 1.4 percent; 1969, 2.8 percent; 1970, 1.7 percent; 1971, 2.8 percent. Even without the element of disguised unemployment inherent in this irregular pattern of labour force growth, measured unemployment was very substantial. Significantly, in my view, this high rate of unemployment did not occur for the first time in 1967; notwithstanding the general economic recovery of the first half of the 1960s, it is characteristic of a long period starting in 1958.

The rate of unemployment in Quebec is lower today than in 1960 and 1961, when it exceeded 9 percent of the labour force on an annual basis. But it is increasing: it was 6.9 percent in 1969, 7.9 percent in 1970, and 8.2 percent in September, 1971. The fact of the matter is that, throughout the 1960s, unemployment in Quebec was at a recession level, with a low point of 4.7 percent of the labour force in 1966. In relative terms, unemployment in Quebec was typically two percentage points higher than in Ontario throughout the entire period 1941-57. After 1958, the gap widened to an average of 3.5 percent; and in 1969, unemployment was 3.8 percent higher in Quebec than in Ontario; in 1970, 3.6 percent. This is one of the most disturbing aspects of present-day Quebec, particularly in view of its broad ramifications. The relatively poor employment situation preceded by at least five years the deterioration in the political and social climate. In other words, the economic problems preceded the political ones, not the reverse.

Another disturbing feature of the Quebec economy concerns investments, and particularly, although not exclusively investments in manufacturing. The average annual increase in total private and public investments during the period 1961-66 was 10.6 percent in Quebec, 12.2

percent in Ontario, and 11.8 percent in Canada as a whole; it fell to 1 percent annually in Quebec during the period 1967-70. The year 1967 marked a down-turn in employment, and a natural correlation in investment. Subsequently, the rate of investment in manufacturing has oscillated still more dramatically. While it increased 15 percent annually in Quebec and 18 percent in Ontario from 1961 to 1966, the rate of increase fell in the period 1967-70 to .9 percent in Quebec and 7 percent in Ontario. On the other hand, a marked improvement was evident in 1971, with a 16.3 percent increase in investments in Quebec, compared to 7.2 percent in Ontario.

Comparisons of investment to manufacturing output in Quebec reveal such a poor situation that, paradoxically perhaps at first glance one can only feel optimistic about the future. Notwithstanding the considerably reduced investment rate, increase in output appears to have been largely maintained. Between 1965 and 1969, for instance, the Quebec proportion of total Canadian manufacturing did not decline at all; on the contrary, it rose by 0.2 percent. Given the relatively slow growth of employment in Quebec, this output performance indicates a higher than average increase in productivity. This high rate of productivity, and the low investment in recent years, suggests that there will be a substantial demand for new equipment in the future. Accordingly, brighter economic prospects can be anticipated than are reflected in the present wave of pessimism.

From this brief review of the main short-term indicators, I conclude that Quebec has been experiencing, and continues to experience, a recession. Furthermore, I believe that, thanks to the vigourous expansionist policies adopted belatedly by the federal government in mid-1970, we reached the low point of the cycle in 1971.

Structural Characteristics

An appropriate perspective on an economy and an accurate assessment of its potential for growth require a longer period of examination than a single phase of a short-run cycle. A different amalgam of problems must also be studied.

An economy can be easily and vividly portrayed in descriptive terms by outlining its industrial components (see Table 2). Quebec has been analyzed in this manner by the Wonnacotts, John Dales, Gordon Bertram, Claude Dauphin, Gilles Lebel, the Economic Council of Canada, and many others, myself included. In these studies, comparisons have usually been made with Ontario and with some regions of the United

Table 2
GNP by Industrial Sectors As A Percentage
of Total GNP, Constant $, 1951-69

SECTORS	1951		1961		1969	
	Quebec	Canada	Quebec	Canada	Quebec	Canada
Primary	13.2	19.3	6.6	9.8	5.7	9.0
Agriculture, forestry, fisheries	9.8	15.2	3.8	5.7	3.1	5.2
Mines, quarries	3.4	4.1	2.8	4.1	2.6	3.8
Secondary	41.6	34.0	37.3	31.9	33.6	30.4
Manufacturing	36.7	29.2	31.0	26.1	28.1	24.3
Construction	4.9	4.8	6.3	5.8	5.5	6.1
Infrastructure	12.2	11.8	13.1	12.6	12.6	11.7
Transportation	7.8	7.6	7.1	6.9	6.7	6.1
Storage	0.3	0.2	0.3	0.2	0.2	0.2
Communication	1.9	1.8	2.6	2.5	2.8	2.6
Electric Power	2.2	2.2	3.1	3.0	2.9	2.8
Tertiary	40.00	34.9	43.0	45.7	48.1	48.9
Wholesale trade	3.8	3.8	4.5	4.9	4.7	5.0
Retail trade	6.7	7.2	7.7	7.9	7.6	7.4
Finance, insurance and real estate	8.6	8.4	12.2	11.4	11.1	11.0
Public administration and defence	4.3	5.6	5.1	7.3	5.6	7.3
Services	9.6	9.9	13.5	14.2	19.1	18.2
Total	100.0	100.0	100.0	100.0	100.0	100.0

Sources: Statistics Canada and Department of Industry and Commerce, Government of Quebec.

States. In general terms, the province has a relatively high concentration of resource and light consumer goods industries. Agricultural, durable goods, and producers' goods industries are much weaker. This means that there is a relatively large proportion of workers in slow-growth and low labour productivity industries. On the other hand, the overall rate of growth in manufacturing output has remained approximately the same ever since 1870 in both Quebec and Ontario. A fairly wide consensus exists on the reasons for these developments. The first is obviously the natural resource base of Quebec, together with a favourable world demand and a high level of technological competence. The availability of hydro-electric power, wood pulp, and a wide variety of minerals has led to substantial exports, large capital requirements, and a number of induced secondary manufacturing industries.

The second major factor is the Canadian tariff. Recent penetrating studies, particularly those by John Dales, have shown the extraordinary impact of the tariff on foreign trade, on the location of industry, and on population growth and productivity. Since labour was abundant and therefore cheap 'in Quebec when the National Policy was introduced by the Canadian Government in the late 1870s, labour-intensive industries protected by the tariff developed rapidly, and became a significant part of the economy by the turn of the century. These industries were established to serve the Canadian market, and they attained that goal. Today, 15 percent of Quebec's manufactured products are sold abroad and 31 percent are sold in other provinces, for a total of 46 percent. The protected industries account for only a small proportion of the foreign sales, but a high proportion of the exports to other provinces, including soft beverages, textiles, clothing, leather, furniture, tobacco, and rubber goods.

Employment opportunities offered by the tariff contributed to a more rapid growth in Quebec's population than would otherwise have been the case; for most of this century, the increase has been higher than in Ontario, a phenomenon reflected in persistently lower salaries. A current theory holds that present difficulties in maintaining a high level of employment might be associated with the reduction or at least the erosion (through higher prices and increased competition from under-developed or semi-developed countries) of the protection offered by the tariff to Quebec industry. If this theory is correct, Quebec has a need for a major reconversion in the near future. But it remains to be seen if the alternatives in 1971 are the same as they were in 1871, that is, between increased protection in order to protect jobs and population, and rapid long-term growth in standards of living to be attained by allowing effective protection to diminish. Something more than that bleak trade-off should be possible, for instance, through a so-called industrial strategy and regional programmes.

Medium-Term Forecast

A useful way to examine an economy is to estimate its expected per-formance during some future period. Three years ago, I carried out an exercise for the forecast period 1967-75, using a base period of either one full cycle from 1957 to 1966, or two full cycles from 1948 to 1966. The results are given in Table 3. In the aggregate, they indicate a basically sound and strong economy. Predicted output per worker is especially encouraging. In manufacturing, output per worker increased

Table 3
Growth Rate of Macro-Economic Indicators
(Observed and Required)
Quebec 1957-75

(Percentage annual growth rate)

	Observed (1957-66)	Required* Hypothesis A	Hypothesis B
Capital Stock	9.3**	Required in 1970: 4.8 Billion 1975: 6.8 Billion	Required in 1970: 3.5 Billion
Real GNP	4.9	5.8	5.1
Output Per Worker	2.0	2.8	2.8
Employment	2.7	2.8	2.2
Labour Force	2.6	2.2	2.2

* Hypothesis A: The assumed magnitudes in this case imply no unemployment by 1975.
Hypothesis B: The assumed magnitudes in this case imply 4.7 percent unemployment by 1975, and require 50,000 new jobs a year starting in 1967 and 75,000 new jobs a year starting in 1971.
** 1947-66.

---

at a rapid rate of 4.4 percent a year from 1957 to 1966; the projection until 1975 indicates a rate of 4.5 percent (see Table 3).

Other estimates are less optimistic than mine. Recent experience has not met my expectations, but I am still confident that the first half of the 1970s will witness a repetition of the conditions in the first half of the 1960s. Concerning savings and investments, the magnitude of capital requirements may be somewhat frightening, and, in the current state of public opinion, the federal and provincial governments may not be able to allow private enterprise to increase profits to the extent necessary to achieve the employment goals.

Social Background

Examination of the basic data on Quebec's economy reveals serious problems; but it explains neither the frequent gloomy predictions and diagnoses nor the intensity of dissatisfaction felt by Quebecers with their present economic situation. Relatively high unemployment and reconversion problems are not unique to Quebec, and in comparative terms, are not particularly severe. Scotland, the Atlantic Provinces, Appalachia, and *la Wallonie* are probably in a poorer long-term situation than Quebec, yet they are not usually described on the basis of their unfavourable economic environments as political powder kegs.

Thus, we must look elsewhere for the economic causes of present discontent in Quebec. Even though the basic data I examined are strictly economic, I have included under the heading of social background two further dimensions: distribution of income and ownership of enterprises. I believe that they are the most important economic factors contributing to the rise of the present vocal nationalism in Quebec.

My contention is, first, that the unequal access of French Canadians to high-income and high-power jobs in the private sector of Quebec's economy is related specifically to ethnic factors and is reflected in the relative income levels of French Canadians both in Canada and within Quebec. Second, I agree that these factors should be reflected in any explanation of recent developments such as increasing popular support for separatism, and belief, widespread among French Canadian élites, that action by the state is the best, if indeed not the only way to solve Quebec's economic and social problems. While the economist's tools are unsuitable for testing the second part of my hypothesis, they offer a very useful framework to approach the first part. Accordingly, I shall first analyze the distribution of income by ethnic group, and then provide some data on the distribution of economic power.

Distribution of Income

Regional income disparities in Canada have been well documented but do not accurately reflect ethnic differences. Income per capita has been shown to be about 25 percent lower in Quebec than in Ontario, for instance, and there is fragmentary evidence that the gap has not narrowed since 1926, or even since 1870. While these figures are important – mainly because they are so well known – they are less important than more detailed analyses according to ethnic groups.

Some basic demographic features of the Canadian mosaic are worth recalling at the outset. In 1961, Canadians of British origin comprised 45 percent of the population, Canadians of French origin 28 percent, Germans 5.6 percent, Italians 3.4 percent, Jews 1.3 percent, and other groups still smaller percentages. In Quebec, French Canadians constituted 76 percent of the population, Canadians of British origin 12 percent, and all others 12 percent, of the total population of about 5.2 millions.

The distribution of total income in Canada in 1961 by ethnic groups and labour income is shown in Table 4. The absolute difference in

Table 4
Index of Total and Labour Income
Male Labour Force – Canada, 1961

	Total Income	Labour Income
Total	100.0	100.0
British	109.0	110.6
French	88.9	87.0
German	94.1	96.1
Italian	82.6	82.3
Jewish	171.9	159.5
Ukrainian	92.4	94.4
Others	94.8	94.9

Source: Census of Canada 1961.

average annual income between British and French Canadians was 980 dollars in total income and 960 dollars in labour income: The differential in percentages is 20 percent.

The most remarkable fact revealed by these figures is that French Canadian labour income was 12 percent below the overall average in every province except Quebec, where it was 40 percent below the over-all provincial average. In absolute terms, the gap was about 1,000 dollars a year in Canada as a whole, and 2,000 dollars in Quebec.

To isolate the influence of ethnicity on incomes, the influence of a host of other income determinants must be held constant. In my studies, I eliminated, either by regression analysis or by considering only certain subgroups such as full-time gainfully employed males, the possible influence of several factors: age; sex composition of the labour force; education; occupation; employment status; region; and labour force participation. Over all, the predutive power of some 80 variables – plus ethnicity – is similar in magnitude to that shown in similar studies, for example, Morgan, et al., in Income and Welfare in the U.S. (R^2 of .325 and .340 respectively). My analysis showed that variables other than ethnicity explained less than 50 percent of the differences in income between French Canadians and Canadians of English and Scottish descent. They eliminated most of the differential between Jews and Italians on the one hand, and French Canadians on the other. Thus, the influence of ethnicity on earnings, shown in Column 2 of Table 5, was the sum of the influence of all other measurable factors.

In 1961, Anglo-Scots earned 1,319 dollars more than the average, and French Canadians 330 dollars less than the average; the observed disparity between these two groups was thus 1,649 dollars per annum. When all other factors were held constant, Anglo-Scots were 606 dollars above the average and French Canadians 267 dollars below the average; the net disparity was reduced from 1,649 dollars to 873 dollars. The

Table 5
Net Influence of Ethnicity on Income

	Deviation from the observed mean ($4,433)	Net effect of ethnicity
Anglo-Scottish	+ $1,319	+ $606
Irish	+ 1,012	+ 468
Scandinavian	+ 1,201	+ 303
German	+ 387	+ 65*
Italian	− 961	− 370
Jewish	+ 878	+ 9*
Eastern-European	− 100	− 480
French	− 330	− 267
Others	− 311	− 334

Note:* non-significant

figure 873 dollars was the net contribution of ethnicity to the income differential, and the balance, 776 dollars, was the net contribution of other factors such as age and schooling. In other words, even if he heeded the traditional advice to invest in himself through schooling, migration, and so on, a French Canadian could still look forward to an income about 15 percent lower than that of his counterpart of British descent.

One more point is worth mentioning. In my regressions, both unemployment and underemployment were excluded by pre-adjusting the figures for the number of weeks worked in the year. However, adjustment itself provided a direct arithmetic measure of the influence of underemployment on the level of income. (Those who were unemployed for the 12 months preceding the census were not included in this adjustment). (See Table VI.)

Table 6
Underemployment, and Wages and Salaries

	Percentage who worked from 49 to 52 weeks	Influence of underemployment on labour income	
		$	%
Anglo-Scottish	85.2	–	–
French	73.9	240	13.2
Irish	82.0	125	30.0
Scandinavian	83.1	90	38.0
Italian	65.2	283	11.6
Jewish	74.8	402	72.5
Eastern-European	75.0	239	15.5
German	80.6	92	9.2
Others	72.8	291	16.0

While all the results obtained from these data do not prove that widespread discrimination is practiced against French Canadians in Canadian labour markets, they suggest that it is possible, particularly when examined in conjunction with the evidence of ownership of capital and control of firms, or what I have called the distribution of power.

The Control of Industry

Moving from income disparities to power disparities, a very different set of circumstances is observed. French Canadians are not satisfied with their present share of high-prestige, high-income and high-power occupations in the federal public service and large business enterprises. But this analysis of relative incomes is only one particular aspect of our study. I now wish to introduce the question of the economic power enjoyed by entrepreneurs and capitalists through ownership and control of industry. French Canadians resent the fact that in the Province of Quebec, where they constitute a large majority of the population, they do not own and control more business firms. I have conducted a survey to establish the basic facts on the extent and nature of this problem.

For this purpose, firms in Quebec have been classified according to three categories of ownership: French Canadian, Other Canadian, and Foreign. In establishing the classification, two major considerations have been taken into account: place of residence and ethnic origin or language of owners; and the names of members of boards of directors. The residence of the ultimate owner of 50 percent or more of the capital stock was used to establish whether a firm was foreign or Canadian. In the agricultural sector only two categories of heads of farms were used, French Canadian and Other Canadian (note that the head of a farm is not necessarily the owner). In the service sector, as in agriculture, only the two Canadian categories were used because the Statistics Canada data provide a breakdown only on a language basis. In the other sectors, the classification of French against Other Canadian firms is based on the names of the members of the boards of directors and their apparent origin. This method is somewhat questionable in principle; in practice it is justifiable since, perhaps surprisingly, there are no mixed boards in Quebec industry. The typical board of a large English-language firm has 15 members, only one or two of whom are French Canadian. The same is true in reverse for French-language firms, except that the total board membership is smaller. Out of some 10,000 cases examined, only about ten cases could not be classified in this manner. Where the directors of the firms were French Canadian, the owners

Table 7

Percentage of Labour Force in Selected Industries by
Employment in Establishments under French Canadian,
Other Canadian and Foreign Ownership
Quebec 1961

	Establishments Controlled by:				
	French Canadians	Other Canadians	Foreign Interests	Total percentage	Total number of establishment
1. Agriculture	91.3%	8.7%	–	100	1,312
2. Mining	6.5	53.1	40.4	100	259
3. Manufacturing	21.8	46.9	31.3	100	4,683
4. Construction	50.7	35.2	14.1	100	1,264
5. Transport and Communications (Private Sector)	37.5	49.4	13.1	100	1,024
6. Wholesale Trade	34.1	47.2	18.7	100	693
7. Retail Trade	56.7	35.8	7.5	100	1,787
8. Finance	25.8	53.1	21.1	100	622
9. Services	71.4	28.6	–	100	3,509
%of Total	47.3	37.6	15.0	100	15,153

The total above excludes the labour force in forestry, fishing, trapping, the public sector and non-classified.

Table 8
Percentage Distribution of Value Added in
Manufacturing Industries. Quebec 1961

	Establishments Controlled by:			
	French Canadians	Other Canadians	Foreign Interests	Total
1.a Food Products	30.9	32.0	38.1	100
1.b Beverages	4.7	64.9	30.4	100
2. Tobacco products	0.9	31.2	67.9	100
3. Rubber products	8.0	37.5	54.5	100
4. Leather products	49.4	46.3	4.3	100
5. Textiles	2.1	68.3	29.6	100
6. Knitted goods	24.7	53.2	22.1	100
7. Clothing	8.2	88.6	3.2	100
8. Wood products	83.9	13.2	2.8	100
9. Furniture	39.4	53.6	7.0	100
10.a Pulp and Newsprint	4.8	53.3	41.9	100
10.b Paper products	22.0	41.2	33.8	100
11. Printing and Publishing	28.2	65.7	6.1	100
12.a Iron and Steel Products	11.7	28.9	59.4	100
12.b Non-ferrous Metals	3.7	11.6	84.7	100
13. Metal products	23.7	35.9	40.4	100
14. Machinery	18.3	17.0	64.7	100
15. Transportation Equipment	6.4	14.4	79.2	100
16. Electrical Appliances and Supplies	6.6	58.0	35.4	100
17. Non-metallic Mineral products	14.8	51.2	34.0	100
18. Petroleum and Coal products	0.0	0.0	100.0	100
19. Chemical products	6.5	16.4	77.1	100
20.a Precision Instruments	4.6	23.5	71.9	100
20.b Miscellaneous	24.5	41.3	34.2	100
Total	15.4	42.8	41.8	100

Sources: Statistics Canada and Census of Canada.

were also French Canadian, except in cases where a transfer of ownership had occurred not long before the survey.

The survey covered the whole economy except forestry, fishing and
trapping. The public service and Crown corporations were dealt with
separately, and will not be considered here. Table 7 indicates the general
situation; the 9 categories are an aggregation of 52 different industries,
numbering about 15,000 establishments.

Our results, summarized in Tables, 7, 8 and 9, provide a general
picture of the extent of French Canadian ownership of business firms in
Quebec. In the case of the whole Canadian economy, the only available
index was used, the number of employees. For manufacturing, however,
Statistics Canada supplied figures on value of shipments, value added,
wages and salaries, and number of male and female employees. The
Quebec Bureau of Statistics supplied figures on exports to other provinces
and to foreign countries. A comparison was thus achieved between the
three categories of establishments according to size, output per man-year,
average labour earnings, and exports.

The distribution of establishments among industries is interesting.
French Canadian establishments were at the one extreme in every
respect, Foreign establishments at the other extreme in every respect,
and Other Canadian establishments were in between. With regard to
size, Foreign establishments were seven times larger than French Canadian, and four times larger than Other Canadian by value added. The
average output per man was 6,500, 8,400, and 12,000 dollars respectively for French Canadian, Other Canadian and Foreign establishments. Wages and salaries in French Canadian establishments were 30
percent below those in Foreign, and 12 percent below those in Other
Canadian establishments. With regard to exports, food and beverages,
and pulp and paper, were not found to be useful indicators since they
were exported by all three groups; but the four other leading export
industries of each ownership group were established as follows: French
Canadian: leather products, clothing, wood, and furniture; Other Canadian: primary metallic products; textiles; and supplies; Foreign: primary
metallic products, transportation equipment, chemical products, and petro-
leum products.

Ownership of firms according to ethnic groups is not a standard
feature of economic analysis. However, recent developments, mainly in
the field of communications,[2] enables us to link our findings on
ownership to those on relative incomes of French Canadians. This
approach also helps to understand why important structural changes
("French only" policies, separatism, nationalizations) are perceived by
many in Quebec as essential pre-conditions to the progress of French

Table 9

Exports 1961

| | Establishments controlled by | | | |
	French Canadians	Other Canadians	Foreign interests	Total
Exports as % of total exports	4.5	44.0	51.5	100
Exports as % of output of each group	22.0	48.6	59.5	
% of which exports to foreign countries	3.8	17.7	19.6	

Canadians. The "model" goes something like this: job-seeking by individuals is not without cost, nor is personnel recruitment by business firms. The cost per job filled may well be directly related to the salary the job pays and to the responsibilities it entails. To minimize hiring costs, employers engage the services of outside specialists – both formal and informal. The very existence of large specialized personnel agencies implies the existence of economies of scale in the labour market information industry.

Quebec relies on imported capital and technology. The institutionalized networks dealing with information on high-level jobs, both for the employer and the employee, were built up largely outside the French Canadian community. In other words, *ceteris paribus,* entrepreneurs know less about prospective French Canadian than English-speaking employees, and vice versa. These networks are essentially engaged in a screening process, and in that capacity they are more likely to reject whatever is unfamiliar to them because it is more costly to handle. The well-known links between English-language universities and the business community in Quebec are an example of attempts by firms to reduce their search costs by dealing almost exclusively (and even becoming deeply involved) with institutions familiar to them. One result of these links is to lower demand for French Canadian university graduates. French Canadians have been criticized in the past for choosing the "wrong" field of study, and concentrating on law, medicine and a few other fields of specialization. The explanation for this situation may lie, not in any fundamental, cultural trait, but in rational decisions to obtain specialized training in fields where upward mobility was less restricted.

Although they are often expressed in a confused manner, current assertions that important constraints related to ethnic considerations are hindering access to high-level jobs could well be solidly based on facts.

Even within a purely economic perspective, ownership of firms in Quebec is a relevant consideration; it is a determining factor with regard to the consistently lower incomes of French Canadians, and the widespread discontent that is generated by the inequitable situation. Our knowledge of the economic dimensions of the unfavourable situation of French Canadians is still somewhat limited but it is sufficient to enable us to dismiss suggestions that the present agitation and demands for change are based solely on ideological or strictly political fantasies.

Notes

1. For further details, see: *Report of the Royal Commission on Bilingualism and Biculturalism; Book III. The Work World.* Ottawa, 1969.
2. See Jean-Luc Migué, "Le nationalisme, l'unité nationale et la théorie économique de l'information," *The Canadian Journal of Economics,* Vol. III, No. 2 (May, 1970).

10
Quebec and the Demographic Dilemma of French Canadian Society
by Jacques Henripin

The political situation of the Province of Quebec cannot be fully understood unless the demographic situation of French Canadians is taken into consideration. The French Canadian community and the Province of Quebec are not synonomous, but one of the basic realities underlying Quebec's political problems is the fact that 76 percent of Canadians of French origin, and 82 percent of those whose mother tongue is French, live in the province, and, numbering about five million, constitute four-fifths of its total population. A community of such a size, with all the political powers of a Canadian province, cannot be easily swept away. Yet recent demographic trends indicate that the French Canadian society is losing ground, not only compared with Canada as a whole, but even within the Province of Quebec itself. This situation merits close examination.

The Demographic Erosion of French Canadian Society

In Canada, no other important ethnic or linguistic group is concentrated to the same extent in a single province. French Canadians have migrated from the St. Lawrence valley to other parts of Canada (as well as to the United States), but Canadian studies leave no doubt about what has happened to them when they have settled too far from "home": they or their children have gradually adopted English as their mother tongue. Consequently, in 1961, while 23.6 percent of Canadians of French origin were living outside Quebec, only 17.8 percent still claimed French as their mother tongue. Exceptions to this general situation are to be found in a few' areas such as northern New Brunswick, the Ottawa River valley, and north-eastern Ontario, where French Canadians are relatively concentrated; but even in these regions, the number of Canadians of French origin who have adopted English as their mother tongue is far from negligible.

As a matter of fact, in all provinces except Quebec, this trend has

Table 1

Percentage of Canadians of French Origin Who Have Adopted English as Their Mother Tongue, by Province, 1961

Province	Percentage of English Mother Tongue	Province	Percentage of English Mother Tongue
Newfoundland	85.0	Ontario	38.0
Prince Edward Is.	55.0	Manitoba	30.0
Nova Scotia	57.0	Saskatchewan	43.0
New Brunswick	12.0	Alberta	50.0
Quebec	1.6	British Columbia	65.0
		Total Canada	9.9

Source: Statistics Canada, *1961 Census of Canada*, Bulletin 1.3-5, Tables 95 and 96.

been accelerating since 1921 in practically a geometric progression. Table 1 shows the results of this process.

By projecting this trend until 1981, we can estimate that six provinces will have an assimilation rate above 75 percent and two others will have a rate between 50 and 60 percent. These percentages only refer to Canadians of French origin who claim English as their mother tongue. According to the definition used by Statistics Canada, the mother tongue is the first language learned during infancy, provided it is still understood. However, many persons living outside Quebec whose mother tongue is French use English predominantly in their daily lives. In other words, the level of assimilation to English is still higher than is indicated when the mother tongue is used as the basis of measurement.

According to one estimate, both the proportion of French-speaking persons, and their absolute numbers, will decline in almost all provinces in the immediate future.[1] A study of these trends leads to the conclusion that, if there is any hope of a French-speaking community's surviving in North America, this can only be in the Province of Quebec. They lend credence to the growing opinion that the five million French-speaking persons living in Quebec must consider themselves the only viable group capable of maintaining the French Canadian culture. Most are strongly identified with that culture; they want it to survive and continue to develop; and they insist on having the political and economic power necessary to ensure that it does. These facts and opinions do not prove the absolute necessity for political independence, but they certainly constitute arguments towards that political option. To a large proportion of Quebecers, they prove that there is a real danger of the French-speaking population being swallowed up by the Anglo-Saxon majority of the North American continent.

This threat is not new; French Canadians have probably always been threatened by their neighbours and their neighbours' culture. What is perhaps somewhat new is that this threat is becoming evident within the fortress itself, that is, within the Province of Quebec. Demographically and linguistically, Quebec is far from homogeneous. The metropolitan area of Montreal contains about 40 percent of the total population, and will probably contain 50 percent in the year 2000. And it is precisely in Montreal that one finds most of the non-French population: nearly 80 percent of them live there. This demographic concentration has great political significance; Montreal is the economic and intellectual centre of the whole Province (although Quebec City remains important too). And yet French Canadians make up only two-thirds of the city's population and may well fall to between 53 and 60 percent by the year 2000. This trend is largely due to the fact that most immigrants to Quebec settle in Montreal, and choose to integrate into the English community.

Throughout their history, French Canadians have had to face the constant and very significant threat of being over-run, if not completely eliminated, by the English-speaking population and English culture of North America. In earlier years, French Canadians resorted to an exceptionally high birth rate in order to counterbalance the inflow of immigrants, who were either English-speaking or generally adopted the English language. While this strategy was successful for some time, it has faltered since World War II. It also had draw-backs: there is a high cost associated with an excessive fertility rate – for instance, in terms of standards of education, health, and economic well-being. French Canadian society still faces the same dilemma: it can maintain its relative demographic position within Canada, or at least within Quebec, by continuing to bear the economic costs of a higher fertility rate; or it can allow its birth rate to drop, in which case the cost may well be its very survival as a distinct, organized society.

The Demographic Challenge and Response in Retrospect

Present-day French Canadian society, made up of about five million persons in the Province of Quebec, half a million just outside it, and another half million scattered throughout the rest of Canada, has had a rather unique demographic history. After the founding of the colony in 1608 with a mere 70 settlers, the St. Lawrence valley remained for a century and a half an exclusively French-speaking community (except for the Indians).* The threat to their survival was present from the outset. During the first winter, two settlers died, one was sentenced to death, and three were sent back to France as prisoners. During the second winter, there were 17 deaths. The first married couple arrived in 1616, but both spouses died during the same year. The first marriage was celebrated in 1618, and resulted in the first of an almost fabulous series of births; but both mother and child died almost immediately. Twenty years after the foundation of Quebec, there were still only 30 inhabitants in New France, and only one farm.

The first census, taken in 1666, reported a population of 3200. France wanted to populate the colony, but was most reluctant to send emigrants from France. During the whole French Regime (1608-1760), emigration to Canada amounted to not more than 10,000 persons, or an average of about 65 per year. In 1760, when Canada was ceded to England, there were some 70,000 inhabitants in New France, compared to one million and a half in New England, a ratio of one to twenty. This comparison illustrates the potentially significant political consequences of demographic phenomena. France and England were engaged in a demographic and political struggle during the 17th and early 18th centuries. France had a population twice the size of England's; it had almost the entire North American continent, from the Appalachian to the Rocky Mountains, at its disposal, since it controlled the entrances to the St. Lawrence and Mississippi Rivers. But it failed to occupy that territory. As Alfred Sauvy has put it dramatically: "At the very moment when French was becoming the predominant language in Europe, thanks to its demographic underpinnings, it was losing in the long run on the global plane, because a few more shiploads of illiterate individuals were leaving little England each year."[2]

From 1760 to 1960, the French Canadian population grew at an exceptional rate. The world's population multiplied during these two centuries by three, the population of European origin by five, and the French Canadian population by about 80, notwithstanding a net emigration – mostly to the United States – of about 800,000. But even this remarkable performance was not sufficient to counteract the inflow of immigrants into the territory which is now Canada. After American Independence, a new demographic race began within British North

---

* Another French settlement was founded in Acadia, on the Atlantic coast, at about the same time. It was ceded to England and its population was deported to Louisiana. Some escaped into the woods, and others returned; today their descendants make up most of the French-speaking population of the Maritime Provinces, about 260,000 persons in 1961.

Table 2
Percentage of French Origin in Total Population,
Canada and Quebec, 1760 to 1961

Year	Canada	Quebec
1760	–	100.0**
1806	50.0	–
1827	40.0	75.0**
1850	–	77.0**
1871	31.0	78.0
1901	30.7	80.1
1921	27.9 (26.6)*	80.0 (79.2)*
1951	30.8 (29.0)*	82.0 (82.5)*
1961	30.4 (28.1)*	80.6 (81.1)*

* Percentage of French Mother Tongue, according to Canadian census statistics.
** Rough unpublished estimates, made by H. Charbonneau. Calculations exclude natives.

America. United Empire Loyalists from New England and immigrants from the British Isles flowed into the area. By 1806, the English-speaking and French-speaking populations were about equal; by 1871, as indicated in Table 2, a state of equilibrium had been reached both in Canada as a whole, and in the Province of Quebec. Since that time, the proportion of persons of French origin has been approximately 30 percent throughout Canada, 80 percent in Quebec.

This remarkable stability over the last century, reflected in Table 2, is largely the result of two counter-balancing factors: migration flows which favoured the English-language community, and a differential fertility which favoured the French-language community.

Another important factor favouring the English-language community is the tendency, even in the Province of Quebec, for the majority of immigrants whose origin is neither French nor English to adopt English for themselves and their children. The ratio is approximately three to one in favour of English (throughout Canada, it is roughly nine to one). There are indications that this trend is increasing. For instance, until recently, one immigrant group at least – the Italians – had been more favourable to French, but they now send three-quarters of their children to English schools in Montreal, where most of them are concentrated. The figures in Table 3 reflect this situation. Comparing British and French origins, and the corresponding mother tongue, we note that the French group did not gain many adherents from other groups, while the English group gained 130,000 persons, an increment of nearly 25 percent.

Table 3

Population Distribution of the Province of Quebec, by Ethnic Origin and Mother Tongue, 1961 (by thousands)

Ethnic Origin	Population	Mother Tongue	Population
French	4,241	French	4,269
British	567	English	697
Italian	109	Italian	90
Jewish	75	Yiddish	35
German	39	German	32
Others	228	Others	136
Total	5,259	Total	5,259

Source: Statistics Canada, *1961 Census of Canada*, Bulletin 1.2-5, Table 36, and Bulletin 1.2-9, Table 64.

The impact of the factor of fertility, which favoured the French Canadians on the other hand, is reflected in Table 4.

It will be noted that the excess fertility of French-speaking ever-married women is greater in the Province of Quebec than in Canada as a whole; in Quebec, it is twice as great for women of 50 years and over. These women were born before 1911 and had most of their children before 1950. After that date, the excess fertility ratio decreases progressively. We can conclude that, before that date, the price that French Canadians had to pay to counterbalance the English-oriented immigration was to have about twice as many children as English-language families. That price has been reduced since World War ɪɪ; in 1961

Table 4

Ratio of French to English Mother Tongue Fertility,* by Five-Year Age Group, Canada and Province of Quebec, 1961

Age Group in 1961	Canada	Province of Quebec
30-34 years	1.18	1.26
35-39 years	1.35	1.47
40-44 years	1.51	1.64
45-49 years	1.62	1.81
50-54 years	1.78	1.99
55-59 years	1.88	2.13
60-64 years	1.92	2.14
65 years +	1.98	2.05

* Number of children born per ever-married woman.

Source: Statistics Canada, *1961 Census of Canada*, Bulletin 4.1-8, Table H-9.

the excess fertility was about 50 percent for Quebec women aged 35-39 years, and it is probably still less for younger families. That means that the challenge of English immigration is no longer being met, and that the French-speaking proportion of the population will decline even in the Province of Quebec, and more particularly in Montreal.

Some commentators have predicted that there will soon be an English-language majority in Montreal. This seems quite improbable in the near future, but such statements are sometimes accepted at face value. Consequently there is a widespread feeling that the survival of the French Canadian community is threatened, even in Quebec, and that something has to be done. Suggested counter-measures include political independence, with a panoply of miracles flowing therefrom; the elimination of English-language schools; compulsory French-language education for immigrant children; and the imposition of French as the working language at all levels in private firms.

Is the threat serious? Is there a real possibility that the French-speaking population will lose their demographic majority status in Montreal, or even in the whole province? Two colleagues and I have tried to project an answer for the next 30 years.[3] We have not tried to make predictions, but rather hypothetical projections, which are as realistic as possible. The task has been difficult because of the absence of relevant information about linguistic groups, mortality and fertility rates, and migration flows between Montreal and the rest of the Province, and between Quebec and the other provinces and other countries.

We have made the assumption that the excess natality of French Canadians throughout Quebec will continue to decrease, and will disappear by 1985. For the Montreal metropolitan area, there was already no natality differential in 1956-61, and we have assumed that this situation will persist. Possible mortality differentials have also been disregarded. As for migrations, we have used two sets of hypotheses: one favourable to the English-Canadians, and estimating a net annual immigration of 30,000, with only 15 percent French-speaking; the other as favourable to the French-speaking group as seemed plausible, with a net annual immigration of 13,000, 30 percent of it French-speaking. The results appear in Table 5. With both sets of hypotheses, the percentage of French-speaking persons continues to decrease. In Montreal, neither set of hypotheses leads to a reversal of the majority-minority linguistic relationship, but the first, the most unfavourable to French Canadians, predicts a situation not far from it in the year 2000.

These projections have not taken into account all possible future developments; in fact, any radical changes in demographic trends have been deliberately excluded. For instance, we rejected the possibility of a

Table 5

Percentage of French Mother Tongue in the Province of Quebec
and in Montreal Metropolitan Area, 1961 to 2000,
According to Two Sets of Hypotheses

Year	Province of Quebec		Montreal	
	A	B	A	B
1961	82.3	82.3	66.4	66.4
1971	80.7	81.8	64.9	66.0
1981	77.6	80.8	60.5	64.3
2000	71.6	79.2	52.7	60.0

substantial excess fertility within the French-speaking population on the grounds that it is unlikely to recur. But other radical changes might intervene, such as policies that would lead immigrants to adopt the French instead of the English language. Or conditions might arise that would induce non-French-speaking Quebecers to leave the Province. While we do not suggest this as a solution, it is a possible outcome. And it may even have become manifest in the last two or three years. During the period 1960-66, the average annual net immigration in Quebec was 14,000. It was 14,000 again in 1967. But in the following three years, there was an increasing net *emigration* of 5,000 in 1968, 13,000 in 1969, and 34,000 in 1970. And according to a rough estimate, about three-quarters of the emigrants in 1970 were English-speaking.

Whatever the outcome of present political uneasiness in Quebec, the old demographic equilibrium has been upset. French Canadian families have ceased to rely on excess fertility to balance English-oriented immigration. And if nothing else changes, they are bound to see their demographic strength decrease, even in the Province of Quebec.

III. The Cost of the *"Revanche des Berceaux"**

While there is widespread opinion in favour of increasing the French Canadian birth-rate again, it seems to us of little real advantage. Any move in that direction would have to affect French Canadian families more than the others and it is difficult to imagine any policy which could ensure this result. To indicate the economic costs of such a step,

---

* A popular expression referring to reaction to the British conquest of New France, which can be translated as "the revenge of the cradle."

Table 6

Crude Birth Rate* for the Provinces of Ontario and Quebec, 1846 to 1966

Period	Ontario	Quebec
1846-56	47.5	45.0
1856-66	46.8	43.0
1866-76	44.8	43.2
1876-86	37.2	42.0
1886-96	31.3	39.3
1896-1906	28.8	38.3
1906-16	29.1	38.0
1916-26	26.3	36.3
1926-30	21.0	30.5
1931-35	18.5	26.6
1936-40	17.5	24.7
1941-45	19.9	28.4
1946-50	24.6	30.4
1951-55	26.1	30.0
1956-60	26.4	28.6
1961-65	23.5	24.0

* Annual number of births per 1000 population.

Sources: 1846-1956—J. Henripin, *Trends and Factors of Fertility in Canada*, Ottawa, Statistics Canada, 1972, p. 366.

1926-1966—Statistics Canada, *Vital Statistics*, annual reports.

---

we shall compare the Provinces of Quebec and Ontario. Although Ontario has achieved a higher level of economic development, both Provinces began to industrialize at about the same time, and had comparable population increases. From the demographic point of view, the main difference was that the population of Ontario increased through a relatively moderate birth rate and an appreciable net immigration, whereas Quebec relied only on its birth rate and experienced a net emigration. Tables 6 and 7 illustrate these phenomena. The differences they reveal imply economic effects and an appreciable inequality of opportunity in economic terms. In this respect, the Province of Quebec was certainly handicapped in comparison to the Province of Ontario.

Three of the many aspects of this problem are examined here:

1. Between 1891 and 1946, a critical period of industrialization for both Provinces, Ontario's population multiplied by 1.94, Quebec's by 2.44. The annual rates of increase were 1.21 and 1.63 percent respectively. But there is an economic cost to population increase:

Table 7

Net Migration* for Ontario and Quebec 1881 to 1966 (by thousands)

Period	Ontario	Quebec
1881-91	− 84	−132
1891-1901	−144	−121
1901-11	+ 74	− 29
1911-21	+ 46	− 99
1921-31	+129	− 10
1931-41	+ 75	− 32
1941-51	+304	− 13
1951-56	+377	+ 96
1956-61	+308	+109
1961-66	+237	+ 64

* For the period 1881-1941, estimates relate to population 10 years and over only.

Sources: 1881 to 1941 – Nathan Keyfitz, "The Growth of Canadian Population", in *Population Studies*, June, 1950, p. 53-54.

1941 to 1951—Statistics Canada, *1951 Census of Canada*, Vol. X, Table 3.

1951 to 1961—Statistics Canada, *1961 Census of Canada*, Bulletin 7.1-1, Table 2.

1961 to 1966—Statistics Canada, *1966 Census of Canada*, Bulletin S-401, Table 2.

new capital has to be created so that national income increases at least as fast as the population. This new capital is called demographic investments. Only when demographic investments are satisfied can supplementary investments result in an increase in living standards. And the greater the rate of population increase, the greater the demographic investments, and the more difficult it is to devote supplementary investments to improving living standards. To put it more simply, let us assume that both Provinces had been able to increase their total production by 3 percent a year during that period. Population increases would have absorbed 1.21 percent in Ontario and 1.63 percent in Quebec, leaving Ontario with 1.79 percent to increase the living standard, compared to 1.37 percent for Quebec. That is a relative difference of 30 percent, using the Quebec percentage as a base. The reality was not that simple, but our calculation indicates the kind of economic burden that is attached to a rate of population increase such as existed in Quebec in this period.

2. In addition to having a higher rate of population growth

between 1891 and 1946, and thus having to devote a larger share of its production to demographic investments, Quebec also had a smaller proportion of its population in the labour force. The following table indicates the number of persons in the labour force in Quebec and Ontario per 1000 inhabitants for some census years: [4]

	Ontario	Quebec	Difference	Percentage Difference
1911	394	331	63	16.0 %
1931	392	357	35	8.9 %
1951	411	364	47	11.4 %
1961	384	336	48	12.5 %

Three factors explain these differences:

(a) The rates of participation are lower in Quebec than in Ontario. For instance, of the 11.4 percent difference in 1951, 3.5 percent is due to that factor.
(b) A high level of fertility reduces the proportion of adults, and consequently of the labour force. This is another cost to be borne by a population with a high fertility rate.
(c) Net immigration usually increases the proportion of adults. From this point of view, Ontario was definitely in a better situation. According to Nathan Keyfitz, Ontario's net gain from migrations was 324,000 between 1901 and 1941, whereas Quebec had a net loss of 170,000. Keyfitz adds that, of all the provinces of Canada, Quebec has supplied the largest number of persons to other provinces and to the United States.

3. It must be obvious that the most direct economic effect of an excess level of fertility is on the living standard of individual families. Quebec ever-married women born between 1880 to 1911 bore from 58 to 73 percent more children than did Ontario women of the same age group. It can be roughly estimated that this excess burden represented approximately 12 percent of an average family budget, and 10 percent of the total economic production. This burden was bound to have serious effects on living standards, on savings and capital formation, and on the general welfare of the Quebec population. And it is reflected in social indicators for that period, which show that Quebec was consistently behind Ontario with regard to rates of mortality – especially infant mortality rates – levels of schooling, the quality of the labour force and labour productivity, hospital facilities and number of physicians per capital, and the quality of housing. These deficiencies

certainly cannot all be attributed only to the demographic characteristics of the Quebec population. But they are partly related to the economic cost of a very high fertility rate and the raising of children – many of whom later left for other regions.

Such was the price paid by French Canadians for maintaining their relative demographic strength in Canada, and the Province of Quebec. There does not seem to be the slightest hope of such a goal being successfully pursued with regard to the whole of Canada. In the Province of Quebec, the situation is less clear. In all probability the *"revanche des berceaux"* approach has been well and truly abandoned. Accordingly, if recent migration trends continue, and if immigrants continue to opt predominantly for the English language, the French-speaking community of Quebec is bound to see its majority seriously reduced, particularly in Montreal. This would mean losing their only power: that of making laws and electing governments.

There are two possible developments: adoption of policies to induce immigrants to associate themselves with the French community and culture; or, if that demoractic process fails, a turbulent minority could succeed in creating a situation which would force the non-French-speaking population to leave the Province. It must be hoped that the first solution will prevail. But for that to happen, two things are required: an energetic Government, and an unusual measure of good will and wisdom on the part of the English-speaking population.

Notes

1. Robert Maheu, *Les Francophones au Canada,1941-1991,* Montreal: Editions Parti Pris, 1970, pp. 57-59.
2. Preface to Marcel Reinhard, *Histoire de la population mondiale de 1700 à 1948.* Paris: Domat-Montchrestien, 1949, p. 12.
3. H. Charbonneau, J. Henripin and J. Légaré., "L'avenir démographique des francophones au Québec et à Montréal en l'absence de politiques adéquates," in Revue de géographie de Montréal, Vol. XXIV, No. 2, 1970, 199-202.
4. Jacques Henripin, "Population et main d'oeuvre", in André Raynauld, *Croissance et structure économiques de la province de Québec.* Ministère de l'industrie et du commerce de la province de Québec, 1961, p. 258.

II
The Catholic Church in Quebec:
Adapting to Change
by Abbé Norbert Lacoste

Although statistics indicate that the strength of the Roman Catholic Church is being maintained in Quebec, the past few years have been marked by radical changes in the religious attitudes and behaviour of the faithful. The publication in 1971 of the Dumont Report, an examination of the relations between the Church and its lay members carried out at the instigation of the ecclesiastical authorities, reflected a re-assessment by the Church of its role in Quebec society. Its title is meaningful: *The Church of Quebec: a legacy, a prospect.*[1]

The Report outlines the situation of the Church of Quebec, both past and present. In Appendix I, the author Nive Voisine traces its history from 1608 to 1970, identifying five distinct periods:

> 1608-1760, a period of early development, corresponding to the French Régime.
>
> 1760-1838, a period of submission to the civil authorities during the first years of British rule.
>
> 1840-1896, a period of increasing Roman influence, together with the beginning of a Canadian phase.
>
> 1896-1940, a triumphal period, marked by the development of the Church's institutions.
>
> 1940-1970, a period of uncertainty, highlighted by Quebec's two-fold cultural revolution, the lay Quiet Revolution and its religious counterpart, the second Vatican Council, known as Vatican II.

These different periods are, of course, interrelated, and the last, best-known one is the product of the others. What are the characteristic features of Quebec's contemporary Church? From the first period it draws its missionary impetus, its religious institutions, its popular character, and its spirit of independence. To the second period can be traced its will to survive, its sense of hardship, and the great prestige of the bishop, but also some weakening of the faith in certain circles. From the third period it retains the conservatism that is still apparent in some quarters, a sense of organization, wide-spread piety, a militant character, and a high degree of involvement on the part of lay members. The heritage from the triumphal period includes a doctrinal orthodoxy but also a social dimension, an identification with the needs of the people including their need to protest against existing conditions.

With the advent of World War II, the development of modern communications systems integrated Quebec into international society. New values were suddenly introduced that could not be controlled as easily as during the previous period of isolation. Various currents of thought met and cross-fertilized one another; Quebec found itself henceforth exposed to the different ideologies sweeping the world. Some of these currents of thought – for instance, those relating to industrial and technological developments – were communicated through non-secular channels; values of the North American industrial society such as pragmatism and materialism penetrated Quebec's urban population.

Innovations also transformed religious thinking. The organization of Catholic action movements after 1930, and the creation of important new church services from 1935 to 1945, made it possible to draw on the human sciences. These developments also resulted in the organization of social action projects adapted to particular groups such as manual labourers, and, in the 1960s, in a stronger tendency toward political action. The re-assessment of the Church's mission in Quebec carried out in the light of Vatican II contributed to a literal explosion from within. There was a decrease in religious practices, particularly in the badly-organized urban districts, and in the number of priests and other religious personnel. Sub-groups within the Church multiplied rapidly, and family-based groups were displaced progressively by communes or similarly organized groups.

Using the classification established by Normand Wener,[2] Quebec Catholics can be divided into five categories.

a) The conformists, or those Christians who declare themselves in agreement with the stated objectives of the Church as an institution, and the changes it proposes. They submit to the institution and accept the pace of its evolution.

b) The ritualists, who criticize or ignore the objectives of the ecclesiastical institution, while placing value on the means employed to attain them; for instance, those "Sunday Christians" who attend weekly mass, often through habit, without being overly concerned about participating in the life of the Church or applying religious precepts in their daily lives.

c) The innovators, Christians who accept the general objectives of the Church as an institution, but who consider inadequate the means employed to attain them, and who attempt to devise better ways of adapting the Church to modern conditions. This preoccupation with adaptation appears to us to characterize the entire ecclesiastical institution today, as it continues to pursue the same objectives in a Christian manner but tries to adapt itself to new realities. Among the innovators are found many persons who participate in various religious movements.

d) The rebels, who reject both the ends and the means of the Church as an institution, and attempt to substitute others. Included are certain members of new local groups and members of what Americans call the "underground church".

e) The withdrawn, or persons who have entrenched themselves in a negative posture. They simply reject the ends and means of the Church; many have excluded religion from their lives.

Depending on the firmness of their views, it can be predicted that some ritualists and rebels will join the withdrawn, and that some conformists will become innovators. The present cultural conflict in Quebec has divided Catholics, some identifying with existing structures, others with values. Since society cannot exist indefinitely under the resulting tension, a range of possible solutions has been advanced to ensure a greater measure of integration.

The withdrawn persons find themselves being courted by astrologers and ideologists, while the Church as an institution is attempting, in spite of internal contradictions, to find a path through the maze of new values. A possible path was suggested by the Dumont Commission, and accepted by the Episcopate of Quebec.

The abiding concerns of the Church of Quebec in carrying out its pastoral functions can be summarized as follows:

- the solidarity of the Christian community as a whole.
- the essential creativity of the Church's pastoral activities.
- co-ordination of pastoral activities in order to avoid sectionalism and regionalism; and co-operation among all members of the pastorate.
- the development of brotherhood, of relevance, and of service to others.
- recognition of the importance of short-term situations, of the need for flexibility and mobility.
- acceptance of recent cultural trends.
- mindfulness of the significance of day-to-day experiences, leading

to new forms of pastoral ministry.
- the Gospel witness of going first to the poor, the dispossessed, the disadvantaged, the fringe elements of society, the unhappily-married, the unemployed, the uneducated, the disinherited, the powerless, the unheard.
- the training of pastoral workers, priests, religious and lay members of the Church, whether they are already in the field or are preparing to undertake religious work.

These concerns will be manifest in dealing with eight specific milieux: the parish, the educational field, non-practising Catholics, the disadvantaged, social groups in general, the family, youth, and apostolic and religious movements. The success of this new approach cannot yet be determined; it will depend on the successful fusion of these principles with the concrete values of each milieu.

Within each parish there are conformists, ritualists, innovators, rebels and those who have withdrawn. Is it possible to bring together such a wide range of parishioners in support of a specific, joint project? This is a challenge of the same order as attempting to square the circle. The pastor must establish contact with these various types of individuals, and operate on various levels. He must form new groups around different focal points of interest. Internal conflicts can easily be foreseen; for instance, there will certainly be tension between the ritualists and the innovators. To reconcile these extreme positions recourse will be necessary to the Gospel's *nova* and *vetera*, seeking the harmony of the "new and the old". In the face of increasing tension, the rebels will attack and the withdrawn will withdraw further; it will be important to maintain a peaceful atmosphere, avoiding overly emotional reactions. The conformists will have to be convinced of the need to take part in these joint projects, for in doing so they will develop a deeper sense of participation and communion. In the field of education, more emphasis will have been placed on creative activity and research. Here, too, there are ritualists, rebels, and those who have withdrawn, and the same challenge of bringing them together will have to be met. Paradoxical as it may seem at first glance, the Church will be able to carry out its missionary activities with the least tension among non-practising Catholics, since they include neither ritualists nor innovators. Indeed, of the sixteen decrees emanating from Vatican II, the one dealing with missionary activity best reconciles norms and values within organized groups. In other words, by accentuating its missionary and ecumenical roles, the Church will reduce its internal conflicts. The suggestion has been made that, in its work among the disadvantaged, the Church should instigate projects benefiting the poor, and create centres to promote spiritual development, missionary activity, and a greater joint consciousness.

In dealing with youth, the Church should make its presence felt in new ways that will take into account the attractions of transitory considerations, freedom of participation, and the constant search for the meaning of all manner of things.

The activities of the Church of Quebec, carried on heretofore somewhat autonomously within each of the twenty dioceses, will be concentrated around four growth centres: eastern Quebec, Quebec City, Montreal and western Quebec. These large groups of dioceses will be expected to guide the apostolic and religious movements, and the spiritual activities of society as a whole, leaving to the Christian communities the responsibility for the spiritual life of the family. Plainly, the Church's infra-structure to meet the needs of the future is ready, but as with a rocket about to be launched, one can ask: "Will all the parts work?" The outcome depends on Quebecers themselves, on their motivations. What are those motivations? Foremost among those noted by the Dumont Report are the desire for freedom, pleasure, creativity and self-fulfilment. Next, I sense that Quebecers feel the need to rid themselves of a feeling of alienation, in order to participate in a creative manner in their society. Finally, I perceive a desire for redefinition, both as individuals and as a group. To win the support of Quebecers, the Church must identify with these aspirations.

As far as their religious aspirations are concerned, some Quebecers are seeking a return to Christianity, others are motivated by a desire for reform. In this realm, transcending ideologies, it is God who sets the course through the maze of obscure aspirations and the constant search for identity. The mission will establish the link between the institution and daily life, between the Church, the world and the Kingdom of Heaven. The future of the Church of Quebec depends on the spiritual qualities of its members, that is, on their maturity and unity. Rational planning stops there, and yields to the Spirit.

Throughout their history the people of Quebec have been inspired by the Chosen People of God, and there are many affinities between Jews and French Canadians. Will Quebecers place their faith in their numbers and their majority in Quebec, even though their birth-rate is declining, or will they opt for a form of Diaspora, or Dispersion, similar to that of the Jews? Recent Church theology, and the fact that all peoples are becoming minorities in a united world, leads us to believe that they will choose the latter course. If they do, we will see a modified Canadian constitution, within which the Church of Quebec will renew its leadership role.

Notes

1. Commission d'étude sur les laics et l'Eglise: *l'Eglise du Québec: un héritage, un projet*, Montreal: Fides, 1971 (322 pages).
2. Normand Wener, *Croyants du Canada français I. recherches sur les attitudes et les modes d'appartenance*, Montreal: Fides, 1971 (p.45).

12
The Federal Option
by Gilles Lalande

Quebec is one of the ten provinces, or member states, of the Canadian federation. Known as Lower Canada from 1792 to 1867, it was, together with Ontario (Upper Canada), New Brunswick and Nova Scotia, a founding member of the federal union commonly called a Confederation which was formed in 1867.

As a member state of this federal system, Quebec is a separate political community, or sub-system, within the Canadian political system; the population, mostly French-speaking, thus escapes many of the consequences of majority rule at the national level. Furthermore, under the British North America Act, 1867, the law of the British Parliament that constitutes the principal document of the Canadian constitution, the province has very broad legislative powers. Quebec's exclusive jurisdiction in certain fields of activity, particularly property and civil rights and, more significantly, education, enables it to preserve its cultural identity. At the same time, as one of the original members of Confederation, it has been – and remains – in a position to have a strong impact on Canadian political life, particularly through the main Canadian political parties. With very few exceptions, a parliamentary majority in Ottawa has been possible only with strong Quebec support. Furthermore, the federal Cabinet almost invariably includes several ministers from Quebec, and on three occasions, for a total of twenty-eight years, the Prime Minister himself has been from Quebec (Wilfrid Laurier 1896-1911; Louis St. Laurent, 1948-1957; and Pierre-Elliott Trudeau, since 1968).

Thus, within the Canadian federal system, the population of Quebec has both a regional government, largely autonomous and even sovereign in important areas of jurisdiction; and a federal government in which traditionally it has had a large enough representation in terms of numbers and often even of quality, to have a clear voice and effective participation in the formulation of national policies.

The Quebec Government and French-speaking Canadians

It is sometimes argued, quite rightly, that in view of the composition of its population, Quebec is the principal centre of French life in Canada. In 1971, French was the mother tongue of some 4,867,250 people, 80.7 per cent of Quebec's population. But at the same time, nearly 1,000,000 French-speaking Canadians lived outside Quebec in other Canadian provinces. Specifically, in the 1971 census, 34 percent of the population of New Brunswick (215,727 people), reported French as their mother tongue; 6.3 percent (482,042) in Ontario; 6.1 percent (60,547) in Manitoba; 3.4 percent (31,605) in Saskatchewan; 2.9 percent (46,498) in Alberta and 5 percent (39,333) in Nova Scotia.

Even though in the sociological sense of the term a French Canadian nation does exist, Quebec certainly cannot be considered the national state of French-speaking Canadians; nor can the Government of Quebec be the sole political institution at the disposal of French Canada. In fact, nearly one out of every five French-speaking Canadians is completely outside Quebec's jurisdiction in matters of such great importance for the preservation of their cultural identity as education and civil rights. Conversely, the Government of Quebec has responsibility, in its areas of jurisdiction, for a population one-fifth of which is not French-speaking.[1] Although the Government of Quebec has a primary responsibility for the protection of the language spoken by the vast majority of its population, and although Quebec's initiatives in its fields of jurisdiction have repercussions on the treatment accorded to French-speaking minorities in other Canadian provinces, the fact remains that important responsibilities concerning the whole French-speaking community in Canada devolve upon the federal government.

The Federal Government and the French-speaking Community

It would be at the least incongruous to suggest that a federal government can remain indifferent to the fate of a particular citizen or group of citizens; even more would this be true of its attitude towards a major linguistic or cultural minority group. The French-speaking minority in Canada, which constituted no less than 26.9 percent of the Canadian population in 1971, would not tolerate for long a situation where the central government did not concern itself with their language or with the treatment accorded French-speaking citizens throughout the country. It is true that there have been occasions when the federal government has abstained, for political reasons, from using its constitutional authority to disallow discriminatory legislation: at the end of the nineteenth century, when local authorities tried to abolish the linguistic and religious rights of the French-speaking minority in Manitoba and the right to use the French language in the North-West Territories; and from 1912 to 1916, when the Ontario Department of Education issued the repressive Rule XVII.[2] Yet the same federal government, faced until about 1959-60 with a Quebec Government that showed little interest in education and cultural matters, did not hesitate to take action itself. For instance, it created the Canadian Broadcasting Corporation in the 1930s, the National Film Board in the 1940s, and the Canada Council for the Arts, Humanities and Social Sciences in the 1950s. These organizations have been of undeniable benefit to the French language, the majority language of Quebec, and to the cultural life of French-speaking Canadians.

In the same vein, the federal government has in recent years transformed the Department of the Secretary of State into what amounts to a federal department of cultural affairs. And, in 1968, following a recommendation of the Royal Commission of Inquiry on Bilingualism and Biculturalism, the federal Parliament passed a law guaranteeing the equal official status of French and English in Canada. It thereby committed itself to provision of services in both official languages throughout the country. Subsequently, the federal government launched a far-reaching programme to increase the level of bilingualism in the federal civil service to make French one of the working languages within the federal government. Paradoxically, federal initiatives in such areas as social security, labour and employment, communications, external aid, and scientific research have been the cause of political tension within Confederation since the early 1960s, because they often forestalled or exceeded in scope Government of Quebec projects.

The Division of Powers

Rightly or wrongly, the Government of Canada believes that:

> the Parliament of Canada must have responsibility for the major and inextricably inter-related instruments of economic policy if it is to stimulate employment and control inflation. It must have control over monetary and credit policy, the balance-wheel role in fiscal policy, tariff policy, and balance of payments policy. It must be responsible for inter-provincial and international trade. It must be

able to undertake measures for stimulating the growth of the economy, some of which inevitably and some of which intentionally will affect regional economic growth.

According to the federal authorities,

> without such powers, Canada's federal government would be unable to contribute to many of the central objectives of federalism, including the reduction of regional disparity.[3]

On the other hand, the Government of Quebec has always claimed primary responsibility for the maintenance of the social and cultural identity as well as the distinctive personality of Quebec. The administration of Premier Bourassa, which won 72 of the 108 seats in the Quebec National Assembly in the election of April 29, 1970, considers that

> the question of culture cannot be limited to language alone, since it also affects human activities as a whole: work, recreation, the family, and political, economic and social institutions.[4]

Other Canadian politicians are also inclined to think that Quebec, and presumably the other provinces, must eventually assume full jurisdiction over social affairs, labour and employment, communications, and scientific research, just as in the case of education.

The Challenge of Federalism

But is the main problem facing Canada the internal constitutional division of powers and responsibilities between the Government of Quebec (and the other member states) on the one hand, and the central government on the other? Is this not rather a phenomenon that characterizes any federalist process, namely the balance between the political, economic, and cultural forces at work within any large unit, and is not the main challenge for both federal and provincial governments the rather advanced stage of integration of Canada within the still larger unit, North America?

Most of the major problems facing Quebec have their parallel on the level of Canada as a whole. Compare, for example, the problem of the domination of Quebec s economy by English-speaking businessmen, and the problem of the control of the Canadian economy by foreigners; or the shortage of manufacturing industries in Quebec and the relative weakness of Canada's secondary industries; or again the precarious position of the French language in Quebec and the progressive dilution of Canada's distinctive identity as a result of the American cultural invasion. At the same time, Quebec shares with the rest of Canada a host of problems ranging from strong dependence on foreign markets, both commercial and financial, to control of the environment and various forms of pollution; and including such matters as the recovery of lost ground in the whole field of research and development, and the ensuring of social progress in accordance with popular demands.

Viewed in this perspective, the fundamental challenge of the federal process in Canada appears to be to devise a formula to reconcile the objectives set by the individual provinces with those they have in common as integral parts of the Canadian federation. It is normal for the provinces, in view of the increasing range of their responsibilities, occasionally to demand both a re-allocation of tax resources between the two levels of government and a limit on the (currently unlimited) spending power of the federal parliament. Nor is it surprising that French-speaking Canadians, through the Government of Quebec, periodically demand greater control over activities which affect the very core of their cultural personality. It may even be inevitable that the municipal governments will one day demand a larger share of powers now granted to the provinces by the British North America Act in 1867.

As Carl J. Friedrich of Harvard University wrote in 1964: "Clearly federalism can work in the direction of both integration and differentiation at the same time."[5] According to the Canadian Government, federalism should be a just balance between the extremes of centralization and fragmentation.[6] A federal system of government is the sole form of political organization which can provide maximum protection to a minority group constituting a majority in a particular region. With this fact in mind, Kenneth C. Wheare of Oxford University has declared that federalism is the best guarantee of French Canadian nationality.[7] And Professor W. H. Riker of Rochester University considers that it was the existence of the French Canadian minority which was the basic reason for the federal system in Canada, and the justification for its maintenance to-day.[8]

It will be readily understood, in these circumstances, that Quebec has every advantage in remaining within Canada and in taking advantage of the federal system of government. It will also be recognized that the rest of Canada has every interest in ensuring that Quebec continues, through its distinctive character, to make a special contribution to Canada's cultural identity.

Notes

1. "We do not claim to speak for French-speaking Canadians in other provinces but we wish to speak in the name of all Quebec people, of whom 20% are English-speaking," Hon. Daniel Johnson, Prime Minister of Quebec. Proceedings of the First Meeting of the Constitutional Conference, Ottawa, February 1968, p. 55.

2. "From the beginning of that controversy in 1890 to its settlement in 1897, there was, to say the least, a marked reluctance on the part of the federal politicians, Conservative and Liberal, to take any action which might be represented as an interference with provincial rights." Ramsay Cook, *Provincial Autonomy, Minority Rights and the Compact Theory, 1867-1921*, Study No. 4, Royal Commission on Bilingualism and Biculturalism. Ottawa, 1970, p. 44.

3. *"Federalism for the Future,"* A Statement of Policy by the Government of Canada. The Constitutional Conference, Ottawa, February 5, 6 and 7, 1968, p. 36-37.

4. Hon. Robert Bourassa, Proceedings of the Constitutional Conference, Victoria, British Columbia, June 14, 1971, p. 16.

5. *Tendances nouvelles dans la théorie et dans la pratique du fédéralisme*, Rapport général de Carl J. Friedrich au Sixième congrès mondial de l'Association internationale de Science Politique, Genève, 21-25 septembre 1964 (unofficial translation by the author)

6. *"Federalism for the Future,"* A Statement of Policy by the Government of Canada. The Constitutional Conference, Ottawa, February 5, 6 and 7, 1968, p. 16.

7. Kenneth C. Wheare: "It is in Quebec, however, that they (the French Canadians) are the overwhelming majority and it is through Quebec's existence as an independent unit in the Canadian federation that French Canadian nationality finds its great safeguard in Canada." W. McMahon, ed., *Federalism Mature and Emergent*. 1962, p. 32.

8. William H. Riker, "The main beneficiary in Canada from the beginning has been the French-speaking minority, whose dissidence was the original occasion for adopting federalism and is the justification for retaining it today." *Federalism: Origin, Operation, Significance*. 1964, p. 152.

13
The Independence Option:
Ideological and Empirical Elements
by Daniel Latouche

Since 1960, the struggle for Quebec's independence* has entered a new phase in its historical development.[1] It is now in the forefront of all political discussions, within Canada and within Quebec. It is now so well advanced that more attention can be paid to the political and socio-economic conditions of post-independence Quebec. And finally the struggle has shifted to the electoral arena, where the Parti Québécois is recognized as a major contender. This study is concerned with the last two of these developments, the evolution of independentist ideology since 1960, and the extent of the Parti Québécois' electoral support.

The Evolution of Independentist Ideology during the 1960s

Ideologically, independentist groups have differed in recent years on three major issues: the Canada-Quebec relationship after independence; the socio-economic programme of an independent Quebec; and the political strategy for achieving independence.

On the future political relationship between Canada and a sovereign Quebec, three attitudes have been prevalent. In the early 1960s, groups such as the *Alliance Laurentienne,*[2] led by Raymond Barbeau, and the *Parti Républicain,*[3] led by Marcel Chaput, had not yet recognized the subject as a significant issue; sovereignty seemed so remote and English Canada so much of an enemy that there was no incentive to speculate on it. Another attitude has been to recognize the problem, but to foresee no special Canada-Quebec arrangements after independence.

---

* Throughout this study, we shall use the term "independence" rather than "separatism," which, in addition to its negative overtones, refers to only one aspect of Quebec's struggle, the constitutional break-away of the Province of Quebec from Canada. We shall also use the adjective "independentist," which is becoming increasingly common in both French and English in Quebec.

For example, the *Rassemblement pour l'Indépendance Nationale*[4] saw relations between Canada and Quebec simply as those existing between any two sovereign countries. More recently, political developments have led to a third attitude identified with the *Mouvement Souveraineté-Association*[5] and its successor, the Parti Québécois.[6]

As the 1960s advanced, an increasing number of English Canadians recognized that independence was, if not inevitable, at least a very real possibility; and they became preoccupied with its possible consequences. Anti-separatist propagandists,[7] on the other hand, reacted to the growing popularity of the movement with predictions of economic catastrophe. These gloomy appraisals prompted the M.S.A., and then the Parti Québécois, to stress possible economic cooperation between Canada and a sovereign Quebec as a means of reducing the danger of economic breakdown. A minority of English Canadians and independentists realized that Quebec's separation from Canada would make both countries more vulnerable to the American economic and cultural threat; and they have argued for common Quebec-Canada strategies with regard to foreign investments, culture, and fiscal policies.

As first suggested by the Parti Québécois, this Canada-Quebec economic cooperation could take three possible forms: a customs union to protect Canadian and Quebec products from a tariff war; a common market agreement along the lines of the European Economic Community; and a monetary union with a common currency and a joint publicly-owned bank responsible for administering the debts and setting the monetary policies of both states. Recently, this concern of the Parti Québécois for close economic cooperation with Canada has diminished. In its 1972 manifesto, serious doubts are expressed about the likelihood of a monetary union:

> We have scarcely any illusions. While a customs union is desirable and, so to speak, in the cards, a monetary union remains problematical. [author's translation][8]

Two factors have contributed to this new scepticism. In the aftermath of the October crisis of 1970, the leaders of the Parti Québécois are no longer convinced of the feasibility of any Canada-Quebec agreement. That experience shattered their stereotype of English Canadians as cold, rational, unemotional individuals motivated primarily by economic self-interest. They had presumed that English Canada would soon realize that cooperation with a sovereign Quebec was to its economic advantage. The October crisis revealed that, in times of crisis, English Canadian public opinion, probably because of its uncertain sense of nationhood, can be made to support any paranoid response of the federal government advanced in terms of the "national interest." In the wake of Quebec's secession, this public opinion could easily be manipulated into support of an economic boycott, even at great cost to Ontario's secondary industry.

The new trend toward radicalism apparent in the Parti Québécois programme has also caused second thoughts concerning Canada-Quebec cooperation. If this programme is implemented, even within a framework of social democracy, an independent Quebec is not likely to be an acceptable economic partner to the rest of Canada. And there is a growing feeling among independentists that any economic agreements would merely perpetuate the dependence of Quebec on English Canada.

Let us now consider the evolution of independentist ideology with regard to the socio-economic conditions of an independent Quebec. For the *Alliance Laurentienne,* the *Ralliement National** and even the early R.I.N., independence implied an opportunity for Quebec to return to its true self by recognizing the central position of language, faith, and family in the social fabric of Quebec society. But except for occasional references to free enterprise, and to businesses owned by French-speaking Quebecers, they had almost no economic programme. The first coherent and detailed statement of the socio-economic content of independence first appeared in the R.I.N. platform prepared for the 1966 elections. It reflected the climate of modernization brought about by the Quiet Revolution and called for an increased role for the state, non-compulsory planning, administrative decentralization, and economic growth.

The first Parti Québécois programme continued where the R.I.N. had left off. It took the position that the Quebec economy is not under-developed, but merely badly developed. Among its many weaknesses are the shortage of investment in manufacturing, the absence of heavy industries, a badly organized agricultural sector, a high level of unemployment, regional disparities, and the absence of French-speaking Quebecers in the top level of management. To remedy this situation, the Parti Québécois put forward a development plan with five principal objectives: increase of the growth rate; full employment across the Province; satisfaction of the real needs of Quebecers; equitable distribution of the products of economic growth; and an end to regional disparities. To achieve these objectives, a long list of measures, indicative of the party's economic philosophy, was suggested: consolidation of the government procurement policy to favour Quebec industries; government

---

* A splinter group from the R.I.N. which ran candidates in the 1966 election but later joined forces with the P.Q.

support to accelerate the fusion of small business enterprises; government financing of industrial research; government subsidies to promote exports; nationalization of certain sectors of the economy; utilization of the banking system to channel private savings into specific areas of investment; an integrated and aggressive commercial policy; compulsory measures to ensure the use of French by outside investors; government support of high risk investments; and priority to technical aspects of economic growth. This emphasis on planning, government intervention, and efficiency suggests that the Parti Québécois fully accepts the general rules of the economic system in present-day North America. "There can be no healthy capitalism in a sick economy," it has stated.[9] Its objective is to "fully understand the evolution of contemporary capitalism,"[10] and to use this knowledge to ensure the prosperity of the majority of Quebecers.

Since 1970, this economic philosophy has come under attack from a number of quarters, including citizens' groups, trade unions, and most important, from within the party itself. Criticizing the absence of a critical approach to the capitalist system, these groups argue that the system envisioned by the Parti Québécois would not alter the sub-human and alienating conditions under which a majority of Quebecers now have to work and live.[11] As a result of these pressures, the economic programme has been radicalized by including the following elements:

- an investment code prohibiting any foreign investment in a number of strategic sectors such as the steel industry and the mass media;
- nationalization of finance companies and their replacement· by credit unions;
- nationalization of all urban land so that rental costs can be divorced from construction costs;
- compulsory incorporation of banks and insurance companies in Quebec to ensure that they are locally and not foreign based.

Even the apparently sacred concept of "economic growth" has not escaped re-assessment:

The increasing seriousness of environmental problems, the destructive effects of pollution, the increasing quantities of detergents that are a reflection of anarchical and basically sterile trends, must necessarily lead us soon to an agonizing re-appraisal of old concepts of growth.[12]

But, the manifesto continues;

> Before embarking on a re-orientation of economic growth, a certain
> level of conomic well-being is necessary, and adequate control of
> the economy that produces it.[13]

This debate on the form and nature of independence has given rise to
dissension within the independentist movement concerning the strategy to
bring about Quebec's liberation. For militants operating within a political
party, the electoral approach is clearly the most appropriate. This choice
stems from their definition of the "Quebec problem" in terms of political
power. For the Parti Québécois, the recuperation by the Quebec government of the major instruments of political decision-making is essential to
the establishment of a society where all individuals can achieve full self-
determination. Only through national independence will Quebecers find
the imagination, energy and tools to build a new society. Arrived at
through peaceful and democratic means,

> the hour of independence will provide a special opportunity for
> progress and renewal . . . . The Quebecer will not be able to recog-
> nize himself. Belonging to a people that has full responsibility for its
> own destiny cannot help but engender a new sense of responsibility
> and stimulate as never before a spirit of initiative.[14]

Since 1964-65 a number of groups have rejected this strategy of peaceful
change by electoral means. Members of the Front de Libération du
Québec made clear their commitment to a more direct and violent type
of action. Other groups, while not advocating terrorism and violence,
have questioned the bourgeois character of the electoral approach; the
Mouvement de Libération Populaire, the *Ligue Socialiste Ouvrière* and
the *Révolution Québécoise* have suggested that it is a trap set up by
persons who are interested in independence but not in the establishment
of a socialist society. In a manifesto published in 1966, the *Mouvement
de Libération Populaire* rejected the strategy of tactical support for a
bourgeois independence party in favour of the creation of a Revolutionary Workers Party, which, they argued, would be able to enlist the
active cooperation of non-independentist but socialist groups. This plan
was soon abandoned by some of its authors, who eventually advocated
tactical support of the Parti Québécois. Two of them, P. Maheu and G.
Tremblay, explained their action by arguing that independence is the
necessary first step to socialism:

There can be no common strategy between independentist and non-independentist socialists within the same party. There can be no doubt that independence is a necessary priority for Quebec. . . . It is impossible for workers to have a clear understanding of class alienation as long as the colonial situation makes it impossible to distinguish between capitalist and English-Canadian domination of Quebecers.[15]

The recent exchange between Pierre Vallières,[16] a former advocate of violence who now recommends an end to terrorism and support for the Parti Québécois, and his former cell-mate, Charles Gagnon, who favours the creation of a workers' party outside of the Parti Québécois, is an extension of this earlier debate concerning the best organizational strategy for the achievement of a free Quebec.

Table 1
Voting Intention in 1970 in the Montreal Area
by Age Groups (in Percentages)

Voting Intention in 1970	18-25	26-35	36-50	51+
Liberal	35.8	35.5	33.1	33.0
Union Nationale	5.3	2.5	8.7	6.0
Parti Québécois	35.8	29.8	24.4	19.0
Others*	4.3	2.5	1.6	4.0
D.K/N.A/A.**	18.9	29.7	32.3	38.0 ·
Total	100.1	100.0	100.1	100.0
Number	(95)	(121)	(127)	(100)

* New Democratic Party, Ralliement Créditiste, other candidates

** Don't know, No answer, Abstention

Table 2
Voting Intention in 1970 in the Montreal Area According to Total Annual
Family Revenues (in Percentages)

Voting Intention in 1970	$0-3,999	$4,000-7,999	$8.000+
Liberal	23.3	33.6	43.2
Union Nationale	3.3	9.4	4.9
Parti Québécois	40.0	28.1	32.1
Others	6.7	3.1	2.5
D.K/N.A/A.	26.6	25.8	17.3
Total	99.9	100.0	100.0
Number	(30)	(128)	(162)

During the past dozen years, the independence movement has taken two apparently contradictory directions: towards an increased radicalism of its socio-economic program, and towards an electoral approach as the best means to achieve independence. Does this paradoxical situation, which finds something of a parallel in Chile, herald the end of the struggle? Or does the future lie in the electoral approach of the Parti Québécois?

Electoral Support for the Parti Québécois in the Montreal Area.

Some empirical studies[17] have established that Parti Québécois supporters tend to be male, young, better-educated, and in the upper professional brackets. These findings create an image of the Parti Québécois as a party of intellectuals with hardly any roots among the working population. Our own data, collected in the Montreal area on the eve of the 1970 elections by the Survey Research Center of the University of Montreal,[18] confirm some of these findings. They reveal, for instance, that support for the Parti Québécois decreases progressively among older age groups (Table 1); and that 42.1 percent of male voters support the Parti Québécois, compared to only 33.3 percent of female voters. But if we consider total family revenues, our findings diverge significantly: we found that, in striking contrast to the Liberal Party, the Parti Québécois had a particularly strong appeal among the lower income groups (Table 2). In other words, in addition to being popular among the young, the intellectuals, and the professional groups, the Parti Québécois receives considerable support from the underprivileged segments of the population, although for different reasons.

Table 2 raises some interesting questions. It has been argued, notably by Prime Minister Trudeau, that a vote for the Parti Québécois should not be interpreted automatically as a vote for independence, but as a protest vote against the inabilities of traditional parties to solve the problems of health, unemployment, housing, and inflation. According to this interpretation, the Parti Québécois derives its electoral strength principally from the fact that it is a new party, and from its socio-economic programme, rather than from its stand in favour of independence. Opponents of this viewpoint argue that, even among the underprivileged, a vote for the Parti Québécois is in fact a vote for independence since these persons are most likely to be aware of the close connections existing between poor socio-economic conditions and Quebec's political servitude. They point out that the Parti Québécois won its most striking victories in 1970 in the poor constituencies of eastern Montreal, and not in the middle-class northern part of the city, where it had run its most prestigious candidates.

The importance of ideology in determining electoral choices is not a new subject, nor is the phenomenon peculiar to Quebec. V. O. Key first raised it in the United States, and suggested that American voters were motivated by programmes and ideological considerations, and not by socio-economic conditioning or long-term partisan ties.[19] In Quebec Hamelin (1959), Dépatie (1965) and, most recently, Pinard[20] have argued that the impact of nationalism on the electoral choice of Quebec voters has been greatly exaggerated. Pinard's analysis has been the most thorough; in his study of the 1962 provincial elections he demonstrated empirically that, on the whole, the Quebec electorate was not influenced by the issue on which the Lesage Administration had called the elections, which was the nationalization of the hydro-electrical power companies. The average Quebec voter gave more importance to party affiliation, the personality of the various party leaders, current economic conditions as they affected his own situation, and the over-all performance of the government. Other students of Quebec electoral behavior, notably Quinn (1963), Rioux (1965), and Regenstreif and Jenson (1970) have taken the opposite view.[21] In a 1969 pre-election survey, Regenstreif and Jenson found no empirical support for Pinard's thesis, and concluded that more Parti Québécois support

is accounted for by the attitude of individuals towards the question of French Canadian nationalism than by their economic and social positions within Quebec.[22]

This subject of electoral motivation is important to the Parti Québécois in terms of electoral strategy and also because of its implications after victory has been won. If the key to success is the socio-economic programme, and not independence, the latter issue should be shelved at least temporarily. On the other hand, if independence is the most popular issue, the socio-economic programme should not be too radical, or potential supporters of independence will be frightened away. This subject is highly relevant as the next elections draw near. In the face of pressures by some members to radicalize the programme, the party leadership argues that independence is a pre-requisite to the implementation of any programme, radical or moderate, and it has denounced

the deceptiveness of short-cuts . . . [and] of a miraculous collective metamorphosis occurring overnight, as it has never happened in any other part of the world.[23]

Table 3

Voting Intention in 1970 in the Montreal Area According to Subjective
Nationality of the Respondent (in Percentages)

Voting Intention in 1970	Canadian	Canadian-Québécois	Québécois
Liberal	46.6	31.4	5.4
Union Nationale	6.9	5.9	1.8
Parti Québécois	7.5	29.9	76.8
Others	2.9	3.5	1.8
D.K/N.A/A.	36.2	29.4	14.3
Total	100.1	100.1	100.1
Number	(174)	(204)	(56)

What are the implications of this subject for the post-victory period? If the Parti Québécois wins an absolute majority* of the popular vote, will it still be required to carry out a referendum to ascertain the wishes of the people on the subject of independence? Or would an electoral decision constitute in itself a satisfactory mandate? To the extent that the Parti Québécois vote is also a vote for independence, a referendum would entail no dangers; otherwise, a referendum might very well reject independence.

A close examination of the available data provides some additional, but indirect, support for the Regenstreif and Jenson thesis stressing the significance of nationalism in determining the Parti Québécois vote. Respondents were asked to locate themselves on a Canadian-Quebec continuum. Table 3 indicates that a majority of those who defined themselves as exclusively or mostly "Canadian" intended to vote for the Liberal Party, while an even larger proportion of those who defined themselves as "Quebecers" intended to vote for the Parti Québécois.

While self-definition on a scale of subjective nationality is not equivalent to nationalist fervour, it is difficult to imagine that the two would not correlate at a very high level. The same cleavages, only more pronounced, are found in Table 4, which provides the reaction of respondents to the idea of Quebec's independence, and in Table 5, which indicates the level of support for the federal system

Eighty-nine percent of those who are highly favourable to independence, and 87.0 percent of those who strongly reject federalism, intended to vote for the Parti Québécois. Predictably, the Parti Québécois is

---

* This is even more true if the majority is only a relative one, or if the P.Q. wins the election without even a plurality of the votes.

Table 4

Voting Intention in 1970 in the Montreal Area According to the Level of Support for Quebec's Independence (in Percentages)

Voting Intention in 1970	Highly Favourable	Favourable	Indifferent	Unfavourable	Highly Unfavourable
Liberal	8.0	28.6	36.4	65.0	86.7
Union Nationale	2.7	11.1	9.1	10.0	6.7
Parti Québécois	84.0	57.1	33.3	15.0	1.9
Others	4.0	3.2	9.1	7.5	1.9
D.K/N.A./A.	1.3	0.0	12.1	2.5	2.9
Total	100.0	100.0	100.0	100.0	100.1
Number	(83)	(85)	(50)	(67)	(148)

Table 5

Voting Intention in 1970 in the Montreal Area According to the Level of Support for Federalism (in Percentages)

Voting Intention in 1970	Highly Favourable	Favourable	Indifferent	Unfavourable	Highly Unfavourable
Liberal	81.8	54.2	26.9	8.7	2.7
Union Nationale	5.5	11.1	11.9	4.3	2.7
Parti Québécois	5.5	29.2	47.8	87.0	89.2
Others	3.6	2.8	3.0	0.0	0.0
D.K/N.A./A.	3.6	2.8	7.5	0.0	0.0
Total	100.0	100.1	99.9	100.0	100.0
Number	(156)	(99)	(99)	(26)	(41)

Table 6

Voting Intention in 1970 in the Montreal Area According to the Respondent's Attitude Towards Bill 63 (in Percentages)

Voting Intention in 1970	Highly Favourable	Favourable	Indifferent	Unfavourable	Highly Unfavourable
Liberal	65.1	58.8	69.6	45.1	21.1
Union Nationale	14.0	5.9	4.3	5.6	8.8
Partie Québécois	18.6	25.5	26.1	46.5	68.4
Others	0.0	7.9	0.0	2.8	1.8
D.K/N.A./A.	2.3	2.0	0.0	0.0	0.0
Total	100.0	100.1	100.0	100.0	100.1
Number	(55)	(64)	(36)	(93)	(72)

particularly strong among voters who approve of independence and reject federalism.

The nationalist appeal of the Parti Québécois is further corroborated by Table 6, which records respondents' attitudes towards Bill 63, authorizing parents to transfer their children across linguistic and religious boundaries when choosing their schools. This legislation came under attack from nationalist forces because immigrants took advantage of it to switch their children from French-language or bilingual to English schools, and it was thus considered a threat to Quebec's cultural survival. In our Montreal sample, 68.4 percent of those who were highly critical of the measure indicated their intention of voting for the Parti Québécois.

Thus, on the basis of these four variables, subjective nationalism, support for independence, support for federalism, and attitudes towards Bill 63, it is plausible to conclude that the Parti Québécois has succeeded in attracting a large majority of the nationalist vote.* Furthermore, Table 7 also indicates that a clear majority (86.0 percent) of party supporters identified the Parti Québécois as the most pro-independence party. Their choice was obviously made with full knowledge of its position, and cannot be considered to have been made in ignorance of its pro-independence stand.

We cannot suggest with the same degree of confidence that a majority, if not all, of the Parti Québécois' electoral support came from voters who were motivated by nationalism. Table 8 reveals that 15.7 percent of the party's supporters are either indifferent or unfavourable to independence.

Similarly, Table 9 shows that 48.8 percent of those who intended to vote for the Parti Québécois either support or are indifferent to Canadian federalism.

Clearly, most of the independentists are Parti Québécois supporters, but not all Parti Québécois supporters are independentists. An analogous situation prevails within the Liberal Party, where 23.7 percent of party supporters are favourable to independence, and 12.5 percent are apparently indifferent or even hostile to Canadian federalism. As for the Union Nationale, its supporters are still more ambivalent with regard to these two options. Even after a bitter electoral campaign, it evidently remained impossible to equate completely support for federalism with support for the Liberal Party, or approval of independence with support for the Parti Québécois. This situation adds to the difficulty of assessing the strength and predicting the progress of the independentist movement.

* A fact which does not necessarily contradict Pinard's thesis.

Table 7
Ranking of the P. Q. on an Independence Scale According to the Voting Intention of the Respondent (in Percentages)

Rank of the P.Q. on an Independence Scale	Voting Intention in 1970		
	Liberal	Union Nationale	Parti Québécois
Most independentist party	69.7	50.0	86.0
2nd most independentist	7.1	19.2	2.5
3rd most independentist	1.9	0.0	1.7
4th most independentist	4.5	7.7	0.0
Least independentist party	3.9	0.0	0.0
D.K/N.A./A.	12.9	23.1	9.9
Total	99.9	100.0	100.1
Number	(155)	(26)	(12)

Table 8
The Level of Support for Independence in 1970 in the Montreal Area According to Voting Intention (in Percentages)

Level of Support for Independence	Voting Intention in 1970		
	Liberal	Union Nationale	Parti Québécois
Favourable	15.5	34.6	81.8
Indifferent	7.7	11.5	9.1
Unfavourable	75.5	42.3	6.6
D.K/N.A/A.	1.3	11.5	2.5
Total	100.0	99.9	100.0
Number	(155)	(26)	(121)

Table 9
Level of Support for Federalism in 1970 in the Montreal Area According to Voting Intention (in Percentages)

Level of Support for Federalism	Voting Intention in 1970		
	Liberal	Union Nationale	Parti Québécois
Favourable	83.3	53.9	22.4
Indifferent	11.6	30.8	26.4
Unfavourable	1.9	7.6	43.8
D.K/N.A./A.	3.2	7.7	7.4
Total	100.0	100.0	100.0
Number	(155)	(26)	(121)

Quebec Society and Politics

This absence of a proper correlation between Parti Québécois support and independentist sentiment reflects in empirical terms the strategic dilemma faced by the party. Should it try to attract outside independentist supporters, or should it concentrate on the outside, non-independentist voters who still constitute the majority of the electorate? In other words, should it strive to consolidate its position as the party of *all* independentists, and hope for victory when a majority of Quebecers have rallied to that cause, even if that approach entails the risk of remaining a minority party forever?* Or should it aim at becoming a majority party as soon as possible by further diluting its independence platform to attract non-independentist voters, thus running the risk of losing some committed independentists, as well as setting the stage for a post-victory intra-party struggle?

There is still another complicating dimension to this situation. We have assumed thus far that, in the minds of the electorate, the independence of Quebec and Canadian federalism are two mutually incompatible options. But this relationship is not fully supported by the data. Table 10 and 11 show that for a sizeable portion of the Montreal electorate, they are both ideal objectives worthy of support in principle.

While this ambivalence creates more strategic problems for the Parti Québécois, it also raises some interesting prospects. It will be noted that 32.1 percent of those who are favourable to independence are also favourable to Canadian federalism (Table 10). Similarly 21.2 percent of those who support federalism also support independence (Table 11). Thus, on the whole, it would seem that there are more disappointed federalists among the independentists than potential independentists among the federalists. Nevertheless, the Parti Québécois should clearly not base its electoral strategy on the expectation that the number of independentists is going to grow rapidly; no more than 26.3 per cent of the federalists can be expected to develop independentist leanings in the short run. Furthermore, Tables 10 and 11 reveal that the idea of federalism is more widely accepted (56.4 percent *vs.* 37.2 percent) and less strongly rejected (14.9 percent *vs.* 47.5 percent) than independence. These statistics lead us to the conclusion that the Parti Québécois will have considerable difficulty in increasing its strength through trying to convert non-independentists to the idea of independence. Even if it succeeded in bringing about such intellectual conversions, there is still no guarantee that they would be translated in Parti Québécois votes.

More encouraging for the Parti Québécois is the fact that the idea of independence leaves fewer people indifferent and unresponsive (15.3 per-

---

* Like the Social Credit or the New Democratic Party on the Canadian federal scene.

Table 10

The Level of Support for Independence by the Level of Support for Federalism
in 1970 in the Montreal Area
(in Percentages)

Support for Federalism	Support for Independence			
	Favourable	Indifferent	Unfavourable	N.A./D.K.
Favourable	32.1	26.0	86.0	52.6
Indifferent	27.9	60.0	8.7	26.4
Unfavourable	33.9	8.0	1.8	10.5
N.A./D.K.	6.1	6.0	3.7	10.5
Total	100.0	100.0	100.2	100.0
Number	(168)	(50)	(215)	(19)

Table 11

The Level of Support for Federalism by the Level of Support for Independence
in 1970 in the Montreal Area
(in Percentages)*

Support for Independence	Support for Federalism			
	Favourable	Indifferent	Unfavourable	N.A./D.K.
Favourable	21.2	47.4	80.5	32.2
Indifferent	5.1	30.3	5.9	32.2
Unfavourable	60.0	20.2	5.9	9.9
N.A./D.K.	13.7	2.1	2.8	25.8
Total	100.0	100.0	100.1	100.1
Number	(255)	(99)	(67)	(31)

* Originally the respondents were given five choices: highly favourable, favourable, indifferent, unfavourable, highly unfavourable. For the sake of simplicity these five were collapsed into three categories: favourable, indifferent and unfavourable to federalism.

Table 12

The Support for the P.Q. and the Liberal Party by the Stand on Federalism and
Independence (in Percentages)

Stand on Federalism and Independence	Parti Québécois	Liberal
Federalist, independentist*	14.2	12.8
Federalist, non-independentist	8.2	70.5
Non-federalist, independentist	67.7	2.3
Non-federalist, non-independentist	9.8	14.1
Total	99.9	99.7
Number	(121)	(155)

* The table reads as follows: 14.2% support both independence and federalism.

Table 13

Support for Independence, Federalism and the Voting Intention in 1970 in the
Montreal Region (in Percentages)

Voting Intention in 1970	Independence Federalism	– Federalism	Independence Federalism	– Federalism
Parti Québécois**	45.9	97.5	8.5	35.3
Liberal	54.1	2.4	91.5	64.7
Total	100.0	99.9	100.0	100.0
Number	(37)	(86)	(119)	(34)

** The table reads as follows: 45.9% of those who express support both for federalism and independence intended to vote for the P.Q. (the U.N. and the other
parties were excluded from the total).

cent) than the idea of federalism (26.5 percent). These figures partially confirm the widely held impression that for the last ten years the tone of the
political debate in Quebec has been set by the partisans of independence
and that, generally speaking, the federalists have been on the defensive.*
Indifference to federalism may well be the first step in the development of
independentist leanings. This could explain why 27.9 percent of the independentists declared themselves to be indifferent to the idea of federalism.
If indifference to federalism is indeed the first step towards support of the
Parti Québécois, the party can find encouragement in the fact that the proportion of those who are indifferent to federalism and favourable to independence (47.4 percent) is larger than the proportion of those who are
indifferent to independence and favourable to federalism (26.0 percent).
That having been said, it is not clear from the available statistics whether
there is any bandwagon effect in favour of independence, nor whether the
switch from federalism to independence is a one-way or a reversible process. A source of concern to the Parti Québécois is the presence in its ranks
of supporters (8.2 percent) who support federalism in principle and who
are either indifferent or unfavourable to independence. The Liberal Party
contains a similar element, but they constitute only 2.3 percent of Liberal
supporters. Apparently there are more Parti Québécois supporters in the
Montreal area who are likely to defect to the Liberal Party than vice versa,
even though both parties have approximately the same percentage of supporters who can be regarded as stable voters. 67.7 percent of Parti Québe-
cois supporters are both independentists and anti-federalists, and 70.5 percent of Liberal supporters are pro-federalists and opposed to independence.

* The appearance of Pierre Trudeau may have changed this situation at the
federal level but not on the level of Quebec politics.

In the final analysis, the evolution of these two groups, the disappointed federalists and the potential independentists, will determine the fate of the independentist struggle on the electoral level.* In 1970 the Liberal Party was particularly successful in attracting voters who supported *both* federalism and independence, or who were hostile to both. It won 54.1 percent of the first and 64.7 percent of the second group. Is this an indication that the Liberal Party is slowly disintegrating from within, or that it has a particularly wide appeal among all groups other than convinced independentists? Only the next provincial elections, which will presumably be held in 1974, will tell.

---

* The indifferent voters and those voters who hold no opinion on either one of the two options also constitute an important parameter (Tables 10 and 11.) For example among these electors who are indifferent to federalism there is a large proportion of voters (47.4%) who are favourable to independence. On the other hand, 26.0% of those who declared themselves indifferent to the idea of independence are favourable to federalism. Will these individuals eventually join the cause of independence, or are these percentages simply the result of the fact that federalism leaves more people indifferent than independence?

Notes

1. On independence movements before 1960, see D. O'Leary, *Le Séparatisme, doctrine constructive,* Montréal: Les Jeunesses Patriotes, 1837; Wilfrid Morin, *L'Indépendance du Québec,* Montréal: Alliance Laurentienne, 1938; Action Française, *Notre Avenir Politique,* Montréal: Action Française, 1923; Maurice Séguin, *L'Idée de l'indépendance au Québec, Genése et Historique,* Trois-Riviéres: Boréal Express, 1968; Fernand Ouellet, "Les Fondements historiques de l'option séparatiste dans le Québec," *Canadian Historical Review,* 11.3 (1962), pp. 185-203.
2. On the *Alliance Laurentienne,* see Raymond Barbeau, *J'ai choisi l'indépendance,* Montréal: Editions de l'Homme, 1961; *La Libération Economique de Québec,* Montréal: Editions de l'Homme, 1963; *Le Québec est-il une colonie?* Montréal: Editions de l'Homme, 1962.
3. On the *Parti Républicain,* see Marcel Chaput, *J'ai choisi de me battre.* Montréal: Club du Livre du Québec, 1965.
4. On the *Rassemblement pour l'Indépendance Nationale,* see M. Lavallé, "Le R.I.N. est d'orientation socialiste," *Socialisme 67, XII.13 (1967), pp. 49-54;* Pierre Renaud, *L'Histoire du* R.I.N, Montréal, Sécrétariat du R.I.N.,, 1964. The R.I.N. disappeared in late 1968 when its leadership recommended that its members join the newly formed Parti Québécois.
5. The *Mouvement Souveraineté-Association* was founded in 1967 by a group of dissidents from the Liberal Party led by René Lévesque; in 1968, it became the Parti Québécois. On the M.S.A., see *Ce Pays qu'on peut bâtir,* Montréal, M.S.A., 1968; "L'option Lévesque," *Parti Pris,* v. 6 (March 1968); René-Lévesque, *Option Québec,* Montréal, Editions de l'Homme, 1967.
6. The list of publications edited by the Parti Québécois is impressive. See *Quand nous serons vraiment chez nous,* Montréal: Les Editions du Parti Québécois, 1972; *Le Programme d'action politique, les statuts et les règlements,* Montréal: Editions du Parti Québécois, 1972; *Le Programme d'action politique, les statuts et les reglements,* Montréal: Editions du Parti Québécois, 1971; *Les dossiers du 4ième congrès national du Parti Québécois,* Montréal: Les Editions du Parti Québécois, 1972; *La Souveraineté et l'Economie,* Montréal, Editions du Jour, 1970.
7. On anti-separatism, see Daniel Latouche, "Anti-séparatisme et messianisme au Québec depuis 1960," *Canadian Journal of Political Science,* Vol. III, No. 4 (1970), pp. 559-579.
8. *Quand nous serons vraiment chez nous,* p. 135.
9. *La Souveraineté et l'Economie,* p. 159.
10. *Idem,* p. 159.
11. See André Larocque, *Défis au Parti Québécois.* Montréal: Editions du Jour, 1971.
12. *Quand nous serons vraiment chez nous,* p. 48.
13. *Ibid.,* p. 49.
14. *Ibid.,* p. 21.
15. Pierre Maheu et Gaétan Tremblay, "L'Indépendance au plus vite!", *Parti Pris,* Vol. IV, Nos. 5-6, (1967), p. 3. On the political history of Quebec in the 1960s, see Luc Racine et Roch Denis, "La conjoncture politique québécoise

depuis 1960," *Socialisme québécois,* 21-22 (1971), pp. 17-79.
16. See his *L'Urgence de choisir.* Montréal: Editions Parti Pris, 1972.
17. This analysis will only sketch the outlines of a more detailed study of independentist electoral support which is to be published in 1973 (J. G. Vaillancourt (ed.), *Les Elections de 1970 au Québec,* Montréal, Presses de l'Université du Québec, (forthcoming). Other empirical studies on recent political attitudes in Quebec include Jane Jenson and Peter Regenstreif, "Some Dimensions of Partisan Choice in Quebec," *Canadian Journal of Political Science,* Vol. II.1 (1970), pp. 308-318; V. Lemieux, *et al., Quatre Elections Provinciales au Québec: 1956-1966,* Quebec: Les Presses de l'Université Laval, 1969; V. Lemieux, M. Gilbert et M. Bellevance, *Une Election de Réalignement,* Montréal: Editions du Jour, 1970.
18. The 70 question survey was conducted by professional interviewers and covered a probabilities sample of eligible voters in the Montreal metropolitan area. 452 questionnaires were finally processed out of a total of 950 individuals selected in the sample. This poor rate of return is the result of the extremely difficult material conditions under which the survey was conducted. This poor rate of return is also responsible for the under-representation of men in the sample. On the other hand, on political characteristics such as the vote, the sample apparently does not suffer from any major bias.
19. V. O. Key, *The Responsible Electorate: Rationality in Presidential Voting, 1936-1960.* Cambridge: Harvard University Press, 1966.
20. Maurice Pinard, "La Ratinalité de l'Electorat: Le cas de 1962" in Vincent Lemieux (ed.), *Quatre Elections Provinciales au Québec:* Les Presses de l'Université Laval, 1969, pp. 179-195; Jean Hamelin et al., "Les Elections Provinciales dans le Québec," *Cahiers de Géographie de Québec,* 4, (1959-1960), pp. 5-207; Francine Dépatie, *Comportement Electoral au Canada Français,* M.A. Thesis, Université de Montréal, 1965.
21. Herbert Quinn, *The Union Nationale: A Study of Quebec Nationalism.* Toronto: University of Toronto Press, 1963; Marcel Rioux, "Conscience Ethnique et Conscience de classe au Québec," *Recherches Sociographiques,* VI.1 (1965), pp. 23-32.
22. Regenstreif and Jenson, *op. cit.,* p. 316.
23. *Quand nous serons vraiment chez nous, p. 36.*

Quebec Society and Politics

14
The Gospel According to Holy Ottawa
by Claude Morin

It would be a serious mistake to attribute the failure of the 1971 Victoria constitutional conference purely to tactical errors by one or other of the negotiating parties. Albeit convenient for the white knights of unconditional federalism, this explanation ignores the real reasons for the fiasco. Nor can it be seriously asserted that the paucity of Quebec's gains over a decade of federal-provincial negotiations is due to inadequate preparation or exorbitant demands on its part.

The Gospel . . .

The explanation is found elsewhere, in the official federal doctrine developed towards the end of the Pearson régime as a reaction to attitudes associated with the Quiet Revolution in Quebec. This doctrine matured with the years to be ready for publication in the first of the federal White Papers distributed during the process of the constitutional review. It appeared in February, 1968; its title was *Federalism for the Future,* and its sub-title – highly evocative but almost unnoticed at the time – *A Statement of Policy by the Government of Canada.* With such a label, it could not be considered simply a "working paper" of items for discussion any more than the subsequent White Papers.

For identification of the continuing strategy of the federal government this first White Paper is by far the most important. It contains a detailed list of federal priorities, since scrupulously observed, and specific statements of policy and principle that cast much light on Ottawa's true objectives. We in Quebec were wrong not to analyze this document more carefully at the time. The vagueness of its title, its highly theoretical character and unctuous style, its polished language and obvious clichés, probably obscured the real content; and so it disturbed no one. But it is all there; the subsequent White Papers merely applied to specific areas the policy positions and postulates found in this first official statement.

Federalism for the Future did not appear overnight in 1968. As early as September, 1966, the Honourable Mitchell Sharp reflected similar ideas in his opening address to a meeting of ministers of finance; and other federal ministers intoned the same hymn. Earlier still, Prime Minister Pearson, even in his most conciliatory period, used the same broad themes in defending his government against the challenge from Quebec. In fact, the White Paper of 1968 – and this is the essential fact to be borne in mind – contains no new political philosophy or views on the distribution of powers within the federal system; it is entirely faithful to traditional theories. Its principal merit lies in having given these theories greater coherence, assembling them in a sort of Canadian Declaration of Federalism, readily accessible and easy to consult. So let us consult it.

The following lengthy extract from the White Paper contains the principles the federal government considers should govern any re-examination of the distribution of legislative powers between Ottawa and the provinces. The italics are ours.

Discussions on the division of powers should take place, in the opinion of the Government of Canada, after the constitutional conferences have considered the other principal elements of the Constitution – the rights of individual Canadians, including linguistic rights, and the central institutions of federalism. We say this because *provincial interests and the interests of Canada's two linguistic groups are not and cannot be represented simply through the device of transferring powers from the federal government to provincial governments*. These interests are and must be reflected as well in constitutional guarantees and in the central institutions of federalism. It follows that a balanced judgement as to the powers required by the provincial governments for the primary purpose of protecting linguistic or provincial interests can only be made in the perspective of the constitutional guarantees and the representation of such interests in the central organs of government. To jeopardize the capacity of the federal government to act for Canada, in the name of protecting linguistic and provincial rights, when what is essential could be accomplished through constitutional guarantees and the institutions of federalism, would be to serve Canadians badly. Furthermore, *the division of powers between orders of government should be guided by principles of functionalism, and not by ethnic considerations*. Such principles can best be applied after issues concerning the protection of linguistic rights have been settled.

The Government of Canada would propose, therefore, that discussions on the division of powers take place at subsequent conferences. However, in anticipation of these discussions, and as a guide to the direction of the Government's thinking we believe we should place before the Conference some of the principles by which we feel we would have to be guided.

First, we are committed to the view that *Canada requires both a strong federal government and strong provincial governments.* The field of government now is so wide, and the problems of government are so many, that it is not a contradiction to speak in these terms. Governments themselves confirm this view when they argue that their spending responsibilities exceed their ability to raise revenues. There is another reason for achieving a balance between the powers of the federal and provincial governments: the freedom of the individual is more likely to be safeguarded if neither order of government is able to acquire a preponderant power over the citizen.

Secondly, the Government of Canada believes that there are certain areas of responsibility which must remain with the federal government if our country is to prosper in the modern world. *The Parliament of Canada must have responsibility for the major and inextricably inter-related instruments of economic policy if it is to stimulate employment and control inflation. It must have control over monetary and credit policy, the balance-wheel role in fiscal policy, tariff policy, and balance of payments policy. It must be responsible for interprovincial and international trade. It must be able to undertake measures for stimulating the growth of the economy, some of which inevitably and some of which intentionally will affect regional economic growth.* Without such powers Canada's federal government would be unable to contribute to many of the central objectives of federalism, including the reduction of regional disparity.

We believe that the *Government of Canada must have the power to redistribute income, between persons and between provinces,* if it is to equalize opportunity across the country. *This would involve,* as it does now, *the rights to make payments to individuals, for the purpose of supporting their income levels – old age security pensions, unemployment insurance, family allowances –* and the right to make payments to provinces, for the purpose of equalizing the level of provincial government services. It must involve, too, the powers of taxation which would enable the federal government to tax those best able to contribute to these equalization measures. Only in this way can the national government contribute to the equalization of opportunity in Canada, and thus supplement and support provincial measures to this end.

The Government of Canada believes it must be able to speak for Canada, internationally, and that it must be able to act for Canada in strengthening the bonds of nationhood. We have said what we think this implies in international matters. Internally it seems to us *to imply an active federal role in the cultural and technological developments which so characterize the 20th century. We acknowledge, of course, that the nourishment of Canada's cultural diversity requires imaginative provincial programmes, as well as federal ones. But there is a role for the Government of Canada, too; indeed cultural and technological developments across the country are as essential to nationhood today as tariffs and railways were one hundred years ago.*

These are central areas of responsibility essential to the apparatus of the modern sovereign state – economic policy, the equalization of opportunity, technological and cultural development, and international affairs. There are among these, of course, areas of responsibility which are shared with the provinces – including cultural matters, regional economic policy, and social security measures. However to catalogue these now, or federal powers generally, would be to depart from a statement of guiding principles and to anticipate the discussions of future conferences.

The third principle which would guide the Government of Canada in discussions *concerning the division of powers is that most services involving the most immediate contact between the citizen and the government, and those which contribute most directly to the traditions and heritages which are uniquely provincial, should generally be provided by Canada's provincial governments. Strong provincial governments, able to adapt public services to the particular needs of their people, are as essential to meet the fact of diversity in Canada as a strong federal government is to the preservation of Canadian unity.*

The governments of the provinces have responsibility for education, and their own power to support technological and cultural development – so often associated with educational institutions. These powers play an important part in the flourishing of Canada's linguistic groups, and of the diverse traditions to be found in our country. We acknowledge, of course, that many of the institutions involved serve the nation as well as the province but this fact should not be allowed to diminish the capacity of the provinces to perform their role.

The Government of Canada believes *that the provinces must*

have the power to provide health and welfare services. For instance, the provincial governments rather than the federal government should operate hospitals or public health clinics and determine the needs of persons requiring social assistance. Provincial administration of services such as these makes possible the variation of levels of service to accord with local priorities. The role of the federal government should be to provide for those transfers of income between people and between provinces which generally support the income of people and the services of governments in the different provinces.

The Government of Canada recognizes too *that the provinces should continue to have the constitutional powers required to enable them to embark upon regional economic development programmes.* Provincial programmes inevitably will affect national policies for economic growth, and vice versa, and the programmes of the several provinces may well be competitive with one another. But the aims and the expectations of people in the several provinces should find expression in provincial as well as federal economic measures. *The provinces must continue, too, to have responsibility for the many intra-provincial matters which call for local rather than national action.*

The Government of Canada holds the view that in the exercise of these responsibilities – which under the present division of powers are at least as wide-ranging as those of the federal government – each province should be able to develop its own unique approach. *The range of powers we would expect the provinces to have would extend, as they do now, into the areas which are vital to the preservation of Canada's several cultural and regional identities.*

We believe, finally, that the provincial governments like the federal government must have taxing powers sufficient to enable them to finance their responsibilities. However, we suspect that in assigning to governments the power of taxation – the capacity for financing public services in Canada – the principle of access to tax powers will supersede the principle of an exact division of tax fields. We would do well to remember that it is as difficult to predict what technological or social or international changes will have increased the role of the provincial or federal governments in thirty years as it would have been to predict the changes between 1938 and 1968.

The fourth generalization we would advance concerning the division of powers has to do with the effect each government's activities inevitably will have upon the activities of the others. This applies both to individidual programmes and to the totality of government activity. For example, federal income redistribution measures inevitably have an effect upon provincial social welfare programmes and provincial resource development policies inevitably affect the rate of growth of the nation's economy. Similarly the aggregate use by the provinces of their spending and borrowing powers inevitably affects federal fiscal, and monetary and balance of payments policies, and the use of the federal spending power affects provincial policies in different ways. Obviously the total volume of spending by each order of government affects the priorities of the other.

We question whether it is any longer realistic to expect that some neat compartmentalization of powers can be found to avoid this. Instead we suspect that the answer is to be found in the processes by which governments consult one another and by which they seek to influence each other before decisions are finally taken. This remedy has been prescribed so often as to appear commonplace. But there is much to be done even in coming to understand the processes of intergovernmental influence, to say nothing of perfecting the machinery by which intergovernmental consultation takes place. Nor will we find the "participation" of provincial governments in federal government decisions, and vice versa, to be an easy answer to the problems of consultation. The federal government must remain responsible to Parliament, and the provincial governments to their legislatures: federal-provincial conferences must, it seems to us, occupy themselves with the art of influence rather than the power of decision-making.

Both federal and provincial governments will recognize, too, the unresolved question as to *whether there should be a federal government role when there is a "national interest" in provincial programmes (or the lack of them), or whether there should be a provincial government role when there is a "provincial interest" in national programmes (or the lack of them).* Examples abound: What the provinces do or do not do about urban development unquestionably affects the national interest, and what the federal government does or does not do about tariff policy affects the provincial interest. *We have to consider seriously whether there should be a way for the federal government to seek to influence the provinces in cases where a national interest is involved, and a way for provincial governments to seek to influence the federal government when a provincial interest is involved.*

There are, we think, no easy solutions. What is required is a comprehensive review of the federal-provincial conferences and committees which now exist, how they function, and how their work is co-ordinated. We must be prepared, it seems to the Government of Canada, to give more systematic recognition to these new forms of federalism.

We must be prepared to consider new methods for bringing provincial influence to bear on developing federal policies, and federal influence on developing provincial policies, before decisions have finally been taken. We must be prepared for innovations in the machinery of government which will enable us to preserve the essence of Canada's two great governmental traditions – federalism and parliamentary government.[1]

Its Exegesis . . .

Many pages could be devoted to analysis of this lengthy excerpt from the White Paper; extracts could also be quoted from other federal White Papers but they would add nothing of real significance. The text reproduced repays careful attention; it is complete in itself and contains a comprehensive statement that should be clearly understood.

a) In the first place, it stipulates that, in a new or revised constitution, the central government should control the key sectors of economic, social, cultural and political activity, or in the words of the White Paper, the "central areas of responsibility essential to the apparatus of the modern sovereign state – economic policy, the equalization of opportunity, technological and cultural development, and international affairs." The language is ambiguous, but clearly the "modern sovereign state" is Canada as a whole, and the federal government the government of this "modern sovereign state." The authors of this text admit that "there are among these, of course, areas of responsibility which are shared with the provinces – including cultural matters, regional economic policy, and social security measures," but they are mentioned only that they may be demarcated more precisely.

b) According to this federal viewpoint, the activities of the provincial governments must be complementary to those of the central government. In other words, the provincial governments are conceived of as regional administrative units, somewhat on the lines of large municipalities. "Most services involving the most immediate contact between the citizen and the government, and those which contribute most directly to the traditions and heritages which are uniquely provincial, should generally be provided by Canada's provincial governments. Strong provincial governments, able to adapt public services to the particular needs of their people, are as essential to meet the facts of diversity in Canada as a strong federal government is to the preservation of Canadian unity." There we have it! One might have expected at the least that all local services would be clearly a provincial responsibility, but no, only "most" of them; and "those which contribute most directly to the traditions and heritages which are uniquely provincial" should "generally" be provided by the provinces. The central government thus keeps the door open for the expansion of its activities. Conversely, note the use of such terms as "uniquely provincial" and "their people" to specify the restricted scope of the provinces; the latter are given no similar room for expansion.

c) The importance of a new and clearer distribution of powers is minimized. "Provincial interests and the interests of Canada's two linguistic groups are not and cannot be represented simply through the device of transferring powers from the federal government to provincial governments." And further on: "The division of powers between orders of government should be guided by principles of functionalism, and not by ethnic considerations." Thus the acquisition by the provinces of powers currently held by the federal government becomes, in the eyes of Ottawa, a matter of expediency; far better, in the federal view, to rely on "principles of functionalism," that is, to entrust each responsibility to the government best prepared to meet it; and since Ottawa, with its present resources and the implicit support of the other provinces, is usually the "best prepared," this line of reasoning leads logically to an increase in the powers of the central authority. This is precisely the possibility that Ottawa wishes to preserve in stating such a "functional" and so conveniently pragmatic a principle.

d) The federal document recognizes that "the governments of the provinces have responsibility for education, and their own power to support technological and cultural development – so often associated with educational institutions." Does Ottawa then consider education an exclusively provincial field of jurisdiction? Not really, since the White Paper also mentions "an active federal role in the cultural and technological developments which so characterize the twentieth century." Why this "active role" in an area admittedly "so often associated with educational institutions"? Because, we are told, "cultural and technological developments across the country are as essential to nationhood today as tariffs and railways were one hundred years ago." Now, tariffs and railways are subjects of exclusively federal jurisdiction. The very fact that such a parallel is being drawn seems to us highly significant, and raises doubts about the permanency of the provinces' exclusive jurisdiction in the field of education.

e) What authority does the federal White Paper leave to the provinces in the field of health and welfare? There is, apparently, no objection to their accepting responsibility for hospitals and public health clinics; but, it is asserted, Ottawa must retain "as it does now, the right to make payments to individuals, for the purpose of supporting their income levels – old age security pensions, unemployment insurance, family allowances."

f) The authors of the White Paper do not believe in a water-tight separation of powers; they maintain their "functional" approach. "We have to consider seriously whether there should be a way for the federal government to seek to influence the provinces in cases where a national interest is involved, and a way for provincial governments to seek to influence the federal government when a provincial interest is involved." In other words, Ottawa wishes to institutionalize the system of reciprocal influence. However, it is easy to see where this form of institutionalization would lead if one bears three considerations in mind: that the federal government has always claimed the right to intervene whenever, in its judgment, a subject becomes of "national interest"; that its fiscal and financial resources, its spending power, enable it to take action at any time; and that the other provinces are far more inclined to cede certain of their present responsibilities to Ottawa than to try to increase them at Ottawa's expense.

g) In the whole of this lengthy excerpt from the White Paper there is not a single reference to Quebec; nothing at all to indicate to the outside observer that Canada's constitutional problem exists because of Quebec, and that Quebec considers the discussion of the division of powers a matter of the highest priority.

... and its Sources

In short, the White Paper is based on a grand design with two components: a central government responsible for just about everything except day-to-day administrative matters; and a set of regional administrative structures, the provinces. Was this plan conceived for the short-term purposes of current constitutional negotiations? Does it constitute an initial bargaining position to be modified according to circumstances and the negotiating ability of the opposing parties? Does it reflect a sinister desire for conquest or is it the result, notwithstanding an impression of guilelessness, of a sort of rational perversity aimed at the political sterilization of Quebec? To all these questions the answer is negative; there is no sinister plan or even evidence of bad faith in the pro-federal arguments of this White Paper, nor in the other White Papers. The present federal government is quite simply being faithful to a well-established historical tradition that can be traced back clearly to statements made by John A. Macdonald at the time of Confederation. Ottawa, adapting its language to time and circumstances, has always said the same thing: the federal government is the government of a country, with all the implications of such a statement. According to this point of view, the only formal distinction between a federal and a unitary system is that, in the one, the regional (provincial) governments are elected and are relatively autonomous in a few areas of local concern, while in the other, the regional administrations are created by the national government; there are differences of form between the two systems, but no significant differences of substance. Viewed in this perspective, the desire of certain Canadian provinces, and of Quebec in particular, to preserve and increase their autonomy and, consequently, their constitutional powers, appears to be a kind of capricious anomaly based on a spirit of narrow regionalism and a lack of understanding of the current trends of history.

Ottawa's mistake is to confuse the regionalism or parochialism of certain provincial administrators with the nationalism of Quebecers; to Ottawa, Quebec nationalism is merely a variation of the regionalism to be found throughout Canada. Federal officials have never seriously considered that Quebec nationalism springs from circumstances entirely different from those which inspire the widespread conservatism of spokesmen of other provinces. It is not claimed that Quebec delegates to federal-provincial conferences have always been imaginative and progressive compared with their opposite numbers from the other provinces. But one idea has to be clearly established: however imprecise the arguments of Alexandre Taschereau and Maurice Duplessis, modern-seeming those of Paul Sauvé, erratically firm those of Antonio Barrette, dynamic those of Jean Lesage, subtle those of Daniel Johnson, traditional those of Jean-Jacques Bertrand, and doctrinaire federalist those of Robert Bourassa, all these men were absolutely faithful (at least in their official declarations as provincial Premiers) to "a certain idea of Quebec." And that "certain idea of Quebec" is simply the concept, long uncertainly and poorly expressed, of a "certain" or clearly identifiable Quebec. In any case, it has nothing to do with any sort of backward regionalism. This is what Ottawa, probably quite honestly, has never understood. The Canadian federal system, like any other living, structured organism, cannot contain more than a certain number of internal contradictions before activating its mechanisms of self-defense. The regional pulls of one province or another can always be neutralized, since the forces of change in the modern world will sooner or later destroy them from inside. But Quebec nationalism, that abiding, instinctive quest for the "country" of Quebec, does not fit into the normal parameters of federalism; as a foreign body, it is automatically rejected before it can establish itself firmly in the system. Federal authorities do not officially acknowledge its existence, hence the habitual circumspection which is reflected in all White Papers and official statements touching on the "Quebec problem." Better, therefore, for federal peace of mind, to regard this nationalism as the aberrant preoccupation of a certain marginal left-wing element and of a very restricted group of Quebec intellectuals ensconced here and there in the "provincial administration of Quebec," in a few university faculties, and in the communications media. The good people of Quebec, realistic, down-to-earth, preoccupied with concrete problems, as certain politicians sometimes imply, do not follow this microscopic minority of unknown false prophets in their esoteric lucubrations. All countries in all ages have had their visionaries; Quebec has its share as well. There is nothing more to it than that; it is not a very serious matter. At least according to the current federal viewpoint.

We have stated that the federal government considers itself the government of a country, but we did not explain one very important consequence of this notion. Above and beyond the obvious implications of this proposition is the desire of Ottawa to consolidate its power, a power that cannot be exercised in the face of obstruction by lower levels of government. For the essential characteristic of a government is to be able to govern, and Ottawa cannot really govern if the provinces have exclusive power in too many areas of jurisdiction, if they control too many fields of activity where administrative and political decisions have broad ramifications. In the White Paper extract analyzed, it will have been remarked how little insistence has been placed by the federal government on the exclusivity of legal powers, how the accent has been placed on reciprocal influence by the two levels of government and on functionalism. It is to be remembered, too, that, in the White Paper, the federal government feels it should control all key instruments of power. In fact, if it were feasible, the ideal of Ottawa would be to have a unitary form of government; unable to attain this ideal completely, every effort is made to approach it as closely as possible. Vast areas of administrative activity remain under provincial responsibility; from the budget point of view, these are impressive, creating the illusion that the provinces together have powers comparable to those of Ottawa. But the comparison is valid only on the budgetary level; if one considers the total impact of the provinces and the central government on Canadian society, it is immediately apparent that the division of powers sought by Ottawa would ensure its undisputed leadership.

Thus in Ottawa's perspective, the provincial governments are a potentially harmful element, except when they are performing time-consuming functions of a local nature under federal supervision. Since it is not politically possible to eliminate this harmful element completely, the White Paper proposals are designed to minimize its effects.

Once again, there is neither federal conspiracy nor cynicism in this situation. The intrinsic logic of the central government leads it inexorably to espousal of the views outlined in its White Papers. Similarly, the Quebec government's intrinsic logic has often led it, too, to aspire to the role of a true government. To the familiar question, "What does Quebec want?", Daniel Johnson answered:

> As the mainstay of a nation, it wants free rein to make its own decisions affecting the growth of its citizens as human beings (*i.e.*, education, social security and health in all respects), their economic development (*i.e.*, the forging of any economic and financial tool deemed necessary), their cultural fulfillment (which takes in not only arts and literature, but the French language as well), and the presence abroad of the Quebec community (*i.e.*, relations with certain countries and international organizations).[2]

So as to clarify the nature of the control over social and cultural affairs which was sought by Quebec, Johnson proposed a re-allocation of resources and functions between the federal government and the Government of Quebec.

> By this process, the Quebec Government would gradually become solely responsible within its territory for all public expenditures on every form of education, old age security, family allowances, health, employment and training of the labour force, regional development and, in particular, municipal aid programmes, research, fine arts, culture, as well as any other social or cultural service within our jurisdiction under the present constitution. Existing federal programmes in these fields would be taken over by Quebec, which would maintain their portability where applicable.[3]

Premiers Lesage, Bertrand and Bourassa have all at one time or another expressed views reflecting the same philosophy, though not always, perhaps, as succinctly.

There is thus an enormous gap between these positions of the federal and Quebec governments; in fact, they are irreconcilable. To become a genuine government, the provincial administration needs to acquire certain powers presently allocated to, or exercised by, the federal government. On the other hand, to actually run the country, Ottawa needs to extend its present authority in two ways: through obtaining legalisation of its control over those areas of activity which it has appropriated in the past with or without the consent of the provinces, and through official assumption of responsibility for the country as a whole, thereby clearly establishing its predominance over the provincial governments. These divergent positions, the outgrowth of natural conditions and historic trends, provide the elements of a major latent conflict.

No other province has ever taken a stand similar to that of Quebec on these questions, for the excellent reason that none has ever felt the need to do so. Not that they have always been satisfied with their lot within Confderation; on the contrary, their complaints have been, and are, numerous; but essentially they have been of an administrative or financial character. In contrast, Quebec's views, with rare exceptions, have been based on considerations of principle, which, tiresome though they may often be to the representatives of the other governments, reflect clearly Quebec's feeling that it is an autonomous territory, that it wishes to increase the measure of autonomy it now possesses, and that it finds its authority regularly threatened by the encroachments of Ottawa. Underlying this situation there is also the historical fact that Quebec is older than the federal government, which, according to some, is the creature of those provinces originally forming Confederation; this argument is sometimes used by Quebec politicians to emphasize that the government of Quebec does not have to submit to Ottawa. At the same time, it so happens that it was the federal government that created the western provinces, a more recent occurrence than the social organization and development of the territory of present-day Quebec. Alberta and Saskatchewan have had provincial status only since 1905, and that only by federal statute. Accordingly, there are two ways of looking at the federal government: for some, it was created by the provinces; for others, the reverse happened. Only rarely does an English "founding" province raise the argument of seniority; Ontario is practically the only one to do so. Quebec is far more attached to this concept because settlements have existed there far longer than in any other province, whether "founders" or more recent creations. Quebecers have lived along the St. Lawrence for over three-and-a-half centures.

In other words, Quebecers, Ontarians, Newfoundlanders, Saskatchewanites, and British Columbians all have different perceptions of the relations of their respective provinces with Ottawa. In the eyes of

French-speaking Quebecers, Ottawa and Quebec have no authority over each other; each administration is autonomous in its areas of jurisdiction; sometimes their activities are complementary, and if conflicts arise, the Government of Quebec is *a priori* in the right. Furthermore, to Quebecers the federal government is traditionally English, and is usually seeking ways to intervene in areas outside its jurisdiction. Many qualifications can be applied to this necessarily crude appraisal of current Quebec feeling, since outlooks vary according to social class and locality; but, in general, it represents the common denominator of Quebec political opinion, both past and present. The common denominator of views in the other provinces is that the federal government is the "national" government; neither the Newfoundlander nor British Columbian questions this basic postulate. They may, of course, very well complain that their "national" government neglects them, and does not understand their regional problems. But in the event of serious conflict between a provincial government and the "national" government, it is not at all certain that their sympathy will be automatically with the provincial government. All politicians in the English-language provinces agree that it is up to Ottawa to establish the broad policies of the country, to set "national" norms, in short to exercise all the authority usually vested in the government of a country, on condition, however, that it does not interfere unduly with their current programmes. Occasionally these politicians protest Ottawa's actions, and, like their opposite numbers in Quebec, even refer to a federal invasion of provincial jurisdictions. But their protests carry much less weight, since they cannot count on the almost automatic support of their population, who also recognize the "national" character of the central government. Furthermore, these protests are often based on electoral considerations, sometimes compounded by political feuds; they arise also, perhaps, from a conservative reaction. Certainly Quebec politicians have also exhibited the same motivations, but in contrast to the repeatedly stressed position of Quebec, clashes between the English-language provinces and Ottawa hardly ever arise from a feeling that Ottawa is threatening the integrity of the provincial governments.

In English-speaking Canada, the federal-provincial relationship is often that of superior and inferior; both Ottawa and the provinces agree on this definition. An English-speaking provincial political figure, even a Premier, is considered to have received a promotion if he becomes a federal Cabinet minister. In Quebec, for a politician to move from the Quebec to the federal arena is no longer necessarily a promotion; the two are considered of similar significance. Moreover, in the eyes of federal politicians and civil servants, the "provincials" do not deserve much respect, occupied as they are with short-term objectives and specific matters of a house-keeping nature. (One can well wonder whether being a "provincial politician" does not restrict a person's political horizon, the "provincial" being, so to speak, restricted to current administration, while the "federal" prepares the future. If this occupational characteristic really exists, as we believe it does, it has serious consequences for the Government of Quebec.)

The federal Gospel, several verses of which we have quoted, thus reflects very accurately the opinion of English Canada concerning the prerogatives and powers of a "national" government. No politician from an English-language province, whatever his party, has ever questioned it. During the abortive process of constitutional review, the whole of English Canada was clearly in agreement with the federal views that we have outlined. In other words, the majority of Canadian citizens identified with them, and found perfectly acceptable the concepts and principles enunciated. Obviously, Quebec did not share this opinion; and the other provincial governments felt that in taking a different stand it was attacking the very foundations of the federal system as understood by them and the people they represented. In practical terms, in order to satisfy Quebec at the constitutional conference the whole of the rest of Canada would have had to abandon its concept of the country and of the central government. And in order to succeed in the present negotiations, preserve its existing powers, and solve certain continuing problems, Quebec would have to bring that about; it would have to force the rest of the country to change its views on the nature of Canada and on the powers which should normally belong to the central government.

Mission impossible? Yes, indeed, and all the more so because no one can blame the English Canadian majority for wanting its "national" government to govern in reality. It is totally absurd to demand that English Canadians share present-day Quebecers' concept of the federal government; that would be asking them to go against their very nature and consequently an exercise in frustration and a waste of energy. It would be like trying to change the course of a river – without a dam.

But if it does not wish to change its perception of the federal government, would English Canada at least agree to an essentially different relationship between Quebec City and Ottawa than between, say, Toronto and Ottawa, or Regina and Ottawa? Not within the present polititical and intellectual framework, whether from fear of Quebec separation or some other reason. The rest of the country is sociologically, historically and politically inclined to the view that its concept of the federal government, valid for Ontario, Saskatchewan or Prince Edward Island, must also be valid for that other province, Quebec.

Notes

1. *Federalism for the Future*, pp. 34ff.
2. "Statement by the Honourable Daniel Johnson," Fourth Meeting of the Tax Structure Committee, Ottawa, September 14, 1966, p. 4.
3. *Ibid.*, p. 7.

15
The Socio-Political Dynamics
of the October Events[1]
by Raymond Breton

The objective of this chapter is to examine the events of October, 1970, in the light of certain characteristics of the socio-political context, the groups present in the socio-political arena, and the relationship among these groups. A basic postulate is that the dynamics of the events cannot be understood without placing them in the general socio-political context of society.

Much of the actual and attempted socio-political change of the last decade or so in Canada, and particularly in Quebec, has involved the redistribution of power and influence among various groups and organizations. Several groups have confronted one another with different models for the reorganization of society, or of a particular institutional sector, and with different plans for the reallocation of power and influence. Matters of power and influence always involve issues concerning the nature of the decisions to be made and the people who will be empowered to make them.

I will first argue that the redistribution of power and influence has been a quasi-general phenomenon in Quebec during the last decade, and that there is hardly a single institutional sphere that has remained unaffected by it. I will then examine some of the factors that have brought about this redistribution, or attempt at redistribution. These considerations will provide the background for the discussion[2] of three questions pertaining to the October events: (a) What are some of the factors related to the occurrence of FLQ violence in Quebec since 1963? (b) Why did the kidnappings, which were, of course, extraordinary happenings in themselves, become a major political event? (c) What were some of the problems associated with the exercise of authority in these circumstances?

Widespread Confrontations over
the Distribution of Power and Influence

There are many ways in which social change can involve the redistribution of power and influence: the centralization or decentralization of decision-making within certain institutional spheres; the appearance of new groups seeking to influence or take over the centres of decision-making; the removal of certain groups or their retreat from positions of power; the transformation of institutional structures and the ensuing reallocation of authority; and the creation of new areas of activity in society as a result of social or technological innovations.

Each of these processes involves groups in conflict with one another over the allocation of influence. That is, each involves the confrontation of groups with different interests and values, and hence different ideas as to the kinds of decisions that should be taken and/or the way in which the institutions should be rearranged. Groups in confrontation differ considerably from one another in terms of their present position in the socio-political structure, their objectives, or the model they propose, and the means they apply to reach their objectives.

Whenever confrontations become intense and widespread, when several social groups and/or institutional spheres are involved, instability results in the social system. This instability stems from redistribution of power and/or from disagreements over the values and norms that should constitute the basis of the subsequent distribution. The redistribution and the accompanying anomie are, of course, a matter of degree. Here I would like to show that Quebec's last decade is characterized by a widespread confrontation between groups over the distribution of power and influence. I do not wish to argue that such confrontations are peculiar to Quebec, although they may be more widespread and intense than in the rest of Canada. Moreover, the ones mentioned below are not the only ones that have occurred, or are now occurring.

1. The most extensive institutional transformation has taken place perhaps in the field of education.[3] Power and influence have been almost completely transferred from the Church to lay teachers and administrators, and to the government bureaucracy; and a similar shift has also occurred from the local authorities to the provincial bureaucracy. This phenomenon can be observed at all levels of the educational system; and, of course, it has produced considerable tension and conflict between the provincial bureaucracy and the local élites, between the bureaucracy and teachers and their associations, and between the bureaucracy and particular schools. The transformations also generated apprehension among the public at large.[4]

214

2. Health and welfare is another institutional sphere where extensive transformations have taken place, particularly in connection with the Church's withdrawal from this sector and the introduction of provincial hospital and medical insurance plans and old age pensions. These transformations have also brought about conflicts between the provincial bureaucracy and hospital administrations, professional groups and the federal government. Again, most of the shift of power has been towards the provincial bureaucracy.

3. Another important arena of conflict has been the federal-provincial network of relationships, a complex arena with a centre and sub-centres, and including policy-making bodies, bureaucracies, political parties, and groups of citizens. Traditionally the distribution of power has followed linguistic lines quite closely, the centre being largely under the control of English-speaking groups and the Quebec sub-centre under the control of French-speaking groups.[5]

Generally, redistribution of power can take place between centre and sub-centre (without modification of their traditional linguistic composition) or between the two linguistic groups within the institutions of the centre and the sub-centre. Both types of change seem to have occurred to a certain extent. On the one hand, Quebec has made considerable gains in the federal-provincial distribution of power; on the other hand, a number of French-speaking groups have gained power and increased their influence within federal institutions.[6]

These changes have had a significant impact on federal-provincial relationships. The usual tensions and confrontation inherent in relations between two levels of government remain, as do many of the tensions and confrontations along the linguistic cleavage. But now there is the added tension and confrontation between groups within the French-speaking community, between various shades of federalists and various shades of provincial autonomists, and between separatists and anti-separatists. Ten years ago, confrontation between these groups was weak compared to what it has become, and probably will become.

A significant change is that some groups of French Canadians have made gains in power and influence at the federal level; thus both federalists and provincial autonomists have a power base to defend. The confrontation is intensifying as more French Canadians have a vested interest in the centre as well as in the sub-centre of political power.[7] Of course, the eventual outcome of this confrontation depends to a large extent on the development of the power base at the federal level and, in particular, in the federal bureaucracy, where much power is located. If the top levels of the bureaucracy are not opened significantly to French-speaking persons, then it is quite easy to predict who will win.

Conversely, groups of French-speaking Canadians will support and defend a federal state to the extent that they have power at stake in it. The last few years have marked the beginning of the development of such a power base.

In this connection, it is important to realize that French-speaking persons in Quebec are developing a new *"Québécois"* identity as opposed to a "French Canadian" identity. Each sub-group is developing new attitudes towards the others. The *"Québécois"* may consider the others less "genuine" or more "assimilated," hence "lost"; other French Canadians are likely to resent these exclusionist attitudes, thinking that the *"Québécois"* aim for a closed society. The nature of these attitudes is of less concern here than the fact that a cleavage is appearing within the French-speaking community, parallel to the evolving dispensation of power and influence. It should be noted, for instance, that a large proportion of French-speaking Canadians in the federal bureaucracy come from outside Quebec.

Finally, in addition to the groups involved in the confrontation, some derive advantages from both sides. For instance, it is better for businessmen to have allies at both provincial and federal levels. I would hypothesize that more and more groups in Quebec are gaining influence at both levels of government.

4. Confrontations and tensions accompanying the redistribution of power have also occurred within labour organizations. Significant events have occurred within unions, between unions, and between unions and management.[8] The past decade has witnessed a significant increase in the incidence of wildcat strikes, and one of their characteristics is that they represent a form of protest by workers against the leadership of their union.[9] The refusal of union members to ratify agreements negotiated by their leaders is another manifestation of intra-union tension.[10]

Another change has occurred within unions during the past decade. According to Dion, "a new intelligentsia has appeared within the labour movement and has managed to create something of a parallel power. It has also oriented unions towards positions and commitments that can jeopardize their internal cohesion so important to such groups."[11] (editor's translation). Moreover, Dion points out, since 1960 the leadership of the unions (CSN, FTQ, CEQ) has changed. As a consequence of these new factors and the increase in membership, "the union movement in Quebec seems to be going through a deep crisis of growth and oreintation. It is involved in both internal and external conflict."[12] (editor's translation). The same point is made by Crispo and Arthurs.[13]

This decade also saw a significant increase in inter-union conflicts.

Dion[14] and Roberge[15] both undertook an analysis of raiding and rivalry among Quebec unions, and showed that the period 1964-67 was a peak period of union feuds. So there have been not only tensions and confrontations within unions, but also between unions competing with each other for power and influence in the field of labour relations. Jamieson[16] points out that between 1900 and 1967 there were at least 250 labour disputes in Canada marked by violence, illegality, and the use of force by the police, and that, of these, about 90 (or 30 percent) occurred during the period 1957-66.

Labour relations in Quebec have also been greatly affected by the expansion of the provincial bureaucracy that resulted from the transformation of the educational system, the increase in public health services, government intervention in the industrial sector, the formation of Hydro-Québec, and growth of the traditional civil service. Now almost 40 percent of unionized workers are in the public sector and negotiate directly or indirectly with the government or with public bodies, mostly at the provincial level.[17]

5. Parallel with the tension between union members and their leaders we can observe an increase in tension between various citizen groups and their governments, whether municipal (for example FRAP) provincial or federal; between citizen groups and the establishment (the F.L.Q. seems to fall into this category); and between students and the faculties and administrations of their institutions. A common theme in these confrontations is the demand for a reallocation of authority, of decision-making power. Whether the slogans are formulated in terms of autonomy, authoritarianism, the decisions affecting one's life, or participation, the demand for more influence and/or power in the decision-making process is common to all.

6. Increased tension is also evident in relations between French Canadians and other ethnic and linguistic groups in Canada. Whether we consider the composition of the population by ethnic origin, mother tongue, or official language, we find that a certain balance between the French and non-French population has been maintained over the years. Among factors affecting this balance were the birthrate of the two linguistic groups, immigration policy, linguistic assimilation of immigrants, the shift of members of the native population from one linguistic group to another, and policies relative to the use, transmission, and diffusion of the two official languages.

These factors underlie the most serious political and social issues confronting Canadian society, because the linguistic distribution of the population is closely linked to the distribution of power in our society. High natality, and programmes to prevent assimilation into the English group, were previously the main socio-political weapons used by the French in the demographic struggle. Immigration and various types of restrictions relative to the use and diffusion of the French language were the main political weapons used by the English group.

One factor that has operated, and still operates, in favour of the English group is the adoption of English rather than French by most immigrants to Canada. The demographic and economic significance of the English language in North America suffices in itself to produce this result.[18]

The declining birth rate among the French population of Quebec, and perhaps in the other provinces as well, is highly relevant. Official statistics show that the birth rate in Quebec is the second lowest in the country, having dropped from 30.0 per thousand during the 1950-55 period to 16.3 per thousand in 1968. At the same time, as far as the French language is concerned, the linguistic characteristics of immigrants have not changed drastically for several decades. The proportion of all immigrants speaking French only has increased a little since 1950 (from 1.1 percent to 3.0 percent), while the proportion speaking either French only or English and French has remained about the same. It is the proportion of immigrants speaking English only that has been decreasing, particularly during the 1951-61 period, with a corresponding increase in the proportion speaking languages other than English and French.

Since most immigrants settle in provinces other than Quebec,[19] most immigrants adopt English as their language even in Quebec, and the French birth rate has declined sharply (and assuming the continuation of these trends), one can hypothesize that the distribution of power in society is threatened demographically, and that the threat is perceived by the élites of the two linguistic groups, but primarily by the French élites. One can thus predict an increasing concern with natality on the part of French socio-political leaders and more attempts to formulate policies and implement programmes to increase the birthrate. The possibilities in this direction seem limited at the moment, however, largely because of the increasing secularization of life and the corresponding difficulty in using a powerful religious ideology in order to promote certain natality objectives.[20] One can also predict a greater emphasis than in the past on measures related to immigration, linguistic assimilation of immigrants, and the use of the two languages, particularly in education and at work. Finally, one can predict an increasing suspicion of, and opposition to, any attempt by the federal government to promote multiculturalism, a policy that reflects the rising power and influence of some ethnic groups. In one respect, the situation is almost ironical: this increase in cultural expectations and claims on the part of other groups seems to have been triggered by the awakening of French Canadians themselves.[21]

It is possible that these demographic trends could be checked, and the present linguistic balance maintained, through the implementation of certain programmes. But it is also possible that the trends are too strong, that the policies arrived at will be too weak, and that, as a result, the French group will start decreasing as a proportion of the total Canadian population. If this occurs, or if the fears of its occurrence increase seriously, and this seems to be the case, then pressures for a different distribution of powers or a complete separation of powers between the two groups are likely to increase. This likelihood is related to the fact that the demographic situation is closely related to the relative power of the two groups. We are assuming that neither side will give up any of its power without proportionate resistance.

7. Increasing concentration of ownership and control of the mass media is another important development. Data show that, in the past few years, two organizations have acquired ownership and control of a large proportion of radio and television stations and newspapers.[22] Together with the government they now constitute the three centres of control of the mass media. It is probably not accidental that this particular concentration of ownership and control has been attacked in a number of publications.[23]

8. The source of influence on mores, social attitudes, and political orientations has also changed in recent years. For instance, the Church has been replaced to a considerable degree by various intellectual and social leaders, particularly those with access to the mass media. This transfer of the Church's influence has occurred not only in lay areas, but in areas seen traditionally as its area of authority. This development is important not only because it involves redistribution of influence, but also because of the people it affects, namely an important segment of the cultural and intellectual élite – writers, journalists, and artists – that has gained considerable importance in Quebec society.

9. Finally, the separatist movement has also witnessed great tension within its own ranks. Since it gained momentum in the early 1960s, a number of potential leaders have attempted to rally people around particular socio-political orientations, solutions and programmes. More than a dozen organizations or political parties were formed,[24] either as

new groups, splinters of existing ones, or mergers of two or more existing associations.

There are two dimensions to the tension between groups in any organization: conflict over the allocation of power; and tension between those whose commitment to the goals of the organization or association (for example, independence) over-rides everything else, and those who are prepared to accept certain expedient compromises in order to facilitate goal attainment. As Hammond and Mitchell point out, one group tries to "maximize goal commitment at the expense of adaptation," while the other tends to "adapt at the expense of goals."[25] The two types of conflict may involve the same groups; that is, the purists or radicals may be the group claiming a greater share of the leadership, while the compromisers or moderates may make a similar claim on the grounds that they have been largely responsible for the success of the organization up to that point. Although all organizations tend to be exposed to such tensions, there are differences of degree. For instance, new organizations[26] and normative organizations are probably more likely to experience tensions than utilitarian or coercive organizations.[27]

The multiplication of associations during the first six to eight years of the separatist movement is indirect evidence of internal tensions – especially in that most separatist associations quite clearly identified themselves in terms of a leftist, centrist, or rightist orientation, the F.L.Q. being the most extreme case. There is also evidence of this type of tension within the Parti Québécois, tension between the leadership (the executive of the party) and the membership, and between the centre and the radical wing.[28] The "events" accentuated these internal tensions.

Some Factors Triggering the Redistribution of Power

It appears, then, that one of the significant dimensions of the socio-political context in which the October events took place is a quasi-generalized redistribution, and attempts at redistribution, of power in Canadian society, particularly in Quebec. This trend did not occur only in one direction; it involved both the centralization or concentration of power and the allocation of influence to groups outside the traditional centres of decision-making.

The FLQ, it should be emphasized, is very much part of this over-all phenomenon. One of the groups contending for influence and power, its aim is to change the social system in accordance with its values. From this point of view (gaining power and influence for the realization of specific goals), it does not differ from any of the other groups involved. Its special characteristics relate to the means it adopts to achieve those aims.

The scope of this essay precludes an analysis of the factors that triggered the processes of reallocation of control and influence over decision-making in the various institutional spheres of society. But, a line of investigation is suggested by the preceding description – that we should be looking for factors that upset the existing, traditional pattern. At least five broad sets can be identified.

(a) The change in the level of opportunities for control and influence resulting from the expansion or contraction of certain institutional spheres; the expansion, for instance, of activities in education, health and welfare, and of other activities made possible by technological innovations. Expansion of this sort has resulted in the emergence in Quebec, largely during the last decade, of a new élite of public administrators, labour leaders, journalists, film and television producers, artists, and writers. And, these new élites, in turn, are bringing about important modifications in the distribution of power.

(b) The Church has withdrawn from a number of fields of organizational activity, such as education, health, and welfare, creating a power vacuum; new groups are competing to replace them. The withdrawal has also been accompanied by a weakening of the Church as a system of values, legitimating institutions and behaviour, creating an ideological vacuum which also has to be filled; various cultural élites (intellectuals and mass media personnel) seek to take advantage of it in order to shape public attitudes and values. This situation in turn has resulted in a large number of ideological confrontations.

(c) As a result of a transformation of social identities, persons at the periphery of institutional decision-making are no longer content to remain there. This situation results from the rise in the level of education, the activities of the new élites, the increasing level of group conflicts, the circulation of social and political ideas accompanying these conflicts, and partisan involvement in them, at least in a psychological sense. Changes occur along many dimensions, but two interrelated ones are of interest here: the individual's conception of his socio-political ability or competence to deal with life's problems, and his conception of himself as an autonomous unit, both of these being enhanced. If they are shared by large numbers of people, these self-conceptions create a massive pressure for control and influence.[29] This phenomenon is almost certainly present in Quebec and requires empirical examination.

(d) There are expansionist tendencies in the organizational centres of power, originating from processes internal to the organizations themselves. As long as no effective opposition makes itself felt, there seems to be no reason why the élites manning particular bureaucracies should not expand their areas of influence as much as they can. The occurrence of such processes is, of course, not peculiar to Quebec; similarly, it is difficult to argue that Quebec bureaucracies would be exempt from them.

(e) Demographic changes have affected the relative sizes of various social groups and the territorial distribution of the population. The demographic changes of interest here are those that impinge on the existing balance of power. For instance, rural-urban migrations are relevant in the present context not because they uproot people, disrupt their traditional social relationships, or disturb their traditional values, but because urbanization may disturb the balance of power. Groups and élites whose power is derived from small communities and rural areas may be threatened by urbanization; or groups and élites in control of urban institutions may be threatened by newcomers. Other demographic factors related to the allocation of control and influence are the birth rate, patterns of immigration and emigration, and patterns and rates of ethnic and linguistic assimilation.

The Use of Violent Means in a Confrontation

The F.L.Q., it was indicated earlier, is only one of the many groups involved in the redistribution of power and influence, but one that has distinguished itself by its tactics, especially the recourse to violence, to affect political decision-making. It is one thing to explain the origin of the confrontation and another to account for the tactics used. As Dahrendorf points out, "the violence of conflict relates rather to its manifestations than to its causes; it is a matter of the weapons that are chosen by conflict groups to express their hostilities."[30] The present section deals with this choice, and attempts to identify some of the factors affecting the propensity to have recourse to violence.

The distinction is not only an analytical one; it also pertains to social perceptions of reality. For example, some people have declared that the violence of the F.L.Q. was inexcusable because there existed legitimate ways of protesting, and of bringing about change; others have said that the use of violence would only be defensible to combat a dictatorial regime.

Quebec Society and Politics

Uncertainties as to the Legitimacy of the Separatist Option

There are three institutional elements that a "conflict group" can challenge: decisions made and enforced, the personal or social qualities of the decision-makers (such as their fairness or representativeness), and the institutional arrangements themselves (the structure, rules, and procedures under which decisions are made). Each type of challenge raises special problems for the groups concerned.

The separatist movement questions the adequacy and legitimacy of Canadian political institutions. It rejects Confederation, and thus the basis of the Canadian political community. Because of its nature, this form of dissent is difficult for the political authorities to cope with positively in a social sense, although not necessarily in a legal sense. There are real difficulties in bringing about changes in the social composition of those who hold positions of authority; but even more in persuading a political community and its authorities to accept its own dismemberment.

Separatists, by the very nature of their option, can easily be excluded, or exclude themselves, from the social bargaining process.[31] For instance, they make no systematic attempt to occupy key positions in the federal decision-making bodies (policy-making, bureaucratic, legislative); to do so would tend to weaken their basic political option. At the same time, federalists who now occupy these positions take great care to keep the separatists out. These are two mutually reinforcing processes. Attempts are made by non-separatists to reach potential separatists, and by integrating them into the existing political structure, to increase their commitment to it; the efficacy of these attempts is difficult to assess. We are witnessing a *dialogue des sourds,* a conversation between the deaf. Federal bureaucrats and politicians complain on the one hand that "these people won't even talk with us." Separatists point on the other hand to the adverse reaction in the English language press over the recommendation made by the federal Public Service Commission to recruit 250 francophones to fill a portion of the 1250 senior positions in the public service.

Separatists and federalists pursue a policy of symbolic exclusion. Separatists accuse French-speaking federalists of having sold out, and declare that French-speaking anti-separatists have rejected their own origins, do not understand the deep aspirations of their own people, are out of touch with the dynamics of current cultural evolution and are not, consequently, the proper authorities. The separatists, the rejoinder is made, are a mere minority, out of tune with the aspirations of the majority of the population, a collection of radical idealists led by outside agitators like de Gaulle, and divided among themselves; hence, they do not constitute a proper political opposition. In short, the federal authorities are not really legitimate in the eyes of the separatists; and the separatists are not part of the legitimate opposition in the eyes of the federalists. The resulting dilemma is serious. Federal authorities cannot deal with the separatists on the latter's terms without calling into question the very basis of their own authority. And yet, if political authorities are to be responsive to dissent, they must consider it legitimate, and as a manifestation of some need that is not being met adequately.

This dilemma is also reflected in the lack of consensus over Quebec's right to separate. A Gallup poll released in April, 1971, contained the question: "Do you accept the principle that Quebec should have the right to separate from Canada, if the majority of its people want to, or do you think that Quebec should be held in Confederation by force, if necessary?" Forty percent of Canadians replied that Quebec should have the right to separate; 46 percent said that it should not be permitted to do so; and 14 percent were undecided. Implicitly, and almost explicitly, the poll raised the issue of the right of one province to secede, and the opposing right of the Canadian political community to maintain its integrity by force. Clearly, the nature of a socio-political option such as separatism makes the usual (legitimate) channels of conflict resolution more difficult to use. And there is a higher probability that some groups *on each side* of the argument will advocate the use of more extreme (non-legitimate) tactics to influence the course of events.

Difficulties Encountered by Separatist Associations in Integrating their Radicals

As mentioned earlier, most organizations have their radicals and, therefore, face the problem of integrating them in some way. "The viable organization finds room for its radicals . . . thereby minimizing disruption that radicals might create without sacrificing their potential insights by excluding them altogether."[32] The same is true for social movements which need groups of highly committed individuals, but must integrate them within their boundaries in such a way that they do not prevent the growth of the movement, destroy its image in the community at large, or disrupt the orderly functioning of its activities.

From the point of view of a social movement or a social group, radicals are both a potential source of dynamism and ideas, and of disruption. From the point of view of the community at large, and of its authorities, they are primarily a potential source of disruption. Both community and social movements have an interest in controlling the behaviour of the movement's radicals, but for different reasons.

It can be hypothesized that the probability of disruptive and violent behaviour is partly related to the inability of a particular association or group of associations to integrate and thus control its radicals.[33] Little evidence is available for testing this hypothesis. In his study of Quebec terrorism,[34] Morf mentions that a number of terrorists had at one time been members of a separatist association, but had quit, dissatisfied with its slow rate of success and the gradualist approach. Since Morf's biographies of the terrorists are not systematic, they do not reveal whether this is a common pattern among F.L.Q. members.

Many reasons can be advanced for the failure to integrate radicals into the associations and parties that are part of the separatist movement. The notion of integration assumes the existence of some structure with an ideological as well as a social centre, and existence of a mainstream indicating the direction of the movement. In the early phase of the separatist movement – and this applies to any movement – the existence of a centre or mainstream is doubtful. The fluid situation generates groups that attempt to define it more precisely, to structure the movement and orient it, in accordance with their respective sets of values and preference. In its initial phases, a social movement has few structural means to cope with potentially disruptive elements.

Once associations are formed with an identifiable leadership and program, other factors become important. Thus, if the association is clearly identified with one person or a small group of persons, persons with different views will have greater difficulty in influencing its leaders, in becoming leaders themselves, and the probability increases of splinter associations being formed.

The tendency for organizations to become too structured, and too rigidly controlled from the top, also creates difficulties, particularly for normative associations such as socio-political groupings. Whether the many separatist associations and parties encountered this problem is hard to ascertain, but judging from articles and letters that have appeared in a number of publications, the Parti Québécois appears to have done so.[35]

Still another difficulty may arise from the diversification of membership that frequently accompanies the growth of an association. For example, initially middle-class (normative) organizations apparently have difficulty in integrating members of working-class origin. This feeling of being left out may stem simply from differences in levels of education and in modes and styles of communication; in some cases, it may result from more or less deliberate attempts to exclude them from important positions.

Differences in social class can also lead to varying preferences in political strategies and tactics and give rise to difficulties. Significantly, ten of the twelve F.L.Q. members analyzed by Morf, and on whom there were class data, were of lower or working-class origin. Several of them started, but did not complete, a university education. The radicalism of some individuals may be a response of upwardly mobile people trying to make it in organizations dominated by people of middle-class origin.

Internal Group Processes

Once radical elements have formed their own groups, their ideology or socio-political orientation develops according to its own logic. A number of possible checks and restrictions are removed, and contacts are established with other radical groups; thus a sub-culture develops with reference groups that endorse radical approaches to social change, including the use of violence.

Radical groups eventually face problems of recruitment and allegiance, and probably in proportion to the extremism of their views and activities. The need for new recruits and ideological development inclines groups to increase their targets and escalate their tactics. We have seen that groups like the F.L.Q. are formed because the progress of non-radical groups is so slow; therefore, the radical group must soon be able to show significant results in order to maintain an appropriate level of commitment. In other words, a group needs a system of rewards consistent with its ideology to recruit new members and sustain their commitment.

Apparently, the F.L.Q. fits this pattern. Its range of targets was broadened progressively from 1963 to 1969. An examination of the F.L.Q. activities reported by Morf reveals that in the first wave,[36] the attacks were restricted almost exclusively to British and/or federal institutions and symbols (Wolfe and Queen Victoria monuments, military buildings, mailboxes, an RCMP building). The second and third waves of activity involved a change of both tactics and targets. Rather than exploding bombs in various places, attempts were made to organize a revolutionary army. The second wave ended with the arrest of six persons calling themselves the *Armée de Libération du Québec*; the third consisted of organizing a military training camp for the *Armée Révolutionnaire du Québec*. According to Morf, a series of camps was to be established right across the province.

The violence of the second and third waves does not appear to have included terrorism, but rather to have been the by-product of attempts to acquire, through robberies, the funds, radio equipment, and armaments required for military operations. Not surprisingly, the targets during both the second and third waves of violence included military depots, banks, a fire-arms store, and a radio station. One interesting aspect was the robbery of a number of French-Canadian establishments, including a *Caisse populaire*, and branches of both the *Banque canadienne nationale* and the *Banque provinciale.*

The fourth wave was marked by robberies to obtain equipment, but, also significantly, by explosions on the property of strike-bound companies. The same elements were present in the fifth wave, with the addition of further new targets: provincial government buildings, provincial political parties (explosions at Liberal and Union Nationale clubs), municipal institutions (Montreal City Hall), and even a moderate labour organization. This last wave preceding the kidnappings was the most intense, both with regard to the number of actual or attempted explosions, and to the range of targets.

On the basis of available evidence, it is difficult to know whether these activities were planned systematically. As Torelli[37] has pointed out, there is a revolutionary literature describing various strategies, and it may have been used to formulate an over-all plan. On the other hand, these developments may have been mainly the result of unplanned group processes, in my view a more likely explanation. Additional evidence, not merely of the kind collected by the police, is necessary to draw a reasonable conclusion.

Choice of Tactics: A Matter of Differential Access

Nieburg states that "the choice of tactics for bargaining and influence is largely a matter of differential access. When influence upon government is sought, there is little difference between the soft word spoken to the President on the golf course by his industrialist friend, and the harsh words echoing shrilly from a demonstration by poor people."[38]

The use of normal channels of access is made more difficult when the very institutional structure of the political community is questioned. One of the bases of the legitimacy of political authority and opposition is weakened. The process of exclusion from channels of influence is already in motion. Moreover, if, for one reason or another, certain sub-groups are not properly integrated within the opposition or the social segment seeking change, they find themselves still further away from the accepted channels of access. And so the need arises for certain groups to devise unusual means of gaining power in the socio-political system.

The escalation in tactics may perhaps result as well from the failure of each of the previous phases of activity. The F.L.Q. was not making real progress. The political authorities defined the terrorists as ordinary criminals, to be dealt with by the police; they did not, or could not, recognize them politically, which is not to say that they were not concerned about them. The initial public reaction to the F.L.Q. activities seems to have been quite negative; then the population accommodated itself to occasional explosions. In other words, the public reaction was similar to that of the authorities: members of the F.L.Q. were seen as crackpots and criminals to be dealt with by the police.

To be ignored or treated as an insignificant entity is a very humiliating experience; it generates anger and can easily stimulate extreme reactions. I would hypothesize that the progressively weaker, even more negative response to the activities of the F.L.Q. contributed to the diversification of targets and escalation of tactics.

Reform and protest groups also reacted negatively to the FLQ, at least in later phases, because the F.L.Q. was providing political ammunition to the establishment – that is, to their adversaries. These opposition groups did attribute political significance to the terrorists, but were increasingly less certain whose interests they were serving. These responses pushed the F.L.Q. still further away from integration into the legitimate opposition and, at the same time, accelerated the evolution of their radicalism.

The "Events": An Arena for Group Confrontations

When the next wave of F.L.Q. activities began, involving new tactics that clearly meant a further escalation, the currently accepted definition of the situation prevailed. The confrontation between the F.L.Q. and the authorities was greatly intensified, but the situation was still basically defined as one that should be dealt with by the police. It was complicated by the fact that the life of James Cross, a representative of another country, was involved; and thus the government was directly concerned. Only in that sense was the situation defined as political, not as a struggle for power. Premier Bourassa's trip to the United States during the kidnapping crisis indicates that he felt secure in his position of authority.

The situation soon changed, assuming the dimensions of a major political event. Yet, that event was not a riot, a revolution, an uprising or a social disorder; it was a kidnapping. It was an act of political violence, but not one of a collective nature in the same category as riots or other manifestations of collective violence. On the other hand, the reaction to it was certainly collective.

F.L.Q. members wanted desperately to be defined as political enemies of the established powers, a goal they had failed to achieve in the past. They wanted to be a power in the social bargaining equation. But even after the kidnapping of James Cross, the political authorities maintained their definition of the situation. There was some disagreement among sub-groups of the F.L.Q., according to some newspaper reports, whether the kidnapping of such a person would suffice to force the government to negotiate seriously with them. Newspaper accounts also suggest that the kidnapping of Pierre Laporte was a further attempt to force the government to bargain. My view is that the kidnappings should be interpreted as a somewhat desperate attempt to affect the distribution of power. They were almost completely outside the power structure, and were seeking, in a final, desperate move, to enter the political arena and to be considered an element to be taken into account.

Another very important process was triggered by the first kidnapping. Extraordinary events, by definition, bring about an unstructured situation, which, in turn, sets in motion a definition-of-situation process, whereby "certain external factors are selectively re-organized and given subjective significance. They are construed as means, obstacles, conditions, and limitations, with reference to the attainment of the dominant desires or values."[39]

Situations do not remain undefined for long. Marked by uncertainties, undefined situations create anxieties and discomfort. More important for the present analysis, they provide an opportunity for interested groups to structure them to their advantage. Groups that view such situations as opportunities to further their cause are also most likely to realize that, if they do not act soon, their political opponents may do so first. Finally, the groups the most likely to take advantage of an undefined situation, or most likely to be suspected of doing so, are the most recent arrivals on the socio-political scene. In other words, people react to undefined situations in terms of their own socio-political goals and interests.

The kidnappings developed into a major political event because the circumstances they created provided an arena for a number of the group confrontations described in the first part of this essay. The events could serve the interests of municipal politicians, or of groups of citizens opposed to them; they could be used to promote the objectives of the police or of the groups opposing the extension of police powers; of the federalists or of the provincial autonomists, of the separatists or of the anti-separatists (whether French or English); they could enhance the influence of the intellectuals, of the mass media, of the political left, right or centre.

Some attempts to take advantage of the situation appear to have been deliberate, for instance, Mayor Drapeau's statements against his political opponents during the municipal election campaign. Other actions were interpreted in this way, whatever their real purpose. The "provisional government" incident and the proclamation of the War Measures Act fall into this category. In such instances, the interpretations of the behaviour of others is at least as important, in determining the course of events, as the objective content of the actions themselves. From my conversations with persons connected with different groups, excluding the F.L.Q., and in reading their statements in the press, I formed the impression that, after the heat of the events, some people felt they had "lost," while others felt they had "won."

In short, the kidnappings became a major political event in part because of, and in terms of, the socio-political context described earlier. They created circumstances which provided various groups involved in the redistribution of power and influence with an arena and a set of opportunities.

Problems in the Exercise of Authority

The redistribution of power and influence, especially if it is widespread, is potentially disruptive of the functioning of the socio-political system. It entails institutional dislocations, the relative withdrawal of old élites and groups in the face of the emergence of new ones, and confrontations of varying intensity between ideologies and groups. These processes may paralyze decision-making almost completely, and prevent role incumbents from pursuing their activities. Various organizations or social institutions may be seriously handicapped in the performance of their functions. Consequently, the processes associated with the redistribution of power and influence tend to trigger social control processes. Potential or actual social disruption raises problems of authority; latent or manifest social confrontations raise problems of regulation.

Among the problems that arise out of this socio-political context is that of integrating the new groups and their élites into the structure of power and the networks of socio-political influence. While they are excluded, the danger of social disruption remains high. This implies that effective social bargaining must occur for orderly social change to take place. Certain types of issues tend to assume an all-or-nothing character, however, and do not lend themselves easily to bargaining. As in the case of wars of religion, the opponent's legitimacy is not conceded; indeed, he is defined as evil.

Quebec Society and Politics

The possibility also exists that the conflict will become violent, that is, excessively damaging to the persons directly concerned and/or to the community. And if group confrontations occur in most of the institutional domains, a given overt confrontation may provide a climate and an opportunity for many latent conflicts to manifest themselves. The conflict situation can become generalized if certain cleavages in society lend themselves to a systematic alignment of groups, thus creating the conditions for a massive confrontation. If the systematic cleavage of this kind concerns people's basic social identities, the confrontation is likely to be not only general, but also quite intense. Whenever basic social identities are involved most people in the community take sides; few remain aloof or psychologically removed from the conflict. In such instances, they are easily drawn into a confrontation.[40]

A widespread redistribution of institutional and social power also raises the level of mistrust in society. The presence of a large number of groups and ideological conflicts generates a considerable amount of uncertainty concerning whose arguments are right, who is simply an opportunist, and whom one can trust. In that sense, authority is weakened. Persons in positions of authority are suspect in the eyes of at least certain segments of the population.

Finally, there exists a high level of discontent and a sense of inequity in segments of Quebec society, attitudes that presumably could be mobilized for either constructive or destructive collective action. Not only is the level of discontent high, it cuts across several institutional domains and strata of the society, and is related to the widespread redistribution of power and influence, and to the access to resources that we discussed earlier.[41]

The argument presented here is that, given the socio-political conditions in Quebec on the eve of the October events, there was a problem of potential social disruption, of potentially uncontrolled social confrontations. Moreover, to the extent that the kidnappings brought about a special set of opportunities for several of the groups in conflict, the possibility of uncontrolled confrontations became still greater.[42] In other words, problems of social control and social regulation existed. Even before the October events there was a problem of authority, and it was accentuated by them.[43]

Problems also existed with regard to the exercise of authority, which can be weakened or strengthened by persons who deploy it. Authority is weakened whenever some of the basic values of the community are seriously offended by the measures adopted. Police actions in awakening people in the middle of the night, or keeping them in jail without shoes, are unlikely to weaken authority, but systematic police brutality might well do so. Measures that result in the arrest of large numbers of innocent persons are likely to generate mistrust, as are measures with a diffuse, rather than a specific, target. Measures clearly disproportionate to the severity of the danger cast doubt on the trustworthiness of the authorities, at least after the event. The application of the War Measures Act appears to have been marked by the arrest of innocent persons, the target was diffuse, and the measures adopted were somewhat disproportionate to the danger.[44] On the other hand, terrorist organizations, by their very nature, do not provide an easily identifiable target; they disperse themselves throughout the population and form loose networks that are difficult to identify.

Authorities are led to overreact partly because of the crisis situation itself and partly because of conditions brought about by the redistribution of power. By definition, extraordinary situations take people by surprise. Reliable information is scarce; reliable channels of communication are primitive or non-existent. The usual premises for decision-making have to be discarded. As Pye[45] points out, the authorities must take the crucial initial decisions in a vacuum. Not only does the number of unknown factors increase the possibility of panic, but so do the lack of experience and the scarcity of institutionalized mechanisms to cope with such situations. In addition, the legitimacy of those occupying positions of power and/or of the régime itself is questioned by many groups when attempts at redistribution of power are widespread, with the result that the authorities become insecure and highly sensitive to any possibility of social disruption.

A second condition which can be detrimental to the exercise of authority occurs when a measure of social control favours certain groups over others; in the event of widespread group confrontations the consequences can be particularly serious. Whenever groups feel that measures give an advantage to their opponents, they will resent the actions taken by the authorities; if they suspect that the favouritism was intentional, they will resent the authorities themselves. Thus measures may increase the likelihood of uncontrolled group confrontations. On the other hand, some measures could have the opposite effect. For instance, postponement of the municipal elections in Montreal would have contributed more than the War Measures Act to controlling one possible source of disruption, and without increasing the level of mistrust.

Problems relative to the exercise of authority are also raised because frequently people in positions of authority are partisans in social confrontations; they themselves are affected by the redistribution of power and influence, the very process they are responsible for regulating. Similarly, those who are assuming a social leadership role but are not in

232

positions of political authority, for example, those concerned with civil liberties, are frequently also partisans in social confrontations. As Nieburg points out, "the two primary issues of politics – who shall apportion values (authority issues), and how they shall be apportioned (policy issues) – are inextricably involved in all questions of political relationships and can be separated only theoretically."[46]

This particular condition, I argue, was one of the main characteristics of the October events and their aftermath. We noted earlier that, during this period, various groups perceived each other as taking advantage of the situation in terms of their own struggle for power, and imputed motives to one another. The high level of mutual suspicion can be explained by the fact that the actors were simultaneously social leaders or political authorities and partisans in the conflict. Statements issued by the authorities to the effect that public order was threatened were interpreted by some opposition groups as a smoke-screen to dissemble their real intentions. Similarly, the authorities received with suspicion the expressions of concern by some social leaders that any decisions taken should be to the advantage of the community as a whole, and that civil liberties should be protected.

Are there institutional solutions to the problems stemming from the dual role situation, authority-partisan or defender-of-community-values-partisan? Is it possible to create conditions for the exercise of authority that would not be exposed to such dilemmas? The social optimism now fairly well rooted in our political culture inclines us to answer in the affirmative. If institutional solutions can be formulated, they will probably involve a third party in some way. Indeed, conflict regulation almost invariably does.[47] Whatever the merit of this approach, the use of institutional mechanisms to assess the danger that social confrontations will escalate out of control, and to cope with such dangers, is a subject that urgently requires research and critical analysis.

Finally, the management of a crisis can strengthen rather than weaken political authority. In socio-psychological terms, crises generate uncertainty and raise the level of anxiety in the population. Ordinary citizens do not have the means to cope with a crisis, and their feeling of powerlessness raises the level of anxiety still further. Consequently, any authority that deals effectively with the crisis will gain the confidence of the population.

This socio-psychological climate contains two kinds of dangers for the authorities. They are tempted to take unfair advantage of the public's anxieties to extend their system of controls through measures such as identity cards, investigation of course content in schools, and legislation to facilitate police searches.[48] In the face of violence and a sense of crisis, the public may feel that these are necessary and acquiesce in the strengthening of the authorities' hands. If the political authorities take advantage of a crisis to institutionalize counter-measures, rather than limiting themselves to temporary actions, the outcome will be accentuated.

The second danger for the authorities concerns the possible consequences of failure to act. In a confrontation, the behaviour of one of the parties is a very important determinant of the response of the other. Thus, failure to act is likely to encourage the other party to act in certain directions. In the socio-psychological climate we have described, with the crisis becoming an arena of confrontation for various groups in conflict, failure to act, or to act in time, may result in the situation getting out of control and authority being weakened considerably. Until methods are devised for rapid assessment of the dangers of a crisis situation – providing this is possible – political authorities will have to judge whether there are more dangers in introducing special measures than in not doing so. Our point is that both alternatives entail considerable danger.

Notes

1. Slightly revised version of an article which appeared in the *Canadian Review of Sociology and Anthropology*, Vol. IX, No. 1 (1972). Reprinted with permission. I wish to express my thanks to Albert Breton, S. D. Clark, Linda Gerber, Jos Lennards, and Maurice Pinard for their helpful comments and suggestions.
2. A precautionary note is in order at this point. The statements made in this essay should be taken as hypothetical, even though this is not always explicitly recognized. Moreover, some pieces of data are presented at different points of the discussion. Although the presentation of these data is not accompanied by a methodological discussion, it is recognized that, like any piece of empirical evidence, they have their limitations.
3. See Dandurand (1970) for a discussion of aspects of the restructuring of power and authority in Quebec's educational system.
4. For example, some analysts have attributed the electoral defeat of the Lesage government in 1966 to dissatisfaction with the disruption of local institutions and authority structure by the "technocrats of Quebec City."
5. It also followed ethnic lines. That is, within the English-speaking segment power was held almost exclusively by people of British origin.
6. The gains have been very uneven. For example, the linguistic composition of the senior levels of the federal bureaucracy does not seem to have changed significantly. Moreover, socially meaningful estimates may be quite unrelated to what is happening in fact. For instance, English-speaking groups who feel threatened tend to exaggerate gains made by French-speaking groups. On the other hand, French Canadian separatists tend to write off the gain as tokenism and/or to believe that the gains are not real, because they involve people who have sold out.
7. My hypothesis is that a similar process is also taking place to a certain extent in financial, industrial, and commercial sectors, that is, a simultaneous expansion of power in Quebec and an increasing integration into the Canadian and North American system.
8. John H. Crispo and H. W. Arthurs, "Industrial Unrest in Canada: A Diagnosis of Recent Experience," *Relations industrielles*, Vol. 23 (1968), pp. 237-262. See also, S. Jamieson, "The Third Wave of Labour Unrest and Industrial Conflict in Canada: 1900-1967," *Relations industrielles*, Vol. 25 (1970), pp. 22-31.
9. M. Flood, *Wildcat Strike in Lake City*. Ottawa: Task Force on Labour Relations Study No. 15, 1968.
10. W. E. Simkin, "Refusals to Ratify Contracts," *Industrial and Labour Relations*, Vol. 21 (1968), pp. 518-540.
11. G. Dion, "Les Relations patronales-ouvrières sous la 'révolution tranquille,'" *Relations*, No. 344 (December, 1969), p. 335.
12. *Ibid.*
13. Crispo and Arthurs, *op. cit.*, p. 243.
14. G. Dion, "La concurrence syndicale au Québec," *Relations industrielles*, Vol. 22 (1967), pp. 74-84.
15. P. Roberge, "Les conflits intersyndicaux au Québec, 1907-1967," *Relations industrielles*, Vol. 24 (1969), pp. 521-556.
16. Jamieson, *op. cit.*

17. Dion, 1969, *op. cit.*
18. Léon Dion, "French as an adopted language in Quebec." Lecture delivered at the colloquium on languages and cultures in a multi-cultural society, under the auspices of the Slavic-Canadian Inter-University Committee, Ottawa, 1971. See also: Richard J. Joy, *Languages in Conflict*, Ottawa: published by the author, 1967; Royal Commission on Bilingualism and Biculturalism, *The Official Languages*, Ottawa: Queen's Printer, 1967.
19. During the entire period 1946-1967, a little over 604,000 out of a total of about 2,922,000 immigrants gave Quebec as their intended destination – that is, about 20 percent (on the basis of the relative size of the Quebec population 29 percent was expected).
20. It is my contention that the interest of the French Canadian elite in a high birth rate has always been primarily related to the linguistic balance in the society – that is, essentially a political interest – and that the religious ideology has been used as a means to that end.
21. It is probably obvious to everyone who is following the events in Quebec and Ottawa that there is already a lot going on in the direction of these hypotheses.
22. J. Guay, "Une presse asservie: des faits," *Socialisme 69* (April-May-June 1969), pp. 67-73. See also, G. Maistre, *"Aperçu Socio-économique de la presse quotidienne québécoise," Recherces sociographique XII* (1971), pp. 105-115.
23. *Le Magazine MacLean,* November, 1967; *Maintenant,* May, 1969; *Socialisme* 69, April-May-June, 1969.
24. J. W. Hagy, "Quebec Separatists: The First Twelve Years," *Queen's Quarterly* LXXVI (1969), pp. 229-238.
25. P. E. Hammond and R. E. Mitchell, "Segmentation of Radicalism – the Case of the Protestant Campus Minister," *American Journal of Sociology* LXXI (1965), p. 134.
26. Many people interpret conflicts within organizations in the process of establishing themselves as a sign of weakness: "They can't even agree among the embryonic structure, but in other cases, the tensions may be a source of dynamic growth and innovation. There is no doubt, however, that internal tension makes the organization more vulnerable. Opposing groups, for instance, may use strategies aimed at accentuating the conflicts in order to weaken their adversaries. Also, the more organizations have to cope with internal conflicts, the less resources, time and energy they have for the pursuit of their goals.
27. In Etzioni's typology of organizations, "normative organizations are organizations in which normative power is the major source of control over the participants. . . . Compliance in normative organizations rests principally on internalization of directives accepted as legitimate. Leadership, rituals, manipulation of social and prestige symbols, and resocialization are among the most important techniques of control used" (1961, p. 40).
28. See, for example, the report on the February meeting of the Party in *Point de Mire,* and a letter to the editor in the same issue (March 5, 1971). See also the statement of Mr. Charron (Parti Québécois deputy) in *Le Devoir* (February 12, 1971), as well as the daily reports on the February meeting. Another illustration is provided by a communication by Charles Gagnon in

Socialisme 69 (April-May-June issue) in which he attacks René Lévesque and the Parti Québécois.

29. I have the impression that expressions such as the "rise of expectations," "the breakdown of traditional values and authority," "a condition of anomie or normlessness," are really meant to refer to the change in people's conceptions of themselves along the socio-political ability and autonomy dimensions and the resulting change in their conceptions of the way they should relate to authority, that is, to the centers of decision-making in all or in particular institutional spheres.

30. R. Dahrendorf, *Class and Class Conflict in Industrial Society*. Stanford: Stanford University Press, 1959, p. 212.

31. N. L. Nieburg, *Political Violence: The Behavioural Process*. New York: St. Martin's Press, 1969.

32. Hammond and Mitchell, *op. cit.*, p. 134.

33. I hope no one will interpret this hypothesis as a way of putting the blame on separatist associations for the violence of the F.L.Q. Trying to understand a set of behaviours in terms of various social processes that operate or fail to operate in certain circumstances is *not* the same thing as trying to decide who is responsible for these behaviours. The confusion about the role of values and ideology in social science is partly a confusion about the issue of the identification of social process versus the assignment of moral responsibility for events and situations.

34. G. Morf, *Le Terrorisme Québécois*. Montréal: Les Editions de l'Homme, 1970.

35. See n. 14.

36. The waves referred to here are those identified by Morf in his description of the terrorism between 1963 and 1969. A good chronology of the FLQ's activities also appears in Pelletier's book (1971).

37. Torelli, M., *Conférence sur les événements d'Octobre*. Montreal: mimeo, 1971, p. 20.

38. Neiburg, *op. cit.*, p. 64.

39. R. M. MacIver, "Subjective Meaning in the Social Situation," in L. A. Coser and B. Rosenberg (eds.), *Sociological Theory*, 2nd Ed. New York: The Macmillan Co., 1964, p. 256.

40. James S. Coleman, *Community Conflict*. Glencoe, Ill.: The Free Press, 1957. 1957.

41. The extent to which political and economic elites are responsible for such discontent for having failed to bring about appropriate reforms and the extent to which the discontent is an unanticipated consequence of the introduction of certain reforms (as seems to be the case with the discontent brought about by educational reforms), form a crucial issue which, however, is beyond the concern of this essay.

42. I am not arguing that the circumstances justified the judgment of an apprehended insurrection, nor am I arguing that they did not justify that judgment. In order to argue this, I would need to know the intentions of the legislators is using the notion of insurrection. Moreover, I am not trying to find out whether or not a notion used in a particular piece of legislation is appropriate for sociological analysis.

43. The present analysis appears to parallel the one made by Mr. Claude Ryan

during the events. His highly controversial intervention apparently resulted from a judgment on his part that the situation was far from being under control.

44. The defensive statement of the government to the effect that it was the only legal means at its disposal to cope with the situation seems to reflect the feeling that "the War Measures Act was not really appropriate for the situation, but ... " A statement by the Prime Minister in the House of Commons on October 16 is clear on this: "The absence both of adequate time to take other steps and of alternative legislative authority dictated the use of the War Measures Act. After informing the leaders of the opposition parties of our intention to act in this fashion, and following receipt of the letters that I tabled a moment ago, the Government proclaimed the act.

"The Government recognizes that the authority contained in the act is much broader than is required in the present situation, notwithstanding the seriousness of the events. For that reason the regulations which were adopted permit the exercise of only a limited number of the powers available under the act. Nevertheless, I wish to make it clear today that the Government regards the use of the War Measures Act as only an interim and, in the sense mentioned above, somewhat unsatisfactory measure." *Globe and Mail*, October 17, 1970, "Trudeau's Explanation in the Commons for Invoking the War Measures Act."

45. Lucian W. Pye, "The Roots of Insurgency and the Commencement of Rebellions," in H. Eckstein (ed.), *Internal War*. New York: The Free Press of Glencoe, 1969, pp. 167-173.

46. Nieburg, *op. cit.*, p. 111.

47. Dahrendorf, *op. cit.*, pp. 229-230. In spite of the rather unfortunate terminology, the idea of a provisional government was not an intrinsically bad idea. On the contrary, there may be more potential in it than appears at first sight. That is, the formation of a group of "prominent citizens" not involved in the confrontation, at least not directly, to act as mediator or arbitrator may have facilitated the exercise of authority. Of course, it is crucial that such a group be composed of people outside the established political power structure, the political opposition, and the groups contending for power. For example, the leader of the Parti Québécois or someone from a municipal administration which had been a target of the F.L.Q. would be particularly bad choices.

48. In the last few years F.L.Q. violence has been instrumental in prompting three acts: The Explosives Act permits searches without warrants; the Fire Investigation Act permits witnesses to be held without bail, and requires witnesses to give evidence even if it is self-incriminating; and the Coroners Act also permits witnesses to be held without bail and requires that possibly self-incriminating evidence be given. The Coroners Act also requires the coroner to state in his verdict if he is of the opinion that a crime has been committed and, if possible, the name of the presumed criminal.

16
Quebec and International Affairs
by Gilles Lalande

Quebec's venture into the field of foreign relations has often been perceived in the last few years as a threat to Canadian unity. Whether such a threat ever existed and, if it did, to what extent it was really serious, is a matter still open to investigation.

What is certain is that the federal government has taken the unequivocal stand that Canada can have "only one international personality" and that consequently "the Government of Canada [must] continue to have full responsibility for Canada's foreign policy and for the representation abroad of Canadian interests."[1] The federal government has also consistently defended the position that it is responsible for the negotiation and conclusion of treaties and other international agreements.[2] On the other hand, Quebec authorities since 1965 have maintained that the Province needs direct contacts with the French-speaking community of nations in order to strengthen the precarious position of the French Canadian group in Canada, and of the French language in North America. A more fundamental concern of the representatives of Quebec appears to have been to forestall the entry of the federal government, through its indisputable right to conclude international agreements for the whole of Canada, into fields of exclusive provincial jurisdiction such as education.[3] Incidentally, no Quebec government has yet challenged the constitutional authority of the federal government over the general field of foreign policy.[4]

Quite apart from recent disagreements between Ottawa and Quebec over this whole question, the right of the provinces to conduct their own international relations has long been a lively issue. Over the years, a certain number of Canadian provinces have maintained offices, or sent missions abroad, for immigration, commercial or financial purposes. And as far back as 1937, a very important ruling of the Judicial Committee of the Imperial Privy Council, at that time still the court of last resort for Canada, established clearly (in the Labour Relations case) that the federal government could not legislate to implement a treaty if the particular subject of such a treaty was under provincial jurisdiction. In fact, many of Quebec's recent initiatives in the field of international relations have been based on long-standing precedents, both as to their form and their content.

Historical Background

Historically, the story of Quebec's international relations antedates the birth of the Canadian nation. As early as 1859, eight years before Confederation, the United Province of Canada, made up of Lower (Quebec) and Upper (Ontario) Canada, successfully asserted the right to control its own tariff. "And the practice was also well established" before Confederation, according to R. MacGregor Dawson, "that the provinces would be allowed to send representatives abroad to discuss informally commercial relations with foreign countries."[5] The enactment of the British North America Act of 1867, transforming the three Provinces of United Canada, New Brunswick and Nova Scotia into the Dominion of Canada, made no significant change in this situation. Contrary to what might have been expected, the Act contained no specific provision for the exercise by the Government of Canada of increased authority in foreign affairs. Only one section, Article 132, referred to the subject. It reads as follows:

> The Parliament and Government of Canada shall have all Powers necessary or proper for performing the Obligations of Canada or of any Province thereof, as part of the British Empire, towards Foreign countries, arising under Treaties between the Empire and such Foreign Countries.

It will be noted that this provision dealt essentially with the treaty obligations of Canada as part of the British Empire, not as a separate nation. There was therefore no suggestion that the Dominion of Canada would ever possess treaty-making powers, or ever conduct its own international relations.

Approximately a year after Confederation, on October 30, 1868, the Canadian government and the Governments of Ontario, Quebec and New Brunswick concluded an interim agreement outlining the division of responsibilities abroad in the field of immigration. According to this agreement, the former was to maintain an immigration office in London, England, and in any other British city it chose. The three provincial governments secured for their part the right to appoint their own representatives in Europe, including Great Britain, should they so desire, as long as such representatives were accredited by the federal government.

The federal government appointed Canadian immigration officers in Liverpool in 1866, and in Antwerp in 1869. Two years later, the Government of Quebec sent two officials on a tour of Europe, one to Belgium, France and Germany, the other to the United Kingdom, in search of rural immigrants. Operating more or less on their own, both of Quebec's representatives found it expedient to avail themselves of the good offices of the Allan Company, a shipping firm servicing the Liverpool-Montreal run, especially for the distribution of an official brochure prepared by the Quebec authorities entitled *La Province de Québec et l'émigration européenne*. In the same year, a Catholic priest, Father Chartier, was acting as immigration agent for Quebec in New England. By 1872, the Quebec authorities had decided to extend their search for immigrants in Europe. Because of difficulties encountered in France, they turned first to Father Verbist, a Belgian Catholic missionary who had just been visiting Quebec, and second to J. H. O'Neill, a newspaperman well-known in Quebec for his writings on the Irish question, entrusting them with the task of seeking out immigrants in Belgium and the United Kingdom. They also appointed James Whyte, a recent immigrant who settled in Cookshire, Quebec, immigration agent in Scotland.

In the mid-1870s, Quebec's preoccupations in the field of international affairs underwent a subtle change. Quebec's first priority appeared to shift from the search for immigrants to attracting investments, primarily for the construction of new railway lines. Joseph Gibb Robertson, the provincial Treasurer, went to London in 1874 and in negotiating the first loan from British financiers, established direct contact between the Quebec government and foreign investors. This new orientation was confirmed in 1875 when all provincial governments, including Quebec, agreed to the disbandment of their immigration offices abroad in exchange for a standing invitation to place representatives in the overseas offices of the federal Department of Agriculture, which had been made responsible for attracting immigrants to Canada. In 1878, the Government of Quebec, using the Bank of Montreal as an intermediary, secured a $3,000,000 loan on the New York market, and in 1880, a loan was secured on the French market, this time through the good offices of the French government representatives in Quebec City. Subsequently, Quebec's interests abroad were widened still further to include commercial markets as well as sources of foreign investments.

Following the establishment of a High Commission in London in 1879, the Canadian government decided in 1882 to open an all-purpose mission in Paris, designated as a *Commissariat général,* and to appoint Hector Fabre, former owner of the Quebec City newspaper, *l'Evènement,* as Head of Mission. Following an understanding between the two governments, Fabre also became Agent General for the Province of Quebec, or more specifically "commercial and financial agent of Quebec in Paris." He was paid by the federal Secretary of State.

In 1891, the Premier of Quebec, Honoré Mercier, made an official trip to Europe together with Joseph Schyn, the provincial Treasurer, primarily to secure additional funds for railway construction and public financing. This visit was regarded at the time as particularly significant in terms of prestige and symbolic value. During the three-and-a-half months Mercier spent in France, Belgium and Italy, the Premier of Quebec was the official guest of French President Carnot, who made him a Commander of the Legion of Honour. He called on the King of Belgium, who made him a Commander of the Order of Leopold, and in Rome Pope Leon XIII bestowed on him the rare Roman Catholic title of hereditary Palatinate Count. On his return to Quebec City, Premier Mercier received what was described as a hero's welcome.

In the early twentieth century, the Legislature of Quebec enacted a law authorizing a commercial mission in the United Kingdom. It was actually opened in 1911. A similar law was passed in 1915 to establish a mission in Belgium. In the meantime, Hector Fabre had died in 1910, and the federal government appointed Philippe Roy, a French Canadian from Alberta, as his successor in Paris. However, Philippe Roy was accredited in France simply as the Agent General for Canada and not as "commercial and financial agent of Quebec in Paris," Fabre's second title. It is interesting to note that this change came a short time after the establishment in 1909 of a Department of External Affairs in Ottawa.

During the economic depression of the 1930s, Quebec's commercial missions in Europe were closed, the one in Belgium in 1933, the one in London in 1935. In 1936, as if to make sure such missions would not re-appear in the future, the new Union Nationale government under Premier Maurice Duplessis enacted a law abolishing all Quebec's permanent delegations abroad. But, somewhat unexpectedly, when the Liberals were returned to power in 1939 under the leadership of Adelard Godbout, another law was passed authorizing the appointment of agents general outside the province, "for the promotion of tourism, trade and industry." Ironically, the first such mission was opened in Ottawa in 1940, to deal specifically with war contracts. It was followed by a mission in New York in 1943. That remained the extent of Quebec's external relations for the next two decades.

A suddenly renewed interest in international relations arose out of the

Quiet Revolution following the formation of a Liberal government under Jean Lesage in 1960. In the context of a broad range of new initiatives, including the radical step, for Quebec, of creating in 1964 a Department of Education, the proposal naturally emerged that direct contacts with countries abroad should be resumed. Premier Lesage lent his personal prestige to this venture when he travelled to Paris in 1961 to take part in the inauguration of Quebec's first *délégation générale* abroad. Soon afterward, the commercial mission established in New York City in 1943 was raised to equivalent status. In 1962, a third *délégation générale*, or Quebec House, was established in London, England. Other missions were subsequently opened by Quebec primarily for commercial purposes in Milan, Italy, in 1965, in Frankfurt, West Germany in 1968 (later to be transferred to Dusseldorf), in Chicago in 1969, in Boston, Dallas and Los Angeles in 1970, and in Brussels, Belgium in 1972. The fact that this trend persisted despite changes of government in 1966 and 1970 suggests a deeper interest by Quebec than heretofore in conducting its own international relations.

The Ottawa-Quebec Imbroglio

Jean Lesage's early visit to Paris in 1961 indicated that the Quebec government had singled out France as the country with which it felt it needed a special kind of relationship. The Quebec Premier reinforced this impression in 1963 and 1964 by making further official visits to Paris, where he was received at the Elysée Palace by General de Gaulle and treated with the honours usually reserved for heads of state. It was, however, a series of much more down-to-earth initiatives by Quebec and France that led to a bitter clash between Ottawa and Quebec City.

The first in this series was an exchange of letters approved by the federal government, in January and February, 1964, between a semi-official French group called the *Association pour l'organisation des stages en France* and the Quebec Minister of Youth to promote educational tours and the exchange of students and technicians. Such an initiative was quickly followed by a similar exchange of letters between the Canadian Secretary of State for External Affairs and the French Minister of Foreign Affairs making provision for Canadian civil servants to attend the French *Ecole Nationale d'Administration Publique*. The second and more significant event was the signature of an entente on February 27, 1965, by the French and Quebec Ministers of Education providing for a programme of exchanges and other forms of cooperation in the field of education. This entente also authorized the creation of a permanent Franco-Quebec commission of cooperation. Once again, Ottawa reacted quickly with an exchange of notes with the French government, giving the sanction of international law to this arrangement.[6] Next, on November 17, 1965, a general agreement was concluded between Ottawa and Paris to promote cultural, scientific, technical and artistic exchanges between Canada and France. It enabled Quebec, or any other province for that matter, to sign its own ententes with the French government providing they referred to this general agreement between the two national governments; or, failing this, had the prior approval of Ottawa. Just one week later, on November 24, 1965, Quebec and Paris signed another entente for cultural cooperation, which made no reference to the general agreement between Ottawa and Paris. This situation was regularized from Ottawa's standpoint by an exchange of notes on the same day between the French Ambassador to Canada and the Canadian Minister for External Affairs, which endorsed the terms of the entente.

In retrospect, the period 1964-65 appears to have been crucial in the Ottawa-Quebec dispute over Quebec's international relations. Statements made between April and November, 1965, by spokesmen of the Quebec and Ottawa governments in support of their respective positions undoubtedly brought the points at issue into focus. Quebec's viewpoint was first enunciated by Paul Gérin-Lajoie, Deputy Prime Minister and Minister of Education, in a speech to the Consular Corps in Montreal on April 12, 1965. This senior member of the Lesage government made it clear that Quebec was seeking a freer hand in its dealings with foreign governments, and that these dealings would include the conclusion of international agreements covering all fields of provincial jurisdiction. Indeed he warned that Quebec rejected in advance whatever attempts the federal authorities might make to exercise any form of surveillance over its relations with foreign governments as long as these were restricted to subjects of provincial competence according to the constitution.[7] Furthermore, he stated, Quebec wanted the right to participate in the activities of international organizations of a non-political character. Reacting quickly to these unusual claims, Paul Martin, Secretary of State for External Affairs, asserted clearly that "only the Government of Canada has the power or the authority to enter into treaties with other countries."[8] He also stressed that "there is no federal state in the world whose constitution allows its members to make treaties freely and independently of the federal authorities." Finally, Martin summed up the concern of the federal authorities by adding that "a federal state whose members actually possess such powers would be neither a federal union nor a state. It would be an association of sovereign powers." Whatever the merits of the two sets of arguments, the point at issue clearly had strong constitutional over-tones.

The de Gaulle "Bomb"

In 1967, two important events occurred in close succession: the visit of Premier Daniel Johnson to Paris in May, and the visit of President de Gaulle to Canada in July. Premier Johnson's five-day stay in Paris was designed specifically to promote scientific, technical and economic cooperation between Quebec and France. It was the occasion for the two governments to decide on cooperation in the field of satellite communications, and to form a study group to look into the possibilities of French investments in Quebec, and eventually Quebec investments in France. Agreement was also reached on the following points: participation of young Quebec engineers in research work at the Saclay nuclear center near Paris; participation of French engineers and technicians in Hydro-Quebec's new research institute; training of top Quebec civil servants in French planning bodies; and cooperation in preparing an exhibition on French Canadian civilization to be shown throughout France in 1969.

General de Gaulle's return visit to Quebec two months later surpassed in many ways Johnson's sojourn in Paris. Scheduled as part of the Canadian centennial celebrations, it reached its climax in Montreal on July 24 with the French President's historic but controversial cry *"Vive le Québec libre"* from the balcony of the Hotel de Ville. Not unexpectedly, such an appeal provoked a number of contradictory reactions in Canada. The federal government, naturally enough, considered it an intolerable intrusion in Canadian domestic affairs. The Quebec Premier, on the other hand, issued a statement calling the de Gaulle visit "unforgettable" and expressing satisfaction that the French President was courageous and lucid enough to go right to the heart of the French Canadian problem.[9] Premier Johnson seized this opportunity to confirm that his government intended to pursue another of his fundamental objectives, the adoption of a new Canadian constitution giving full recognition to "the French-Canadian nation"[10] and consequently, one is led to believe, to its right to conduct its own international relations. The statement issued by the French Government after de Gaulle's return to Paris merely served to exacerbate the tension which had been created in Montreal.[11]

The rest of 1967 and the early part of 1968 were marked by further manoeuvering on the part of Quebec, with the apparently unsolicited assistance of the French government, to establish direct contacts with foreign governments. The most noteworthy incident concerned invitations from the Government of Gabon to Quebec's Minister of Education to attend two meetings of Ministers of Education of French-speaking countries, one in Libreville in February, 1968, and a second in Paris in April, 1968. To Ottawa's manifest annoyance, the invitations were sent directly and exclusively to the Government of Quebec. In an attempt to find a way out of this awkward situation, Prime Minister Pearson wrote no less than three times to Premier Johnson – on December 1, 1967; March 8, 1968; and April 5, 1968.[12] He received only one reply, dated April 9, 1968, the day before the announcement of Quebec's decision to participate in the Paris conference. The federal government again decided to react strongly to such manoeuvering and suspended diplomatic relations with the Republic of Gabon, accusing it of acting "in a way which is neither in conformity with the principle of international law nor with the maintenance of close and friendly relations between our two countries."[13] In the opinion of Ivan Head, professor of international law at the University of Alberta, the Gabonese action "may have been one of the most serious international threats to the integrity of Canada . . . " because it could have opened the way for Quebec to attain sovereign status by the same gradual process adopted by Canada in gaining independence from the United Kingdom.[14] On the other hand, F. R. Scott, a leading professor of constitutional law at McGill University, cast serious doubts on this analogy, suggesting that the matter of provincial representation at international gatherings could be simply resolved by the inclusion of provincial appointees as members of a single Canadian delegation.[15] This is precisely what did happen subsequently.

Establishment of a Francophone Agency

In early 1969 the Government of the Republic of Niger issued invitations to a conference to consider the creation of a new international agency designed to promote cooperation within the French-speaking community of nations. In contrast to the conduct of its neighbor Gabon a year earlier, Niger's invitation was addressed to the Government of Canada, not directly to Quebec. Although the Government of Quebec was on record as favouring the principle of one Canadian "representation" at international conferences composed, however, of one or more governmental "delegations,"[16] an understanding was reached in March between Ottawa and Quebec which ensured the indivisibility of the Canadian representation at the first Niamey Conference, with the proviso that it include members appointed by Quebec. It was further agreed that Quebec would have the right to sign any agreement reached at the Conference, and would have adequate representation as well as effective participation in the new international agency.[17] This agreement proved highly workable, and the conference proved a success, notwithstanding tensions generated by conflict of personalities. A year later, at the second Niamey Conference in March 1970, it was decided formally to establish the international agency, the *Agence de coopération culturelle et technique.* Its Charter was signed by a delegate of the federal government, as well as by delegates of Quebec and other provinces represented in the Canadian delegation.

The distinctive character of Quebec's participation in the new Agency was the subject of intense negotiations at the second Niamey Conference. Article 3.3 of the Charter embodies the agreement between Ottawa and Quebec; it states that "any government can be admitted as a participating government to the various institutions, activities, and pro-grammes of the Agency, subject to the approval of the member state controlling the territory over which the participating government concerned exercises its authority, and according to the arrangements agreed upon by that government and the member state" (author's unofficial translation). This novel distinction between a "participating government" and a full-fledged member of an international organization was made fully operational through a further agreement concluded on October 1, 1971, between Ottawa and Premier Bourassa's Liberal government, specifying the conditions of Quebec's participation in the Agency. This agreement authorizes Quebec government representation in all the Agency's institutions, and obliges Ottawa and Quebec to consult each other before the appointment of Canadian representatives. It specifically allocates "one of the two seats reserved for Canada" on the "Executive Council" to a representative of Quebec. And it stipulates that Quebec will pay half of Canada's share of the cost of the Secretariat. Finally, the agreement confirms that "the participation of the Government of Quebec in official conferences and meetings of the Agency is assured by the presence of a group of ministers and officials within the Canadian delegation . . . " (Art. 11).[18] It also, however, implicitly confirms that the federal government is to remain solely responsible for the important share (33 percent) of the Agency's general budget subscribed by Canada.

Quebec's renewed interest in immigration

The agreement between Ottawa and Quebec reflects the spirit of a parallel accommodation reached several months earlier on immigration.

On May 18, 1971, the Quebec Minister of Immigration and the federal Minister of Manpower and Immigration had concluded another agreement, this accommodation authorizing Quebec to station immigration agents and interpreters in federal immigration offices abroad. At the moment, this arrangement is being implemented in Athens, Beirut, Lisbon, and Rome, and negotiations are under way to extend it to Brussels. Significantly, the text specifies that "the contracting parties will not be bound by the present agreement if the countries concerned raise objections to its application," and that "a Quebec presence in a federal office is not intended, and will not in fact, place Quebec, relative to the other provinces, in a privileged position concerning the recruitment and selection of immigrants."

Conclusion

This brief historical survey shows clearly that Quebec's involvement in international relations has grown steadily over the years. A century after Confederation, the government is still preoccupied with economic development, and thus with the search for foreign investments and new foreign markets. The stimulation of a flow of carefully selected immigrants to strengthen the distinctive traits of Quebec's population also continues to be an important objective. This increase in contacts of all kinds between Quebec and the outside world is hardly surprising in view of the innovations in communications facilities in the twentieth century. The same trend is evident in the external relations of the Canadian government and the other provinces, but Quebec puts greater emphasis on governmental, as opposed to non-governmental, participation in international affairs.

The personal style of Quebec's politicians, and of its Premiers in particular, clearly plays a large part in the tenor and conduct of its international relations. Honoré Mercier, Jean Lesage, Daniel Johnson and others took a personal interest, albeit for varying reasons, in stimulating Franco-Quebec relations. Adélard Godbout, Jean-Jacques Bertrand and Robert Bourassa, on the other hand, have adopted an essentially functional and pragmatic attitude towards Quebec's relations with other countries. Since taking office in May, 1970, the Bourassa government has shown a tendency to orient the *délégations générales* according to the Province's domestic economic priorities. But it has continued at the same time the search begun in the early 1960s for a distinctive Quebec identity in international society, particularly in provincial areas of constitutional jurisdiction.

Two additional factors could have a determining influence on Quebec's future international relations. The first is related to the hazards of provincial politics: all of Quebec's recent international initiatives could be called into question if a new team of politicians interested more in domestic than external affairs were to take power. The second factor is related to the possible resumption of federal-provincial negotiations on the constitution, which could lead to a re-allocation of legislative power and fiscal resources between the two levels of government. In this case Quebec's international relations might once again be placed in their proper perspective: that of a Canadian province or a member state of a federation.

Notes

1. *Federalism for the Future. A Statement of Policy by the Government of Canada.* The Constitutional Conference, 1968, p. 30.
2. "The Constitutional Authority to negotiate and conclude treaties is part of the Royal Prerogative, which in practice is exercised in the name of the Crown by the Governor-General in Council on the advice of the Secretary of State for External Affairs, who is responsible (under the Department of External Affairs Act, R.S.C., 1952, c. 68) for the negotiation and conclusion of treaties and other international agreements." Paragraph 2 of a Canadian Government Memorandum of July 21st, 1952 to the United Nations, United Nations Legislative Series, ST/LEG/SER/B, p. 24-25.
3. " . . . if the federal government were to have a monopoly on international affairs, it would gradually take over *de facto* – if not *de jure* – internal jurisdiction over matters which, constitutionally, do not fall within its competence." Proposals submitted by the Government of Quebec to the Continuing Committee of Officials, Constitutional Conference, July 17, 1968.
4. "We wish to reiterate for the record that Quebec has never questioned the federal government's jurisdiction in matters of foreign policy." Memorandum submitted by the Government of Quebec to the first meeting of the Constitutional Conference, February, 1968.
5. R. MacGregor Dawson, *The Government of Canada,* Fifth Edition. Toronto: University of Toronto Press, 1970, p. 45.
6. "The exchange of notes was a type of umbrella agreement between the two Governments under which international effect was given to an arrangement which otherwise would have had no standing in international law", Statement by Hon. Paul Martin, Secretary of State for External Affairs, House of Commons, April 27, 1965, *Debates,* p. 629.
7. Paul Gérin-Lajoie, " . . . Il n'est plus admissible non plus que l'Etat fédéral puisse exercer une sorte de surveillance et de contrôle d'opportunité sur les relations internationales du Québec . . . "
8. Written statement issued by Hon. Paul Martin, Secretary of State for External Affairs, April 23, 1965. Reproduced in *External Affairs,* Vol. XVII, No. 7 (July, 1965).

9. "Courageux et lucide, le président de Gaulle a été avec nous au fond des choses . . . " Statement by Premier Johnson, July 28, 1967. Quoted in *La Presse*, July 29, 1967.

10. "Le gouvernement du Québec poursuivra l'objectif fondamental qu'il s'est fixé: l'adoption d'une nouvelle constitution qui consacrera la reconnaissance juridique et politique de la nation canadienne-française et qui confie au Québec, compte tenu de l'interdépendance caractéristique de notre époque, toutes les compétences nécessaires à l'épanouissement de son identité." Quoted in *La Presse*, July 29, 1967.

11. "He (de Gaulle) was able to judge their (French Canadians) determination to decide their own affairs in all respects . . . and unmistakably told the French-speaking Canadians and their government that France intended to help them to realize the freedom aims they have set themselves. . . . " Excerpt from the French Government's official statement of July 31, 1967.

12. For full text of these letters, see Annexes of Hon. Mitchell Sharp: *Federalism and International Conferences in Education*, Queen's Printer, 1968.

13. *Note Verbale* from the Government of Canada to the Government of the Republic of Gabon, March, 1968.

14. *The Montreal Star*, March 18, 1968.

15. *The Montreal Star*, March 22, 1968.

16. *Document de travail sur les relations avec l'étranger*, submitted on February 5, 1969, by the Quebec delegation to the Continuing Committee of Officials of the Constitutional Conference.

17. Maurice Torrelli, "Les relations extérieures du Québec," *Annuaire français de droit international*, XVI (1970), p. 299.

18. " . . . il est très clair que, par ces modalités, le Québec n'est pas devenu membre à part entière de l'Agence. Seul le Canada jouit de ce privilège. Le Québec ne siège pas d'une manière indépendante aux conférences mais y participe au sein de la délégation du Canada," Louis Sabourin, "Québec et Ottawa dans l'Agence: une coopération à inventer," in *International Perspectives*, January February, 1972, p. 21.

17
Quebec and the Future of Canada*
by Léon Dion

People began talking openly about the "crisis" of Canadian Confederation in 1962. The Royal Commission on Bilingualism and Biculturalism, set up in July, 1963, "to investigate and report on the present state of bilingualism and biculturalism in Canada," held twenty-three regional meetings throughout the country in 1964. Its extensive Preliminary Report, published in February 1965, was designed to alert Canadians to the seriousness of the situation. It presented the following diagnosis:

> All that we have seen and heard has led us to the conviction that Canada is in the most critical period of its history since Confederation. We believe that there is a crisis, in the sense that Canada has come to a time when decisions must be taken and developments must occur leading either to its break-up, or to a new set of conditions for its future existence. We do not know whether the crisis will be short or long. We are convinced that it is here. . . . The crisis has reached a point where there is a danger that the will of the people to go on may begin to fail.
>
> This is an initial diagnosis, not a prophecy. . . . What is at stake is the very fact of Canada: what kind of country will it be? Will it continue to exist?. . . . The chief protagonists, whether they are entirely conscious of it or not, are French-speaking Quebec and English-speaking Canada. And it seems to us to be no longer the traditional conflict between a majority and a minority. It is rather a conflict between two majorities: that which is a majority in all Canada, and that which is a majority in the entity of Quebec.[1]

At the time, most of the country paid little attention to these words. French-speaking Quebecers welcomed the Report, which they felt accurately reflected their current state of mind. Yet they had reached a point where only concrete proposals for reforms of direct and immediate

---

* Text presented in French as a brief to the Special Joint Committee of the Senate and of the House of Commons on the Constitution of Canada, March 30, 1971.

interest to *them* – proposals which were lacking in the Report because of its "preliminary" character – could attract their full attention. Most English-speaking Canadians, to whom the warning was directed particularly, were unimpressed for a variety of reasons: scepticism about the validity of the diagnosis; faith in the healing powers of time; confidence in the ability of the Canadian political system to withstand attacks from all quarters. These reactions and others along similar lines revealed that the Commission had not achieved its objective of stirring the English-speaking population to action.

Six years have elapsed since the publication of the Preliminary Report. Where do Canadians now stand? More specifically, following the terrorist activities of October, 1970, are they ready to take whatever measures are necessary, in the words of the Order in Council creating the Royal Commission, "to develop the Canadian Confederation on the basis of an equal partnership between the two founding races"?

It is indeed regrettable that, in bringing their investigation to an end in 1971, the Commissioners were unable to agree on an approach to the major political and constitutional problems dividing Canadians. However, their failure in this regard does not detract from their considerable achievements, and should not be misconstrued. If ten people of widely recognized ability, working under the most favourable conditions and far from the heat of action, were unable to reconcile their differences, how can the Canadian people and their spokesmen be expected to do so when they are faced with the realities of political life? What is the real reason for the failure of the Commissioners to agree on a prescription to treat a disease which, in their own opinion, could prove fatal? More than any other factor, the evolution of the situation with regard to bilingualism in Canada accounts for the inability of the Commission to carry out the whole programme it set itself during the two years following its establishment in 1963. By 1967, the crisis had assumed proportions that went far beyond the Commissioners' initial thinking and the research outlined in 1964. Thus, when they tried to find common ground to tackle those major questions they had agreed to hold in abeyance until the end of their mandate, they did not have the facts and criteria on which to base their analyses.

Not only do the symptoms of crisis so lucidly diagnosed in 1965 still persist; they have become more pronounced. And new and particularly disturbing signs have appeared. In order to describe the new situation and prescribe an appropriate treatment, we must re-state the task faced by the Commission. While neither a lengthy analysis of the underlying circumstances nor a study of constitutional reform is practical at this juncture, we can outline the objectives that must serve as guideposts for the creation of a new constitutional order.

We must have the courage to face the new situation squarely. The alternatives are harsh: to advocate a series of radical corrective measures and try to persuade Canadians to accept them at whatever cost and with no prior guarantee that they will be enough to save Confederation; or to accept the inevitability of Quebec's separation and try in good faith to find ways and means of minimizing its harmful impact. The time for half-measures is past.

The situation has changed greatly over the past four years. Any serious diagnosis of the Canadian crisis reveals new considerations with weighty implications. First of all, since the fall of 1968 we have witnessed a rising tide of dissent against the established order. Indeed, it would be inconceivable to speak of the crisis of Canadian federalism without mentioning that other crisis which, perhaps more radically, is shaking the very foundations of Canada's socio-political order. In Quebec, where liberal institutions and values have been introduced only recently, and where socio-political structures are particularly frail because of the lack of organization of the middle class, the forces of dissent against the liberal order are able, apparently, to win over the greatest number of adepts and to have an effective impact. The two crises are undoubtedly quite different, and it would probably be a mistake to assume that the solution of one would lead inevitably to the disappearance of the other; yet the events of October, 1970, demonstrated clearly that they are likely to become indistinguishable in the minds of the persons involved. Thus the Canadian crisis takes on an added dimension. The challenge is no longer directed against federalism alone; the socio-political system itself is being questioned. Not all Quebec separatists are opposed to the present liberal type of régime, but in Quebec as elsewhere in Canada, a good number of non-separatists are also against the régime and, under certain circumstances, the two groups could join forces. It is therefore necessary, in the attempt to reform the structure and operation of the Canadian political system, to strive for a fairer socio-political order for all sectors of the population and all regions, and for the pre-conditions of genuine participatory democracy, as well as for a new *modus operandi* between the two main cultural groups, and between Quebec and the rest of the country.

The growth of governmental activities over the past thirty years has led to qualitative changes in our society. Politics has not only intruded into the daily life of individuals, but is rapidly becoming the main factor in a large number of personal, family, and professional decisions. This new situation is calling into question old concepts of the role of politics under a liberal régime. People require of their governments both flexibility and strength: flexibility in order to adjust to widely varying sectional and regional conditions; and strength to respond rapidly and firmly to the expectations of both individuals and groups. This new political setting, together with new political organizations, will bring about deep changes in both the theory and practice of Canadian federalism.

In their search for flexible yet strong centres of political power, Canadians will turn either to the federal government or to their respective provincial governments. In some provinces they will doubtless place their trust more in the federal government, and this preference will have to be taken into account; in other provinces, they may prefer to entrust themselves to their own provincial government, and this wish must be respected as well. In this regard, French-speaking Quebecers made their choice long ago. All available information is quite clear on this point: in the fields of education, recreation, social security, labour, regional expansion, and social and economic development, the overwhelming majority turn to the government of Quebec, which they consider more responsive to their needs and aspirations, and more directly under their control. With regard to the reform of Canadian federalism, the basic question that must be asked is whether it is possible to have, within a single political system, a strong federal government co-existing with some weak and some strong provincial governments. And following from that question: if one province wishes to extend its activities into the all-important social and economic sectors, how can such a policy be reconciled with the equally legitimate desire of the federal government to intervene in the same sectors of activity? And how can the other provinces be induced to accept the special status for that particular province implicit in such a situation?

The evident growth of Quebec separatism since 1967 provides a major component of the new situation. The fact that an unquestionably legitimate party is now engaged in promoting the separatist cause by means completely acceptable in a liberal democracy, and may conceivably win power through regular elections, is a singularly complicating factor. Now is the time to find ways and means of reconciling two different sets of values: normal aspirations towards political stability; and the greatest possible degree of freedom within the unavoidable constraints imposed by the community on individuals and groups within it. In the past, most liberal societies faced with such serious internal contradictions have either collapsed or have gradually abandoned their liberal creed.

These developments, and others of a similar nature which are likely to occur during the next few years, require much more understanding on all sides than was thought necessary in 1962; and yet, Canadians then were already found to be lacking in clear-sightedness and wisdom. Had we taken the necessary decisions at that time, we would probably not be in the difficult situation we know today; the range of possibilities has narrowed dangerously during the last four years. On the other hand, precisely because they have become more urgent than ever, the options are more clear-cut. Canadians must stop wallowing in sterile discussions about abstract concepts like "two nations," "special status for Quebec," "associate states," and the like.

No force in the world can prevent French-speaking Quebecers from considering themselves a society and a nation distinct from Canada as a whole. Conversely, few English-speaking Canadians see themselves as constituting a separate nation within the Canadian context. Quebecers understand this situation very well, and the best-informed among them have discarded, or will soon discard, the concept of "two nations" which has led to so much useless debate within the various groups and political parties and has had so little success at the polls. The same goes for the concepts of "special status for Quebec" and "associate states." The principal task is to agree on matters of substance; names will follow.

I know of only one principle which could rally the support of all Canadians, and even serve as the cornerstone for the political reality of tomorrow, and that is the principle of self-determination for Quebec and for any other province wishing to adopt it. In the general introduction to its Report, the Royal Commission on Bilingualism and Biculturalism noted that either one of the two societies in Canada can exercise a degree of self-determination with regard to the other, and it established no limits on the application of this principle, even considering that it could imply the creation of a separate state. This principle of self-determination has the advantage of being both normative and functional. The present uncertainty is becoming increasingly untenable for a growing number of Canadians; demands are being made on all sides to clarify the situation one way or another. The principle of self-determination entails no judgment on the sociological character of the country or its constituent parts, nor on the future of Canadian federalism; it does not suggest a certain situation, but indicates the existence of a right to be acknowledged, which can be translated into specific conditions.

The solemn proclamation of the principle of self-determination for Quebec would not mean automatic separation from the rest of the country, although that possibility could not be discounted. It could happen that, on reflection and in view of the new attitude which would no doubt appear in the rest of the country, Quebec would decide on its own to remain, under certain conditions, in a re-cast Confederation. Once adopted, the principle of self-determination would require that a serious and systematic attempt be made at long last to change radically the conditions which maintain Quebecers in state of inferiority that they find irritating and even intolerable. I am aware of the steps that the Government of Canada, the Public Service Commission, and various federal departments have taken during the last few years to improve this situation. I am equally aware that these various measures have borne fruit and that others, still under study, will result in even more significant improvements. I also believe that the federal government is on the right track; a functional and practical approach, even without being comprehensive, has greater chances of success than a more imposing programme based on legalistic considerations. However, there is an urgent need to re-examine the premises underlying these efforts at reform, to speed up the process, and to extend it to other sectors. The objective remains the same: to restore Quebec's confidence in federal institutions without creating a counter-feeling in the rest of the country that the measures adopted are overly detrimental there. It is quite possible that such measures would be unacceptable elsewhere: the social and political consequences of the current economic slow-down, and other unfavourable circumstances including growing American control over Canada's economy and culture, tend to restrict the magnanimity of English-speaking Canadians. Yet magnanimity is essential for the adoption of sufficiently strong corrective measures. The harsh fact is that the existence of a reformed Confederation will place a heavy burden on the physical and moral resources of Canadians. As the material and psychological situation deteriorates and impatience grows on all sides, it is becoming more difficult day by day to achieve equality of real opportunities for both French- and English-speaking Canadians within Confederation.

In my opinion, an adequate response under present conditions should include the following elements:

1. Recognition of the need to maintain a large proportion of monolingual French-speaking persons in Quebec as a prerequisite for the survival of the French language in Canada. The proportion of French-speaking persons there now stands at 75 percent, but, within an urban industrial society, it might decrease rapidly if control over the economy remains out of reach of French-speaking Quebecers, and if the burden of bilingualism rests almost exclusively upon them, as has been the case until now. Thirteen out of every one hundred Canadians are bilingual, but, of these, 80 percent are French-speaking and 20 percent English-speaking; under normal conditions, the proportions should be reversed.

The English-speaking population of Quebec does furnish an increasing proportion of the pool of bilingual people needed by Canada. But ways must be found to free French-speaking Quebecers from the need to learn English in order to lead a normal life in Quebec and within federal institutions. Once that is achieved, only the prospect of greater mobility and a wider choice of careers should have to motivate them to learn a second language. The same criteria should also apply to English-speaking Canadians.

2. The promotion of institutional rather than individual bilingualism, that is to say, ensuring that federal government services, and not just individual civil servants, function in both languages, and devising ways of implementing institutional bilingualism in the federal government. If such a policy were adopted unequivocally, the federal public service would be considered equally French and English, not vaguely "bilingual" as at present (which in practice can only mean the overwhelming predominance of the English language).

3. Precise determination of the number of federal civil servants occupying posts designated as "middle level", and creation of a programme to recruit French-speaking Quebecers to ensure that the proportion of French speakers reaches 30 percent of this group in ten years. According to the Royal Commission on Bilingualism and Biculturalism, these middle-level positions constitute about 25 percent of the federal civil service or more than 100,000 jobs; but less than 15 percent of them are held by French-speakers at the present time. This means that 1,500 additional French recruits would have to be hired each year to reach a level of 30 percent in ten years; yet this is the minimum number required to create a French working environment and an adequate pool of talent from which to draw French-speaking senior officials. If this goal is achieved, it would be possible to abandon the current practice of recruiting French-speaking senior officials outside the public service, which has serious drawbacks. Later, efforts should be made to increase this proportion of middle-level French-speakers to 35 and even 40 percent, a proportion which has been reached, and even exceeded, in Switzerland. French-speaking Quebecers would then identify with the federal public service and would have more confidence in the capacity of the federal government to further their interests and aspirations. I recognize that the implementation of such a sweeping programme would entail enormous practical difficulties, particularly since for budgetary reasons the total increase in middle-level jobs was restricted to less than 1,500 in 1971. A closer examination of these middle-level positions

would probably make it possible to identify less than 100,000 strategically more important ones, and the annual number of additional French-speaking recruits could be reduced accordingly. However, several hundreds would still be required. This, then, is the very high price that must be paid to compensate for decades of neglect.

4. Creation of wholly French-language administrative units to enable officials to work and pursue their careers without hindrance in their mother tongue if they so desire. For such units to be valid, there must be a sufficient number of monolingual French-speaking civil servants; otherwise, there will be a temptation to force all of them to be bilingual. A certain number of bilingual officials would be necessary, of course, to ensure coordination among the monolingual French and English units and to fill senior administrative positions. A sufficiently large number of English- and French-speaking officials would decide on their own to learn the other language because of the prestige attached to positions requiring bilingualism, and the Public Service Commission would have to adapt its existing language training programmes to meet that situation. One advantage of this proposal would be that English-speaking public servants who have learned French would no longer be "obliged" to continue working almost exclusively in English, as is often the case today.

5. Creation of separate French and English advanced training programmes for civil servants. In the past, these programmes have been conducted mostly in English, with only a few courses given in French. This situation has led to considerable frustration for French-speaking Quebecers, who run the risk of falling two or three years behind in their careers because they must learn English and then, having completed a programme, find that they have become so accustomed to working in that language that they are no longer able to pursue their careers in French, even if they were required to do so. Care must be taken to ensure that these programmes have the same prerequisites and standards in both French and English, and that their content is similar. It is high time that the Bureau of Staff Development and Training took steps to correct a state of affairs which is unfair and intolerable for French-speaking civil servants.

6. Administrative decentralization with a view to maintaining in Montreal those government services that can operate exclusively in French. A number of federal offices are already situated in Montreal, but I do not believe that they are thought of as vehicles for increasing the French

proportion of the civil service. More are required, and they should become more self-contained than at present. The establishment of further units in Montreal could be part of a general policy of administrative decentralization throughout all parts of the country, or it could be part of a comprehensive programme designed to give greater scope to the French language in the public service. Once the requirements of administrative efficiency are met, the establishment of decentralized administrative services in Montreal would have the dual advantage of placing them in a cultural setting more favourable to the use of French as a working language than Ottawa or Hull, and of strengthening French as the working language of Montreal itself.

7. Improvement of the communications network between Ottawa and Quebec, and more particularly between federal civil servants on the one hand, and Quebec civil servants and the university community on the other. On both sides there is a serious need for relevant information on a wider range of subjects. Few people in key posts in Quebec know their counterparts in Ottawa intimately, and, conversely, few leading personalities in the federal services know the officials and university personnel in Quebec well enough to telephone them for discussions and really involve them in the development of federal policy. There result hollow regrets and pious wishes on the part of federal officials and ministers, frustration among Quebec officials and university personnel, and much suspicion on both sides. The only way to improve communications between Ottawa and Quebec is to increase more rapidly the number of French-speaking Quebecers in federal middle-level positions, and to promote the best of them to senior positions: people who know and appreciate each other communicate spontaneously.

8. Better alignment of federal and provincial policies in order to ensure close coordination of social and economic development. In key sectors, particularly fiscal and financial matters, consultation should be compulsory, and in some cases, it should have the same weight as executive decisions. In this way, working methods more conducive to cooperation and a climate of mutual confidence would be established without having to re-allocate the powers of the two levels of government; this would avoid the risk of weakening the whole structure of the Canadian state at a time when, on the contrary, it should be strengthened. The present system cannot endure. Many of Quebec's carefully prepared projects in the past few years have been side-lined following the publication of reports covering the same areas prepared independently by the federal government. Many initiatives, taken unilaterally by one side or the

other, have not been carried to a satisfactory conclusion because of the bad faith of the side which had not been consulted and thus felt wronged. The malaise resulting from the lack of genuine official consultation is not peculiar to Quebec; other provinces share that feeling. However, when added to other sources of frustration, it takes on special importance in Quebec. Quebec officials and ministers are exasperated by the feeling of ineffectualness, of being the pawn of a federal government which takes undue advantage of its broad taxing and spending powers. Lack of co-ordination between federal and provincial programmes seriously reduces the capacity of the Canadian political system to tackle current problems. Unfortunately, unlike other countries such as Great Britain and Sweden, Canada suffers from a number of unwarranted prejudices that can only be explained as a result of ignorance of the great possibilities which this approach, properly applied, can bring to a political system like Canada's.

9. Direct federal government support to the Province of Quebec in its efforts to promote the French language and culture. The federal government should make French the main working language in all its operations in Quebec; it should deal with the French-speaking population in their own language, and project a French image of itself both in Quebec and in French-speaking countries. Praiseworthy efforts in this direction have been made in the last few years, and the results are already evident, but they are still not enough. The federal government should also support Quebec's efforts to convince Ontario and foreign businessmen, particularly Americans, that French should be the main working language in the economic life of Quebec.

10. An effort to rally Canadians around some great common project in order to mobilize their energies and direct them into constructive channels. An attempt to give concrete meaning to the expression "participatory democracy" is the approach most likely to stir the hopes and dreams of a people who, out of weariness, or even fear, are in danger of becoming apathetic or intransigent. Neither in Quebec nor in the rest of the country does officialdom seem prepared to move in this direction. Inspired by the ideal of participation, underprivileged groups in outlying areas and in large cities have found new hope and have drawn up concrete plans: if they continue to meet with indifference, lack of understanding or active opposition, they will eventually turn against the authorities and against the whole set of liberal values and institutions. Appropriate mechanisms for the practice of true participatory democracy must be devised, and changes in present socio-political institutions

Quebec Society and Politics

must be brought about to implement it. In the present state of human affairs, action must be taken without further delay. Whether it is attempted on the federal or provincial scale, such a wide-ranging reform would have serious, if largely unpredictable, repercussions on the nature and operation of Canadian federalism.

This set of proposals, and other similar concrete steps, could be implemented without immediate changes in Canada's constitutional system. As they took effect, a new political style and a new language of political communication would develop, new realignments of interests would appear, different relationships would be established, and the position of Quebec *vis-à-vis* the federal government and the other provinces would be clarified. Gradually a new *modus vivendi* would occur between the two majorities – the French Canadians in Quebec and the English Canadians elsewhere – and new constitutional arrangements would then be required.

What would be the shape of this possible *modus vivendi?* One of the imponderable and dynamic factors is the right to self-determination.

According to my diagnosis, the Canadian crisis has reached its most critical phase. Conditions could hardly become worse without resulting in the break-up of Confederation. Any remedy aiming merely to reduce the pain without really attacking the underlying causes will only aggravate the situation, generating further disappointment and exasperation. So the remedies must be radical. To the federal government, and to most English Canadians, the remedies will probably seem harsh, but English Canadians should think seriously before rejecting them outright as excessive or impractical. After all, it is simply a question of taking corrective measures to change a discriminatory situation into an equitable situation. If English-speaking Canadians truly accept the principle of equality of *real* opportunities for the two founding peoples, they must accept the full implications of that goal, and the high cost of attaining it.

As for French-speaking Quebecers, it is impossible to forecast what their final choice will be, even under the most favourable circumstances. Many have opted definitively for separation; some are still undecided; others are still panic-stricken in face of the new set of circumstances. Economic recovery, greater participation in the political life of the whole country, a radical change in their place within Confederation – these and other developments could influence them.

No one knows if the desire for co-existence will overcome the desire for separation. It may be that, with the best will in the world, it will prove impossible to establish a climate of confidence between English-speaking Canadians and French-speaking Quebecers, even within the framework of a new Confederation. Perhaps the tide of hatred between the two groups, and the wave of terrorism, cannot be checked, even with the knowledge that combating terrorism would lead to a restriction of fundamental freedoms for all Canadians. No one can wish to maintain Quebec in Confederation at all costs, including virtually permanent military occupation.

Those who do not want Quebec to separate from the rest of the country should adopt all legitimate means to prevent that from happening, but they should also face the fact that such a possibility exists. If it should occur, every effort should be made to maximize the advantages and minimize the costs of separation for all concerned. The costs could run very high, higher perhaps than those entailed in building a new Confederation, not only for Quebec, but for the rest of the country as well, especially Ontario. It is to be hoped that Canadians will have the wisdom to avoid a violent separation, which would result in incalculable physical and human damage. If separation is to take place, one must hope that men will be found in both English and French Canada lucid enough to negotiate in advance its general terms, and to outline the links which could with advantage be maintained by both sides. Otherwise, the weakest group would have to bear the costs.

The reforms required to restore the confidence of French-speaking Quebecers in Confederation will place a heavy burden on Canada's resources. There are still some in Quebec who hope that these reforms can be implemented, and in time. But even they would understand if English Canadians found the cost too high and refused to adopt that course of action. Whatever happens, we must also hope that many English-speaking Canadians will accept and even endorse the choice that will be made by Quebecers.

Come what may, the "founding peoples" will have to continue to examine their common ground.

Index

social-political context of, 213-238
Office de la Langue Française, 91
O'Leary, D., 195*n*
O'Neill, J. H., 241
Ontario, birth rate in, 163; distribution of income in, 146; French speaking in, 9, 155, 174; Government issues Rule XVII, 175; immigration to, 164, 240; investments in, 142; manufacturing output in, 143; population growth in, 144; population in labour force, 165; secondary industry of, 181; seniority of, 209; unemployment in, 141
Operation Dignity, 28, 29, 31, 82, 83
Ouellet, Fernand, 73, 89*n*, 195*n*
Ownership of enterprises, 146, 149-154

P.P.B.S., 95
Papineau, Louis-Joseph, 42, 71
Parent Royal Commission, 21
Parti Québécois, as catalyzing agent, 88; economic philosophy of, 180-183; electoral reform plan of, 115, 116, 118*n*; extent of support of, 132, 179; founding of, 99; Gagnon attacks, 237; and institutions, 75; in Montreal, 121-123; outside Montreal, 124-127; nature of supporters, 108, 184-187; in 1970 elections, 16, 17, 22, 23, 48, 50, 51, 76, 119, 120, 136*n*, 137*n*, 138*n*; program of, 117, publications of, 195*n*; structural problems, 225; supporters of and separatism, 109, 111, 133, 134, 185-193; standing still, 135; tension within, 220; and Union Nationale supporters, 129-131
Parti Républicain, 179

Participation, 29, 62-63, 88, 202, 260
Paternalism, 28, 29, 57
Patronage, 102, 104, 108
Pays, Le, 53
Pearson, Lester B., 15, 197, 198, 246
Pelletier, Gérard, 19, 89*n*
Pinard, Maurice, 119-138, 186, 189*n*, 196*n*
Playfair, W. E., 67*n*
Polsby, Nelson W., 136*n*
Power and influence, distribution of, 213-214, 219, 220; demographic factors of, 218; disruptive, 230, 231; factors triggering
Presse, La, 19
Prestige, 113-115; Quebec's drive for, 74, 101
Prince Edward Island, 57
Public Service of Quebec, 90-98; French-speaking in, 21, 257, 258; history of, 96-97; unionized, 80, 217
Pye, Lucian, 232, 238*n*

Quebec Act of 1774, 41, 64, 70
Quebec City, 12, 48, 81, 94, 96, 105, 111, 171
Quebec House, 50, 243
Quebec, Province of, administrative institutions of, 93-96; birth rate in, 163; center of French life, 12, 23, 155, 174; changes in, 27; history of, 10-12, 39-51, 69-76; "idea" of, 206; impact on Canadian political life, 173; industrialization of, 13, 56; and international affairs, 239-250; migration in, 164; parallels with Canada, 176-7; population of, 9, 155, 160; population of in labour force, 165; restructured, 24
Quebec Resolutions, 52
Quebec Social Insurance Commission, 57

Québécois, 44, 45, 46, 47, 48, 49, 50, 51; replaces French Canadian, 216

Quiet Revolution, 9, 13-20, 22, 63, 97, 112, 118*n*; affects Catholic Church, 167; attitudes associated with, 197; complicates party system, 99; and education, 78; English Canada welcomes, 14, 100; fosters interest in international relations, 243; fosters modernization of Quebec, 181; and labour movement 19; and political institutions, 78; Union Nationale continues, 79

Quinn, Herbert, 186, 196*n*

Racine, Luc, 195*n*

Ralliement Créditiste, distribution of support, 132-134, 138*n* and electoral reform, 116; enters political arena, 99, 119, 135; federalist in orientation, 100; in Montreal, 121-123; outside Montreal, 124-127; provincial elections of 1970, 17, 184; and self-determination, 85; similarities with Union Nationale, 130; split in, 137*n*

Ralliement National, and independence, 181; 1966 election, 75, 79, 119, 120

Rassemblement pour l'Independance Nationale, demands independence, 108, 181; disappears, 195*n*

Rationality, man-centred, 30-31

Raynauld, André, 139-154, 166*n*

Rebellion of 1837, 10-11, 42

Regenstreif, Peter, 186, 187, 196*n*

Regional development, 29, 78, 105, 111

Reinhard, Marcel, 166*n*

Renaud, Pierre, 195*n*

Revenge of the cradle, 12, 21, 45, 162, 166

Révolution Québécoise, 183

Riel, Louis, 12

Riker, William H., 177, 178*n*

Rioux, Marcel, 186, 196*n*

Roberge, P., 217, 235*n*

Robertson, Joseph, 241

Robin, M., 118*n*

Roman Catholic Church, 167-172; cultural conflicts divide, 169; in France, 49; future of, 171; innovations in 167, 168; and labour movement, 18; loses influence, 81, 214-219, 221; missionary role of, 170; political action of, 70, 73, 168; role in Quebec society, 45, 76; and Union Nationale, 102

Rouges, 52

Roy, Maurice Cardinal, 48

Roy, Philippe, 242

Royal Commission on Bilingualism and Biculturalism, 22, 46, 66*n*; 89*n*; creation of, 15; problems facing, 252; Report of, 98, 154*n*, 175, 251, 257; and self-determination, 255

Royal Commission on Constitutional Matters, 67*n*, 77

Royal Commission on Dominion-Provincial Relations, 60, 77

Royal Commission on National Development in the Arts, Letters, and Sciences, 67*n*

Royal Proclamation of 1763, 40, 41, 42, 74

Rule xvii, 175

Ryan, Claude, 22, 239*n*

Sabourin, Louis, 250

Saint Jean-Baptiste Societies, 75

St. Laurent, Louis, clash with Duplessis, 69, 77; denounced as sellout, 12; Lesage in Cabinet of, 14; Prime Minister from

Union Nationale Party, 39, 50, 63, 64, 77, 78, 79, 91, 105, 117, 118n, 120, 132, 133, 135, 137; attitudes towards independence and federalism, 190-194; contradictions in, 108, 109; decline of, 85, 128-130; defeat of in 1960, 104; and electoral reform, 116; losses in 1970, 17; in Montreal, 121-123; nationalist forces in, 16; outside Montreal, 124-127; in power, 101-103; similarities with *Ralliement Créditiste*, 130; supporters of, 100, 121, 184, 187, 188, 189

Unité Quebec, see also Union Nationale; 85, 100, 125, 131, 137n

United Nations, 46, 47, 249

United States, annexation of Canada, 53; Bill of Rights of, 66; exodus of French Canadians to, 12; expansionism of, 43; independence of, 42, 158; Revolution of, 76

University of Montreal, 13, 21, 91, 185

University of Quebec, 21

University of Sherbrooke, 21

Upper and Lower Canada, 10, 42, 70, 173, 240

Vallières, Pierre, 184

Vatican II, 167, 168, 170

Vedel, G., 118n

Victoria, B.C., constitutional conference at, 51, 85, 178n, 197

Violence, *see also* terrorism; characterizes society, 31, 32, 33; escalates, 226, 227; F.L.Q. adopts, 22; shocks Quebecers, 17

War Measures Act, 17, 84, 230, 232; Trudeau on, 238n

Weber, Max, 102, 112, 118n

Wener, Normand, 168, 172

Wheare, K.C., 89n, 177, 178

White Papers, 197, 198, 203, 205, 206, 207

White, Sir Thomas, 57

Whyte, James, 241

World War I, 13; conscription in, 47, 56-57, 59

World War II, 39, 46, 61, 101, 157, 160; conscription in, 77; disruptive effect on Quebec, 13; integrates Quebec into international society, 168